PLOUGHSHARES

Summer 2015 • Vol. 41, No. 2

GUEST EDITOR
Lauren Groff

EDITOR-IN-CHIEF
Ladette Randolph

MANAGING EDITOR
Ellen Duffer

FICTION EDITOR
Margot Livesey

POETRY EDITOR
John Skoyles

FOUNDING EDITOR
DeWitt Henry

FOUNDING PUBLISHER
Peter O'Malley

PRODUCTION MANAGER
Akshay Ahuja

INTERIM PRODUCTION MANAGER
Allison Trujillo

EDITORIAL ASSISTANTS
Michelle Betters, Matt Mullen,
& Marie Sweetman

MARKETING ASSISTANT
Mimi Cook
& Erin Jones

DIGITAL PUBL. ASSISTANT
Jessica Arnold

SENIOR READERS
Sarah Banse, David Goldstein,
& Abby Travis

COPY EDITOR
Carol Farash

BUSINESS & CIRC. MANAGER
David Weinstein

ASSOCIATE BLOG EDITOR
Amelia Hassani

ePUBLISHING CONSULTANT
John Rodzvilla

INTERNS
Anna Buckley, Hayley Gundlach,
Ashley Howard, & Nia Mendy

READERS
Emily Avery-Miller | Jana Lee Balish | Doug Paul Case | Kyle Dacuyan
Diana Filar | John Francisconi | Joshua Garstka | Kristine Greive
Ethan Joella | Eson Kim | Kristina Kopić | Karen Lonzo | Kristian Macaron
Autumn McClintock | Marisela Navarro | Vickery Prongay | June Rockefeller
Wesley Rothman | Michael Schrimper | Charlotte Seley | Alessandra Siraco
Matt Socia | Jordan Stillman | Ross Wagenhofer
Caitlin Walls | Kristen Winstead

ADVISORY BOARD
DeWitt Henry | Alice Hoffman | Ann Leary
Pam Painter | Janet Silver | Marillyn Zacharis

SO-EDH-993

Ploughshares, a journal of new writing, is guest-edited serially by prominent writers who explore different personal visions, aesthetics, and literary circles. *Ploughshares* is published in April, August, and December at Emerson College: 120 Boylston Street, Boston, MA 02116-4624. Telephone: (617) 824-3757. Web address: pshares.org. E-mail: pshares@pshares.org.

Advisory Editors: Sherman Alexie, Neil Astley, Russell Banks, Andrea Barrett, Charles Baxter, Ann Beattie, Madison Smartt Bell, Anne Bernays, Frank Bidart, Amy Bloom, Robert Boswell, Rosellen Brown, Ron Carlson, James Carroll, David Daniel, Peter Ho Davies, Madeline DeFrees, Mark Doty, Rita Dove, Stuart Dybek, Cornelius Eady, Martín Espada, Percival Everett, B. H. Fairchild, Nick Flynn, Carolyn Forché, Richard Ford, Lorrie Goldensohn, Mary Gordon, Jorie Graham, David Gullette, Marilyn Hacker, Donald Hall, Patricia Hampl, Joy Harjo, Kathryn Harrison, Stratis Haviaras, Terrance Hayes, DeWitt Henry, Edward Hirsch, Jane Hirshfield, Tony Hoagland, Alice Hoffman, Fanny Howe, Marie Howe, Major Jackson, Gish Jen, Yusef Komunyakaa, Don Lee, Margot Livesey, Thomas Lux, Gail Mazur, Campbell McGrath, Heather McHugh, James Alan McPherson, Sue Miller, Lorrie Moore, Paul Muldoon, Antonya Nelson, Jay Neugeboren, Howard Norman, Tim O'Brien, Joyce Peseroff, Carl Phillips, Jayne Anne Phillips, Robert Pinsky, Alberto Ríos, Lloyd Schwartz, Jim Shepard, Jane Shore, Charles Simic, Gary Soto, Elizabeth Spires, David St. John, Maura Stanton, Gerald Stern, Mark Strand, Elizabeth Strout, Jean Thompson, Christopher Tilghman, Richard Tillinghast, Colm Tóibín, Chase Twichell, Jean Valentine, Fred Viebahn, Ellen Bryant Voigt, Dan Wakefield, Derek Walcott, Rosanna Warren, Alan Williamson, Eleanor Wilner, Tobias Wolff, C. D. Wright, Al Young, Kevin Young

Subscriptions (ISSN 0048-4474): $35 for one year (3 issues and 1 Solos *Omnibus*), $55 for two years (6 issues and 2 Solos *Omnibuses*), and $70 for three years (9 issues and 3 Solos *Omnibuses*); $50 a year for institutions. Add $35 a year for international postage ($15 for Canada and Mexico).

Upcoming: Solos *Omnibus Volume 3* will be published in October 2015. Winter 2015-16, a staff-edited poetry and prose issue, will be published in January 2016. Spring 2016, a poetry and prose issue edited by Tom Sleigh and Alan Shapiro, will be published in April 2016. Summer 2016, a fiction issue edited by James Wood and Claire Messud, will be published in July 2016.

Submissions: The regular reading period is from June 1 to January 15 (postmark and online dates). All submissions postmarked from January 16 to May 31 will be recycled or returned (if SASE is included) unread. From March 1 to May 15, we also read for our Emerging Writer's Contest. Please see page 205 for editorial and submission policies, or visit our website: pshares.org/submit.

Back-issue, classroom-adoption, and bulk orders may be placed directly through Ploughshares. *Ploughshares* is also available as full-text products from EBSCO, H.W. Wilson, JSTOR, ProQuest, and the Gale Group. Indexed in M.L.A. Bibliography, Humanities International Index, and Book Review Index. Full publishers' index is online at pshares.org. The views and opinions expressed in this journal are solely those of the authors. All rights for individual works revert to the authors upon publication. Ploughshares receives support from the National Endowment for the Arts and the Massachusetts Cultural Council.

Retail distribution by Ingram Periodicals, Media Solutions, Ubiquity, and Disticor Direct in Canada. Printed in the U.S.A. by The Sheridan Press.

The Miracle Years of Little Fork from MUSIC FOR WARTIME: *Stories* by Rebecca Makkai. To be published on June 23, 2015 by Viking, an imprint of Penguin Publishing Group, a division of Penguin Random House LLC. Copyright © 2015 by Rebecca Makkai Freeman.

CONTENTS

Summer 2015

Cover: Lesley Dill, *Small Poem Dress*, 1993, lithograph on newspress, 10" x 10.5".
Courtesy of the artist.

PLOUGHSHARES PATRONS

This nonprofit publication would not be possible without the support of our readers and the generosity of the following individuals and organizations.

CO-PUBLISHERS
Marillyn Zacharis, in memory of Robert E. Courtemanche
The Green Angel Foundation

COUNCIL
Denis and Ann Leary
Hunter C. Bourne III

PATRONS
W. Timothy Carey
Carol Davis
Drs. Jay A. and Mary Anne Jackson
Elizabeth R. Rea of the Dungannon Foundation
Eugenia Gladstone Vogel

FRIENDS
Michael J. and Lynne A. MacWade
James Tilley

ORGANIZATIONS
Emerson College
Massachusetts Cultural Council
National Endowment for the Arts

Co-Publisher: $10,000 for two lifetime subscriptions and acknowledgment in the journal for five years.

Council: $3,500 for two lifetime subscriptions and acknowledgment in the journal for three years.

Patron: $1,000 for a lifetime subscription and acknowledgment in the journal for two years.

Friend: $500 for acknowledgment in the journal for one year.

LAUREN GROFF
Introduction

I chose this life I'm inhabiting, the mousy isolation of a writer who distantly teaches, the husband and two small children and the house with its monthly measure of death called a mortgage. Still, I'm wary of accumulation; my impulse is to pare to the bone. We have seasonal fits of surrendering goods, giving away, editing out. When they sense a spasm coming on, my little boys have learned to hide their toys.

Here's my hypothesis: the less mess there is, the less one has to worry about outside life, and the less outside life to worry about, the more time one has to do nothing. It seems essential that a writer have unlimited time to faff about, to think things through, to fill the days with silence and space. I support this hypothesis with the fact that the only things that are exempt from my mania for whittling are books, because a book is a dream guided by another mind. The simpler life becomes, the freer I feel to complicate my brain with dreams.

I find, in this time of relative personal smoothness, that I'm turning toward reading work that pushes against the calm of my life, the small-town softness and isolation I've intentionally spun around myself like a woolly cocoon. I've become hungry for narratives that are raw and passionate and strange. I read restlessly to find writing that subverts and explodes the expected, work that teaches one how to read it as it unrolls. This doesn't necessarily mean formal innovation, which I often love, but which can be as rigid in its adherence to its own kind of convention as a well-crafted literary story that suggests little new. What I mean is that I'm hungry for voices that speak to me with real emotion, because real emotion is always new; I want voices that arrive at my ears through translation, voices that take breathtaking risks, voices that break as much as they build. Give me the short and the sharp, like a slap; give me the long, slow immersion in an alien sea. I am searching for work that is written with blood or bile or choler, not necessarily sweat alone.

The pleasure is mainly in the seeking, but there's also a blip of joy when you find what you're looking for. I thank *Ploughshares* for asking me to be a guest editor, a great honor and source of tremendous pleasure. And I hope every reader of this journal is in his or her own warm, quiet world seeking out the work that makes the blood hum and the heart drum, finding the writing that transfigures everyday life and makes it strange.

OSAMA ALOMAR
Eleven Stories

Translated from the Arabic by the author and C. J. Collins

Peace Agreement

Strong and Weak signed a peace agreement; Weak had the document framed in a gold frame and hung it in the front room of his house. He called a press conference to publicize the event with photographs and articles. He considered it a rebirth for himself. Strong, on the other hand, used his copy to make a diaper for his baby.

Who Leads Whom

The donkey had not walked a few meters carrying his master, the traveling salesman, on his back when he suddenly stopped and would not move. The salesman spurred him with his two feet, but in vain. He got down and pulled him by the bridle with all his strength without result. He began cursing him with every insult that came to mind. The donkey brayed in protest saying, "I think it's your turn to carry me! You know that I won't move from here until you carry me on your back as I have carried you these long years. It's very strange, sir: don't we the community of donkeys deserve to revolt even once against the degradation and shame that we are exposed to throughout our lives? It's not possible to reach an understanding with you on the matter of our rights and how to protect them when you speak a strange language and your voices are the pinnacle of ugliness! There is no means other than this for revolt. If only you could understand this, you who think you belong to a species that is preternaturally smart!"

The Case Against the Earthquake

A destructive earthquake hit the country, annihilating everything in its path. The high functionaries were disturbed by the destruction caused to their palaces and their farms. They decided to bring a lawsuit against the earthquake and they put all their effort toward this end. Finally, they won their case. The earthquake stopped visiting the country and secluded itself far away, cursing the loss of most of its savings.

Empty Stomach

A dry breadcrumb made her way with difficulty into the stomach of a beggar who hadn't tasted food for days. She felt extremely lonely inside the dark and totally empty stomach. The sensation that she had been thrown into solitary confinement without reason pervaded her. She waited a while for some bit of food to fall down on her from above and free her from this terrifying nightmare into which she had been plunged…but in vain. She tried to return from where she had come…without success. She fell into a black depression and died before she was digested.

The Agreement of Feet

In my dream last night I saw a large number of men and women sitting at the great round table of history. They were insulting each other and arguing among themselves with vulgarity. But I noticed that there were agreements being initialed by feet beneath the table. And soon these began to flirt and play while the insults and arguments above became more and more crass and vulgar and finally turned into slapping and punching and even spitting.

Today, during my nap, I saw in my dream that the situation had reversed itself completely. Now the feet were fighting and arguing and the hands were signing agreements in a halo of smiles and kisses.

I wondered about the daring hero who would come from somewhere in this world to pull off the thick mosaic tablecloth and turn the table of history over on itself.

Convoy

The drops go calmly and quietly. The steps move forward in an orderly fashion. Smiles appear on faces. The self is utterly serene. Suddenly, a shrieking horn fills the space. Security forces rush everywhere. Everyone runs in all directions. The body is on the verge of exploding from the pressure of the screams and the shrieks. "Get out of the road! Get out of the road!" The policemen shout. Drops from all levels of society run in terror electrified with dozens of questions. After a few moments, the highway of the Aorta becomes completely empty save for the security personnel contracted on either side. The convoy of the royal drop passes at great speed, and within minutes life returns to its normal course.

Meanwhile, a man has sat down on the closest bench on the street, panting hard and loosening the buttons of his shirt while the sweat pours from him in profusion.

After a few days the same situation repeats itself…shouts of the policemen…the Aortic highway completely emptied of blood…security forces contracted on both sides…the royal convoy with its speed so great the man loses consciousness. He is brought to Intensive Care. A month later the story repeats itself, and he dies of a heart attack.

The Garlic and the Flower

The owner of the house put the bag of garlic he had brought from the market on the table and went into the bedroom to change his clothes. The garlic looked with disgust at a flower on the table saying, "Couldn't that fool have put me anywhere else instead of near this awful smelling thing?"

The Price of Perfume

Samer, a student in second grade, left school happy, having gotten a perfect score in math. He sped up his pace so that he could get home and tell his parents the good news.

At the corner of the street, an old man in his sixties appeared before him. His features seemed like those of an angel. His beard was long and white. When Samer was beside him, the old man leaned in close and said to him in a voice laden with warmth: "Do you want to perfume your hand, little one?"

Samer hesitated…His mother had told him not to talk to strangers…but never mind…the old man seemed good like his grandfather.

"Sure, grandpa," he answered him innocently.

The old man took out a vial of perfume from his pocket and smeared some on the little one's hand. The boy inhaled deeply and flew high through the enchanted air. But after a moment, he fell under the burden of words smeared with muddy threats:

"Give me the price of the perfume!"

Samer looked in the face of the old man and saw that the face of the grandfather had burned away to be replaced by the face of a howling wolf.

He took a few steps back. Swarms of locusts invaded his virgin forests and devoured them in moments. The voice of the wolf shook him again: "Give me the price of the perfume, you little bastard!"

Through the blur of terror, he glimpsed its fangs. He felt as if the whole world had changed into fangs and rabid panting. The shreds of his serenity curled into a ball inside the pupils of the monster. He didn't know how to pull his hand away from its claws. He didn't come to his senses until he was running like a rabbit from a hunter, while the threatening question beat the ground behind him with its paws:

"Are you trying to rob me, you little dog?!"

The perfect score in math burned up…the locusts settled in his soul that had been a beautiful forest…He ran toward the house through the tunnel darkened by the howls of the wolves.

Honeyed Words

Starting from his wide smile, a flood of honeyed words poured out of him day and night. And so he became an easy trap for insects and particles of dust.

Fate

In the midst of a crowd of ants, two were conversing at some distance from the others. The one asked the other, "What is the truth about fate in your view?"

Her friend thought a little, pursing her lips, and said, "I think it is an enormous power, far greater than us, that we cannot escape. What's more, its greatness is such that it can bring you down or lift you up without even being aware of you. Sometimes..."

Just then the enormous foot of a child playing with a ball took them by surprise, crushing a large number of ants. The two of them miraculously escaped the massacre. The child continued playing without feeling a thing. The two friends ran away as fast as possible, trembling in terror. When they reached a safe place and their rapid breathing subsided, the second ant said to her friend, "That is fate, my dear, that is fate."

The Dark Side

The moon wished to punish humans for the many transgressions and frightful crimes they commit against each other and against nature. She decided to hide her lighted side so that they would return to reason and curb their behavior...and so the eclipse took place. But great was the surprise of the moon when she saw millions of people coming out of their houses to enjoy the view of her dark side.

RAMONA AUSUBEL
Fresh Water from the Sea

The woman was weeks away. Maybe even days away.

The phone calls at first were difficult to understand. "You shouldn't worry about this, but I'm getting thinner," she said to her daughter, but instead of the note of excitement the girl expected, the woman sounded lost. "There's less of me." The girl imagined an old woman, her spine collapsing in on itself, giving in to gravity.

"Shrinking?" she asked.

"I'm losing myself," the mother tried. The girl thought of her mother sitting on the floor of her apartment, the expensive rug covered in the puzzle pieces of her body. "It's not like that," the woman explained. "It's like I'm vanishing. Like I am a thick fog, burning off."

The girl flew across the world, LAX, JFK, then east, across the Atlantic, across the Mediterranean. The mother answered the door. She was slightly wispy. Where she had once been a precise oil painting, now she was a watercolor. "It's good of you to come." She looked the girl up and down, and the girl knew her mother was disappointed to see that the girl still looked the way she always had. "Any boyfriends?"

"No boyfriends." The girl tried to smile, tried to keep the old joke alive.

Reluctantly, the woman hugged her, and the girl thought, *My goodness, has she always had all of those bones?*

The mother sat down on the couch in front of the huge windows, looking out at the city and the sea beyond. She patted the spot next to her. "You see it too, right?" she put her palm up. The girl nodded. It was just the very edges of her mother that were foggy. The girl reached out and held her mother's hand, which felt as if it was coated in sea foam. "Good. I'm not going crazy," the woman said.

They sat there quietly. For two days, since her mother had first called, the girl had tried to imagine what she would look like. She had tried to prepare herself for the worst. The words *my mother is vanishing* had been like a loose piece of metal rattling around the cage of her brain. She had felt a little bit of electricity shoot through her system, a jig of hopefulness. Maybe we will actually say something real to each other, she thought. Now she was wordless. "It's good to see you," the girl said. She stood at the edge, just where she always had.

From her suitcase she removed a jar of peanut butter, a box of cereal bars, oatmeal, pinto beans, and a loaf of whole wheat bread? "A little bit of America."

The girl thought she could see a wisp of her mother disappear right then. "I'm sure it's just...something," she said, trying to stop it. The mother, misty, smiled at her daughter.

Out the window, they could see the tops of buildings, the air-conditioning units and heating tubes and collections of wires. The minaret from the mosque craned its neck. Below, café people were sitting with their legs crossed at the ankle and their faces up to the sun. This part of the city had been crumbled in the last war and was built back all at once, the center of the city turned into an overly cheerful mall. Plaza and clock tower, cobbled streets radiating out with shops.

"It looks just like California," the girl said. She had taken a class on The American Dream in which the students wrote papers about the exporting of culture.

"At least it's intact," her mother said. She gestured to the other window, through which a big hotel stood, its walls yawning with holes, the railings on the balconies mangled. It was so quiet, that bombed-out hotel. How strange, the girl thought, that only the visual evidence of a war is recorded.

Beyond the city, the sea was endless.

The rest of the afternoon, the girl and her mother did what people do: went on in spite of what had changed. They chatted a circle around the outskirts of their lives, they ate something when they got hungry. By the time they went to bed, the woman's blurry edges had become just another fact of the world, a stray cat that, once let in, had made itself at home.

In the morning, the girl and her mother packed up for the doctor's appointment, put on decent-looking clothes. The girl did not say that her mother was a little hazier than she had been the day before. She did not say that when she came close to her mother, the temperature changed, as if the woman were her own weather system.

The doctor refused to look the mother in the eye or smile, as if doing so would break his calm. He asked a lot of questions that seemed like a way of avoiding what else he had to say. He wanted to know whether she'd been sleeping; and how about the chills, had she had any? And whether her snot, which she reported having a little of, was green or yellow.

"Clear," she told him.

He said, "That's great," with conviction that surprised even him. "I mean," he fumbled, "that's good."

The girl raised her eyebrows and nodded. "Her eyes are fine too," she said, "and everything's shipshape with her toenails."

"We'll run some blood tests," he said, and they all knew that he meant *This is a new way to get there, but the end will be the same.*

The girl stood up and left the room. She went into the sterile-smelling bathroom and sat down on the toilet and kicked the wall once, hard. It clanked. There was a rubber mark on the wall from the black sole of her sneaker. She opened the little window where the pee samples were supposed to go. It was empty at the moment. She could see, through plastic curtains, technicians adjusting dials on the machines. They appeared as if underwater, breathing miraculously, collecting and testing out the life around them. Determining the lengths of time everyone had left on this alien land. She wanted to ask for forgiveness or clemency. Her mother hardly knew her at all, and she suspected the reverse was also true. She had always expected some midlife understanding, a trip to India in which they wore a lot of loose white clothing, finally revealed their true selves, said all those unsayables. On one of the little paper pee cups, in the marker that was meant to be used to write your name on the sample, the girl scrawled: *Give us more time, please. As much as you can spare.*

On the second day, the girl left her mother asleep on the couch in the sun and went walking. Ahead of her, the sea was pane-smooth, and in a square looking out at it, a statue of an angel shot full of holes. A taxi driver swerved and honked at an old woman crossing the road and then stopped short to buy a newspaper from a child. The girl remembered the city, but not well. She had visited her grandparents when they were alive, had eaten sugar-syrup pastries in the sun, driven into the mountains, and looked out at the sea. "The cliffs will eventually erode," her grandfather had said, gesturing. "See how the water keeps tugging at them?" There was an underground river of desperation in his voice. This country was not big enough to lose any more ground.

The girl watched boys jump from the sea wall into the deep blue. Families had chairs set up along the boardwalk, lunches, hookahs, children with candy-stuck faces. They were alive and together, and God, whichever god was theirs, had shaken this day out like a crisp sheet for them to lie down on.

The girl sat on a bench and called her sister who was planning, always planning, to worry about someone beside herself. "It really is as if she's fading away," the girl said over the thousands and thousands of miles. It felt strange to say it, and she looked around to see if anyone had overheard her. The girl waited to be carted off, a crazy daughter.

"I just wish I was there," the sister told her.

"You can be. There are airplanes."

"God," she kept sighing, "give Mom a big kiss for me."

"Is this really happening?" the girl asked, but her sister had already hung up.

The story, the way it had always been told, was this: When the woman was eighteen years old, the war had woken back up. Her parents sent her away with a suitcase full of gifts for the relatives in California who had agreed to take her in. "But I don't know who I am anywhere else."

The parents said, "You'll be whoever you become."

In the airplane, the woman had cried until her cheeks were sore, her eyelids swollen, her lips raw. She promised herself to her country, swore she would never love anything or anyone else.

She planned to go home in a year, but her parents matched her up with the boy who lived down the street from the girl. The woman did not fall in love with him, but she married him because it was easier than not marrying him. She pinned photographs of that faraway coastline to the ceiling above her bed, stared up at the relentless blue sea while her husband breathed into her neck. Then the woman was pregnant with twin girls, a pair of anchors that would sink into the sand of their adopted city.

When the girls were young, everything in the house had come from the woman's faraway home. Olives, sweets, citrus, honey. The first thing the daughters learned to draw was the cedar tree, famous and endangered. Inside the house, the family lived in a tiny island of the woman's long lost home. The girl and her sister were taught to be suspicious of everything else, California looming like a high-wire circus that wanted to recruit them. All their lullabies were from home, all their prayers. The mother surrounded herself with the seaside country like it was atmosphere, the only thing keeping her alive on a noxious, foreign planet.

The girl remembered sitting outside her parents' door before her father left, listening to them fight.

"I'm from the same place as you," the father had said.

"But you are not the place itself. You are not my home."

In the afternoon of the third day, the woman and the girl sat on the bed playing two games of solitaire because neither one could remember the rules to anything else. The cloud that was the mother had grown thinner. The air around her was dewy.

Outside, the people, the poor war-battered and future-looking people, were just trying to enjoy a day in the sunshine. They were being good, trying hard. The girl, watching them through the window, thought about rewarding them, throwing chocolate coins or confetti down.

"Would you do something for me?" the mother asked her daughter. "I haven't shaved in days. I can't stand to touch my skin."

The girl filled up a pot with warm water and put on a pair of shorts. She took one of her mother's legs in her hands. Even without shaving cream, the mother's legs were puffs. For a moment, after each stroke, her skin looked like skin, as if all the girl needed to do was sweep the clouds away to find her. But soon the mist gathered, and the woman was ghostly again.

"Why is this happening?" the girl asked.

"I'm sure it's my fault. Maybe I didn't eat enough leafy greens. Maybe I did something awful in a past life. I'm sure I should have loved you better."

"There are worse mothers, and they don't disappear."

"Everybody goes, somehow."

The mother watched while her daughter worked. She looked back and forth between their legs. "Your bone structure, sweetie," she told the girl, "it's very good. Even your ankles; look at how nicely they taper." She reached out and smoothed her finger over the girl's calf.

The mother was gently marking the girl. When, in some future, the girl let a man near her skin again, she knew already that the fingers she'd feel would be her mother's.

The moment the girl and her sister were settled in college, the mother began to shop for an apartment back home. She was a brightened, colored-in version of herself. She sold off the furniture, gave away half her clothes, made her daughters reduce the relics of their childhood to two cardboard boxes, stored in their aunt's garage. Meanwhile, the girl set up pictures on her dorm room desks, organized her sweaters in the drawer. She, too, felt as if she were living in a new country—college was America and nowhere else. She felt as if she had just stepped off a ship for the first time in her life, her body still listing.

The mother called occasionally at the beginning of fall to report the progress settling in, news from friends, restaurants discovered. The girl would return her mother's calls when she got back to the dorm from a series of parties, just drunk enough to feel like talking. "How is your sister?" the woman asked. "Is she still with that What's-His-Name?"

"I have no idea. I don't keep track."

"It's late. You should study."

The girl put a foot on the floor to anchor herself. *Dear Mom,* she thought, *I'm really happy to be alone in the world. Thank you for being far away.* All her life, the mother's unhappiness had been like a magnet for the girl, pulling, pulling. There were so many new things for the girl to love, now that her mother was in the distance.

The girl could hear her new friends in the common room, microwaving something wonderfully horrible to eat. Her life was an unplanted field, and everywhere she looked, something waited to be sown.

On the fourth day, the girl called her sister, knowing it wasn't a good time for her. She would be eating in a new restaurant with a new boyfriend who was probably on the verge of proposing just at the moment the sister would have spotted someone cuter in the yellow streetlight outside. She made the girl tired, the dance of her life. "How *is* she?" the sister said, her voice full of the over-concern of guilt.

"She's less and less," the girl said. The sister sighed. The girl knew she did not believe what was happening—none of them did. It seemed made up, a story they were all pretending. The sister did not comfort the girl and the girl did not comfort her sister. "Are you sure you don't want to come? Consider ten years from now, won't you wish you'd seen her?" On the far end, the voices of many people, awake late at night, clinking their glasses.

"What? It's so loud here."

The girl whispered, "I can hardly hear you either, in all this quiet."

By the fifth day, the mother's skin was practically radiating light. She looked more and more like weather, like a brewing storm. Her face was hairless and glowing. Disappearing was what the mother was now doing, as if disappearing were a job. She was working hard at it, over-achieving as usual.

The girl sat down close to her mother on the couch. She wanted to touch her mother. It was the same temptation she had had on every airplane flight of her life, looking out at those mounded clouds. There was a coolness to her mother, the chill of wet air. The girl felt something hard around her mother's waist. "What is this?" she asked, startled.

"A girdle," the mother said.

The girl paused and ran her hand up the perfect smoothness of the device, which did not give way. "Have you always worn this?"

"I was trying to find something to contain me. To hold me together."

"Let me do it," the girl said. "The last thing we need is a device that's meant to shrink you." The girl moved her hand up the long line of clasps, releasing. She put her arms around her mother's waist, and she held hard. The woman was too weak to wriggle away. For this they both gave silent thanks.

The woman studied the street scene. "I never got around to sorting all my paperwork," she told her daughter. "I still have all my old gas bills in storage. It hardly seems fair that I should disappear yet they remain."

"Are there things I should keep?"

"I have no idea. Ask my accountant. Or maybe there's some kind of packet available. 'What to do with your files when you vanish.'" They both laughed, and then they both stopped laughing. "You should take the fashion magazine subscriptions for yourself. Give the political stuff to your sister."

"Yeah, she'll really love that." The girl imagined her sister with her nose curled up, as if doing so could make her any less stupid, trying to understand even one line of an article about the wars, the elections.

Down below on the street there were clumps of people eating at tables. They had hummus and lamb-flatbread and a bottle of wine. A man wore a T-shirt that said, *Talk to My Agent*. There was a rack of postcards standing on the sidewalk, and a man and woman were taking out one at time and laughing at it. They pointed and then they laughed. The girl imagined the cards: *puppies dressed as policemen, old women, naked but for cat-eye sunglasses and martinis*. The people found this funny. They could be anywhere on earth, any nationality, and the joke would still be the same.

"Tell me something about your life," the mother said.

"A professor asked me out. We had one boring date and a sloppy kiss. I got a B in the class and I was so furious."

The mother put her hand on the girl's. It was too soft.

"I love you," the girl said.

"Let's not do that."

The girl searched the room for something safe to look at. On the counter was a bowl with a fissure straight through, waiting to be glued. It was an old bowl, probably a gift from some beloved. Would she throw it in the garbage? Dead and over? The apartment was full of the souvenirs of a lived life, each one the nail holding a memory in place. The girl wondered, when they passed through her hands and did not jog a memory because neither the objects nor the places they came from belonged to her, if she would want to wrap them carefully in paper and ship them to herself in boxes. Or if she would send them to the poor because they were inanimate and mute and could not revive the woman who used to love them. Would some part of the girl suddenly bloom that knew what to do?

"Throw them away," the mother said, as if she was reading her daughter's mind. "We'll go through the apartment tomorrow and tag the good things—worth money, or very special. You don't want to treasure some piece of art for the next fifty years only to meet me in heaven and discover that I always hated it."

Late at night the girl took the girdle into the guest bedroom where she was sleeping. She wrapped the girdle around herself and hook-and-eyed the long strand. She examined herself in the mirror. She wondered who would hold her in when she began to disperse.

The girl found her phone and scrolled through the contacts, wanting to hear a warm voice. She hit send on her ex, and he answered with a question in his voice. In the background was the din of twenty-something fun. The girl said, "Hey," and the lonesomeness in her voice surprised her. The ex talked for a second, but she was listening to the party behind him. He had no idea how lucky he was to be in a room with a hundred other young bodies, complete bodies, everyone yelling to be heard. The girl hung up without saying goodbye and didn't answer when the boy called back. The room was sick with quiet. The girl took the girdle off and held it to her cheek, her mother's sweat and skin part of the fibers now, pressed together like praying hands.

A week after the girl had arrived, the woman was vapor. She was pure humidity, and the whole apartment was muggy with her. The marble in the bathroom sweated all day. Droplets of condensation fell from the ceiling. The air was heavy. The mother, what was left of her, hovered on the couch. Even her bones were faint. The girl called her sister to say that she didn't think the woman had long.

Someone knocked on the door a few minutes later. It was a pimpled adolescent boy with a huge bouquet. The girl closed the door to a crack. Her first thought was that God had sent these flowers—who else could have gotten them here so quickly? She pictured the all-powerful, trying to negotiate a bouquet without too many carnations. The card said, "Dear Mom: Wishing you the best in this hard time in your life," in the sister's looping script.

And what about your life? the girl thought. *I suppose this is not a hard time for you. Do you have a secret mother waiting to replace this one?*

The girl looked at the almost-nothing that was her mother now. "Look what your daughter sent," she said. The mother looked back. The girl was completely visible, but that was not the same thing as being whole. Inside the girl, there were fractures, fault lines.

The girl stood by the open window, pulled a rose out and threw it. It whirled in slow motion for a few seconds, like the hand on a clock, counting down. A man picked it up, then turned upward, shading his eyes and trying to figure out the source of the bloom. "What are you doing?" the mother asked.

"I guess I'm throwing roses," the girl said, unable to make sense of herself. The mother, barely a mist now, joined her by the window. A little whorl of her trailed behind, and the girl swept her hand through it.

"Can I have one?" The woman tossed it and it felt good. "You can love as many and as much as you want. I thought I had to save my love up, that I would run out. It turns out it's the exact opposite." She paused. "When I was living in California, the only thing I could smell was this city. I would remember the plainest things, some random intersection, and feel an ache to see it. Missing home was sweeter even than being here."

The girl thought of all the leavings a person does over the course of her life. Leaving the womb, growing up and leaving home, letting go of friends, breakups with lovers, divorce, houses packed up and moved out of. She pictured abandoned, grown-out-of skins everywhere.

The girl could already feel the empty space forming around her mother, and its gravity. She knew she would circle it for the rest of her life, orbiting that absence.

"When I walked out of the airport, when I finally came home, I thought *I never have to leave this*. All those years, all I had wanted was to be surrounded by this city, engulfed."

The mother told her daughter about the first weeks, which were all reunions with old friends, picnics by the sea, meals in which every single thing was right—the dreamed-of bread dipped in olive oil, the woman's fingers glistening. She woke in the seaside country, she slept in it. She breathed and it filled her up.

"Soon, I had seen each of my old friends once, and when I called for another date, their voices cooled. 'We're going away soon, and I have a million and one things to do,' one said. 'I'd really love to, but it's a busy time at work.' I used to be a once-every-three-years friend."

The girl thought of the architecture of those lives in which there was a small room for her mother, quiet, off in the corner." The sitting rooms were filled with nearers and dearers, the gardens were at capacity, the bedrooms, certainly, were full.

As the months passed, the mother said she had continued to buy the dreamed-of bread and dip it in olive oil, but she did not close her eyes with pleasure each time anymore. This was not bread from the faraway seaside country anymore—it was just bread, commonplace and unremarkable. The coffee was just coffee, the oranges just oranges. Every bakery had the treats she had eaten as a child; every café the tomato salad. The concentrate that she had spent her whole life brewing, the thick syrup of this place that she had lived on, had been watered down. Every single thing was the war-torn seaside-country.

"How could I love every single thing?" she asked. "It used to be that I *was* my love for this place. With so much of the place, it was like I, too, was being diluted."

The girl thought of her mother, her mostly water body dropped into a deep blue pool, dispersing.

"I wandered, street by street, buying things just so that I could say hello to the shopkeepers. I still felt unseen."

And the next week, she said, she was also unseeable. Just a little bit, at first. The woman kept taking her sunglasses off to clean them, to try and wipe away the fogginess. But the rest of the world was crisp. Her body alone was blurring. "Is this what dying feels like? I wondered. Does everyone have this experience at the end of their lives?"

"I'm sorry you were sent away," the girl said. The girl remembered hearing as a child her mother crying in the other room. Her mother had been lost, the girl knew that much. She was drifting on an unknown sea. Many times, the girl had tried to turn herself into an island on which her mother could land.

The girl threw another rose. A man picked it up, squinted up into the sky, and the woman and the girl could tell that he did not see them this high. The mother and her daughter were nothing more than strange weather.

The girl asked her mother to tell her that they were both going to be all right. That they were both going to be at home wherever they were. She wanted it to be true, something the mother could know from her perch at the edge of life.

Out over the sea, the sun grew hotter. The girl remembered the water cycle: evaporation, condensation, precipitation. The mother closed her eyes. She was almost invisible now. She was just the faintest color, like the rainbows thrown by a crystal in the window. The air hung against the girl's skin, heavy. The woman was the air; the girl breathed her in. She looked around the room and could not see her mother anymore.

A storm broke over the girl, thunderheads, lightning, rain and rain and rain and rain.

The Blueblack Cold

I went to my father's room in the back hall of the boarding house. The door was open a little, and I could see he was asleep. An old sheet was pulled up to his neck, and he lay looking at the white ceiling with his eyes closed, breathing softly. His foot stuck out at the bottom—I know that foot, I thought.

I took it in my hand and stood there while he woke.

On the wall, he had taped up a photograph of my mother. She was wearing a shawl and standing under a row of cypress trees. There weren't any graves in the photograph, but I remember the place. It was a cemetery where we used to go on picnics. But this image was from long before that. My mother is holding a leather case for binoculars, and it dangles by the ground where her brown shoes stand out against the green grass, fifty years later.

It's time to go, I said. If we don't get there early…

He rubbed his eyes and sat up.

Time for work?

No work, I said. No work. Don't you remember?

He shook his head, as old men sometimes do when agreeing with something they don't like.

In fact, we're already a bit late.

I helped him get dressed. A few days before, we had bought him some good trousers and boots, and a strong tightly woven wool shirt and jacket, well made for cold mornings in a poorhouse.

2044, and they still haven't made better cloth than wool, he had said at the store. The young clerk had looked at me, blinking her dark eyes.

They have not, she said to him.

He repeated the remark to me, and I said, A good coat is a shield against the world.

Who said that? he asked softly.

Why, you did. You know very well you did.

We laughed as we left the store. Or smiled slightly. Smiling slightly was our laughing as we left the store.

*

My father leaned against a low wall in the street as I came down the steps.

I'm afraid it's a bit far, I said.

That's all right. We'll just go slowly.

I handed him his cap. I'd folded the photograph and put it in the band.

He set it carefully on his head.

Shall I leave my things there in the room?

I'll collect them later, I said.

Later, he said doubtfully.

*

We went on down the road, me holding under his arm. The morning was overcast where we stood, but in the distance, where we were to walk, a gaping hole had broken in the clouds and light poured through.

We were going down to the city center, just as we had planned the night before.

The night before: the night before, we had argued, and at the end, we decided it was best, after three hours. An argument—me talking and him keeping quiet. We would make an early start and go to the city center. We would go to the city center where they had told us to.

*

At the first bridge crossing, the first of the signs could be seen, a tall broad billboard a hundred feet across.

HUMANITY ABOLISHES AGING 2047.

There was a face beside the text, a proud, beautiful man who had cast off his wrinkles.

All week long on the radio, again and again, the same message. People, too, government servants, had gone about as if it was the census, knocking on doors—knocking on every door, even boarding houses, even poorhouses.

"All persons over the age of seventy-five report to the Foundation Building. 9 a.m. on Thursday the fifth. You will be frozen to stop further aging. We are close to a cure and want no more unnecessary deaths."

My father didn't want to go.

But billboards, signposts, lines, the declaration of a time and place, they have a way of deciding things. If people are waiting in lines, it makes you feel the thing is worth waiting for. Soon you're in the line. And there's nothing finer than a line that's moving along briskly, drawing you surely toward the front. I must have had happy times in lines like that.

As we came over the third bridge, it was close to ten. We'd stopped on four or five occasions for my father to rest. If I'd had fare for a car, I'd have hired one, but I didn't even have change for my father's breakfast, for what might be his last breakfast. Just then we were passing a food stall, and this is how he put it:

I've never been hungry in the morning.

He clapped me on the shoulder. We'd best go on.

*

Over the third bridge then and what did we see:

A line if I have ever seen one, two miles long at least.

The road had been stopped—no traffic permitted, and the street was full, as if from one end of the city to the other. Not a line, but a crowd, but a throng of crowds. And the whole thing stood up on uneasy legs.

What I'm saying is—we were nowhere near the Foundation Building, where some kind of a chamber, like a massive dairy, hall upon hall of chill, elemental air, had been hollowed out or erected, and even without our permission, we were in line. People were coming up behind us. People before us. One had the impression of a parade. All the oldest living to form a parade.

So many, my father said, I had not known death had undone so many.

And if it doesn't need to?

*

He stumbled heavily, and we had to sit.

This is what it comes to, he said. Nearly falling down, and there's not even a reason. I didn't trip over anything. Just my own legs failing.

I want to talk about it, he said. I want to go back to my room and talk about it. We'll put on some tea, and I won't feel hungry. We'll sit and talk it out. The room is still mine, until Wednesday. We've paid through Wednesday. We can go back.

Look, he said. A line like this—you get in it and it doesn't matter when. We might as well be anywhere in the line. There's no pressing need. To join it, I mean.

I shook my head.

I don't know if the walk home is a good idea. We've already come so far. You haven't had a walk like this in years.

Then let's talk here.

His coat was buttoned wrong, one off all the way down. Somehow I hadn't noticed. I fixed it, and we sat there. Now and then, someone would come along and pass us, heading down over the bridge. There wasn't even any place to sit. We were just on the concrete with our legs splayed out. He took off his hat and set it beside him on the ground, gently, as if putting it on a table.

I loved your mother, he said. We had a little house with a stone wall and an herb garden. We didn't have a dog, but we thought about having one, and that was a good thought. We were very proud of you, she and I. When you graduated, she cried and cried. We were so proud.

I always liked going to work, he said. Work, I never liked, but going there, I always felt because of your mother and your brother and you, I always felt I was on the right course. Now they are in the ground.

Father, I said.

And anyway, he said, what is it to be frozen? I don't know that any of the scientists, any of the politicos—are they being frozen themselves? Do they trust it?

I told him I didn't know if they were freezing themselves. I expect not, I said.

But it's the only chance.

He grimaced.

Are you saying I won't last the year?

It's three, I said. 2047. You won't last three.

Even if I did, he said. What would I do, take up dancing? Be unfrozen, cleaned up, and put on dancing shoes?

Father, I said.

He shook me off.

Don't make me go down there.

Father.

I drew a breath.

They've been making speeches, I said. There'll be no more aging. Just peace.

And no children, then?

My father spat on the ground.

Some kind of horn sounded in the distance.

Come along. I took his arm and raised him to his feet.

We walked down the path slowly and joined the line where the bridge met the escarpment.

A man came after a while with a little device. He took our picture.

It's going well, he said, smiling broadly. I expect you'll be at the front by noon.

Noon tomorrow? said my father. Will you still be counting time?

Got some spirit in you, eh? said the man, continuing on.

I looked back. The line now stretched behind us as far as I could see. All of a sudden I could see their faces. Where before I could not, now I could see all of their faces.

Old faces, peering down at me, as if out of an archive of photographs. Everything was yellowing. Everything was brown and faded. What am I looking at? I wondered.

Have you thought about it, said my father. About being frozen too? Have you thought about it? We could go into it together. We could go on together.

LYDIA DAVIS
Unhappy Christmas Tree

An old woman believes that her Christmas tree wants to get married.

Her caretaker says:

—No, it's just a tree. See? Come here! Feel it!

The old woman feels a branch.

—Oh, you're right, it is a tree.

But the old woman is still worried.

—But inside…inside, there is a woman who wants to come out and get married.

The old woman will not be convinced she is wrong. She sits for an hour staring at the tree.

After an hour, the caretaker says:

—Come on, don't worry. It's only a tree.

—But it's so sad, it's so sad for her…With those little things all over her…Are they little men?

—No, don't worry, they're not little men. Those are your ornaments. You've had them for years. Every year, we take them out and hang them on the tree.

—But they're hurting her! They're pinching her! She just wants to come out and get married.

ALEX EPSTEIN
6 Micro Stories

Translated from the Hebrew by Yardenne Greenspan

Harmony

Dreams may be the soul's Autocorrect, but one man dreamt he was sitting in a fridge, freezing and waiting for someone to open the door. Before his savior's identity was revealed, he woke up in complete darkness and was surprised to find it was only 3 a.m. He got up and hurried to the kitchen and took all the groceries off the shelves and out of the drawers of the fridge and squeezed inside and shut the door. When his wife woke up in the morning and left the bedroom, she was horrified to see the entire contents of the fridge strewn on the floor and opened the door. His teeth chattered when he tried to smile at her.

Soviet Psychoanalysis

Our entire life is an improvisation, but giving up, God knows why, is an abomination. And indeed, in the 1930s, in a town that was no longer called Saint Petersburg, if only to test the efficiency of the Soviet postal system, just like the renowned composer Dmitri Shostakovich, my great-grandfather sent himself letters. Most of them arrived. My great-grandmother, who was convinced her husband was hiding all kinds of things from her, stole the others and kept them as incriminating evidence for the time, if and when, they became divorced by force of nature (she always slept with a dagger under her pillow for fear of her childhood's imaginary Cossacks, but that's another story). And so, thanks to her healthy suspicions, the letters eventually reached me: a random reading convinced me that, indeed, my great-grandfather was a little unbalanced. Not to say, a poet. In one letter he asked himself, Why is your soul such a wreck? In another he answered, Because you put a tie around your neck. From a third letter, I copied—God knows why—the opening sentence to this short story.

On the Art of Composing Suicide Notes in the Age of the Social Networks and on the Woman with the Most Beautiful Handwriting in the World

In a study conducted recently at Colorado Springs University—an edifice that seemed to me like a small Medieval fort, the snow-capped ridge of the Rocky Mountains providing it with the exact measure of drama throughout most of the year—it was found that approximately 20 percent of those warning via social networks of their suicidal intentions announce: "For my next illusion I will use wings." But not really. Meanwhile, the woman with the most beautiful handwriting in the world wasted away her talent on crossword puzzles, grocery lists, Christmas cards, etc. I've never met a happier person.

In the General Direction of Mythology

In April 1938—this is a true story that we lost in the passing of years—the authorities at Graz University asked the following question of Erwin Rudolf Josef Alexander Schrödinger: "Do you support National Socialism?" The physicist wrote two short and contradictory responses. And for the avoidance of all doubt, he immediately burned both.

A Wintry Tale

A man helped his old mother change her diaper. He tried to laugh about it. "We've switched places, Mom," he said. She tried to laugh about it too. "Blessed are you Lord who has granted us life, sustained us, and enabled us to reach this occasion," she said. Outside, it began to rain. The rain grew strong. "What a flood," she said. "Just like old times," he said. Suddenly, it was easy to forget.

Absence

The time traveler attended his son's funeral only once.

KEVIN A. GONZÁLEZ
Palau

I met my wife in Palau.

Here's how you find Palau on a map: Look for San Juan, then look for the farthest point from it.

It was a dive trip my father had promised when I started college. By the time I had my BA, we hadn't spoken for nearly ten months. Still, I sent him a letter with the details of the trip. No response, but still, I convinced myself he would come: I'd get off the cab, and he'd be nursing a drink at the lobby bar. I'd be on the boat, and he'd climb aboard, mesh bag in tow, praying not to be paired with a buddy.

But no. To paraphrase from my youth: Wherever I turned, he was not.

That last year at BC, I'd taken to watching football with my thesis adviser, Father Rosen, at Coover's. Always, I kept disguised my depravity and he kept his God in his pocket. But during the season finale, he picked up on something. The Eagles were getting blown out by Miami, it had started to snow, and I drank too much.

"What's eating at you?" he asked me.

Here's what it was: I couldn't wait to cleanse myself of the city of Boston. Whenever I walked past Grant Park, the hogs inside me squealed. Boston, that phlegm green city of Boston. You undo the world's zipper, and there it is: Boston. One second you're cruising down Boylston, and the next you're on your knees in a station stall, being repugnant, worshipping at the altar of Boston.

Here's what I said: "I don't know. I don't feel great."

"What you need to do," Rosen said, "is find something that makes you feel great, and then do that."

My doctor concurred.

I'd become a divemaster before leaving for college. Every summer, I'd returned to San Juan to work on a boat. We'd cram fifteen divers around the walk-around cabin, our tanks light on air, our go-to reef tame as a petting zoo.

But Palau was hardcore. I'm talking reef sharks by the dozen, whitetips grazing my wetsuit, anemones redder than boxing gloves. I sucked down tank after tank like the addict I am. At night, I wrote long, intricate notes in my dive log. I didn't drink, didn't fiend, barely even touched the TV.

Then, on my last day of diving, one of the divemasters was medevaced with the Bends. He was this blond Cali duder with Moorish Idols tattooed on his shoulder. Dove two hundred feet to a wreck, then ran low on air. They stuck him in the decompression chamber in Guam, his joints all tangled like pretzels.

He survived, but I got his job. I flashed my PADI C-cards and my dive log, and the resort hired me on the spot, set me up with the duder's old studio.

I worked the boat with Andy and Swiever, two Palauans who barely spoke English. Andy captained, and Swiever led every dive. During intervals, I did the briefings and switched all the tanks; underwater, I lagged behind, keeping track of our divers. On shore, I rinsed the gear and refilled the tanks while Andy and Swiever chewed betel nuts. Their teeth were stained black; when they opened their mouths, it looked like an oil spill.

After three months, I'd dropped fifteen pounds. My biceps shaped up; my skin tanned darker than it ever had in San Juan. We led three dives a day, and if we got a full moon, we tacked on a night dive. In the late afternoons, Swiever and I would take out the boat and spear jackfish and snapper. He'd bring a pouch with soy sauce and lime, and we'd eat sashimi leaning up on the gunwale.

There came from the diving a touch of narcosis, a wavering dizziness, an ebb and flow like a tango. One day, the air in my tank would be sweet as a pastry, and the next, it'd be stale as a bank vault. I grew lightheaded and faint; always, it was as though I'd just woken up from a blackout. And then I'd look up and there'd be a devil ray like a stealth jet, my bubbles caressing its wings. Who wouldn't find comfort under such royal shadows? At night, I shut my eyes and my head swayed like the tide. The sleep I got! Not a night passes I don't long for that darkness.

Two days a week, I taught the resort course. I mostly got honeymooners, the occasional diver's wife who'd grown tired of tanning. Then, one day, Becca walks into the dive shop. The class is only the two of us: The two of us in the pool, the two of us on the beach, the two of us in the classroom in the back of the dive shop.

She was finishing a tour with the Peace Corps. Two years in Palau and she'd never bitten down on a snorkel.

"Two years? What's wrong with you?" I said, and she laughed. She was a painter, she told me. What little free time she had, she spent on her art.

She'd grown up in Northampton, but when I mentioned BC, she wrinkled her nose. "Boston College?" She deepened her voice. "For real, bro? What frat were you in, bro?"

"Please," I said. "My best friend was a priest. Literally. A Jesuit priest."

"Well, shit," she said. "That's kind of disturbing." She went underwater. We were in the shallow end of the pool. When she came up for air, she said, "So you mean to tell me I had to come to Palau to meet a Catholic fratboy?"

"Wait," I said. "Wait, wait. And *you're* telling *me* I had to come to Palau to meet a Jewish girl from Northampton?"

Here her face went all tense. "I'm not Jewish, you asshole." She went underwater, offended. I was fashioning an apology when she came back to the surface. "Fine!" she said, and threw up her hands. "I'm a Jew! I'm a Jew! I'm a big fucking Jew!"

The next day, on the boat, she spoke to the guys in Palauan. They were laughing and gesturing, and in the middle of everything, she turned to me in amazement. "Holy shit," she said slowly, each word like a sentence.

I stopped opening air valves. "What is it? What happened?"

She widened her eyes. "I just realized I spent two years learning the world's most useless language."

What talent she had! She could catch me off guard and push from both sides and still keep me upright. Uncertain, I said, "Come on. It's not that bad."

"Hector." Now she was feigning annoyance. "More people speak Elvish than fucking Palauan."

She turned to Swiever and said something foreign. She glanced at me as she said it, and I knew I was being spoken of well. There was in her voice a tinge of flirtation, and then, from Swiever, that sly conspiratorial look that men give one another in these situations—half adulation, half spite. Even before I did, he knew she was mine.

That afternoon, I took her out on the boat and speared us a snapper. The next night, she cooked penne alla vodka, and the following day, I woke up beside her.

She had three weeks left on the island, and so we threw ourselves in without hope or suspense. How unfortunate, then, how we enjoyed one another, how cruel each day. Off I went every morning to breathe underwater. What could make a man more mindful of death? A tank is strapped to your back, your waist bound with weights. The air so cool through the hose, and then you look up, and there goes your breath. And later, at night, you turn off the lights and toss and toss in her bed. And all you want is to rise while she sleeps and coat the face of every clock with elastic, and to rouse her awake and trampoline hand in hand, from clock to clock, to the other side of the world.

I can pinpoint the moment, the particular syllable, when I lost myself to this girl. We had ten days left. For the first time, we dressed up for a date. We made reservations, took a cab to Koror, but we were running late. Before leaving, we'd had drinks at her place. The restaurant gave up our table and turned us away. Looking for food, we passed a bar, the type of bar where people go to die violent deaths. Through the door, a pool table showed its green felt.

I stopped. "Let's get a drink," I said.

"I'm starving," she said.

"Just one. There's a pool table in there."

I was having a blast. It was I who'd kept pouring us drinks, making us late. We'd missed our meal, but I preferred it this way. I wanted to drift with her through those streets, stopping for drinks, until the sun stuck its thumbs in our eyes. I wanted to wander all night, looking for a better bar than the last, more sour drinks, bluer neon lights.

Or rather, what I really wanted was to lead her in circles as my father had done to me all my life. One more for the road, one more for the road, one more for the road, God bless you, good night.

We stepped into the bar and she ordered two cans of Red Rooster. Everyone stared. I walked to the pool table and fed it some quarters.

Then two men stepped up. I was racking when one of them picked up the cue ball and spoke in Palauan, all nasal vowels and attitude.

"They're saying the table is theirs," Becca said. "But we can play doubles."

"That's fine." I shrugged at the men. They said something else.

"They want to play for ten dollars."

"All right," I said, "but I break." I touched myself on the chest.

They agreed, then turned away. When they returned, each held a long leather case. They unzipped them and pulled out their pool cues. They screwed them in, chalked the tips, rubbed talc on their hands as if they were seasoning meat. Becca didn't seem fazed, but what could I say? I wished we'd never set foot in that place.

I sank a stripe on the break, made two easy balls, and then missed a bank shot.

The first man came up, and I'll give him this: his shot had finesse. There were sweat stains on his shirt and red scrapes on his arm, and when he bent down to shoot, his T-shirt rode up and his ass crack poked out, but he worked that cue like an archer. He made four straight, then trapped the white ball in a corner.

When he missed, he pulled out a cigarette and broke off the filter. Then he took out a blade, sliced through the paper, and stuffed the tobacco in his mouth.

"Your shot," I said, and gave Becca the house cue.

"All right," she said, but she didn't move.

I circled the table. "The twelve-ball looks good."

"Which one's the twelve-ball?" She seemed perplexed. Her eyes sucked me in like two little drains. "Wait," she said. "How do you play?"

I froze. By now, I should've known; I should've aced every test. Instead, I took her hand and started molding her fingers.

She shook me off. "Move it," she said, and then she went up and ran the whole table.

When she sank the eight, she turned to the men. I don't know what she said, but whatever it was, it was packed with explosives. It was a three-syllable word; the syllables went loud, louder, and loudest. What came from her mouth was a stairway with three steps that began at the top of the world.

ke-Ke-KE!

And by the third syllable, I was hers.

The men shook their heads. They wanted to play us again.

Becca laughed. She collected ten dollars, then said, "How about now you fucking take me to dinner?"

Of course, the Becca of Now is not the Becca of Then. The Becca of Now goes to sleep before ten and rises at dawn, her belly round and warm as a nest. She takes her tea to the basement; all morning, she paints. She teaches two art classes, gardens, runs, reads before bed, and makes a mess out of every expectation I once had of the world.

But I digress. We had ten days left. That fall, she was starting graduate school at the Art Institute of Chicago. "Chicago," I said later that night, after our date. We were in bed; we'd just had sex. "You know, I've been a Cubs fan since I could stand on first base."

"Then you should come with me," she said.

We'd been drinking all night. Her words had been careless, I thought, and so they wouldn't linger, I reached for her breast. "You come with me first," I said, and then started kissing.

A few days later, I was ready when it came up again. "You could come with me," she said, and I said, "There's something I need to tell you."

After I told her, she lowered her chin. "What does that mean?"

I looked away. "It means what it means. I'm addicted to sex."

"OK. But what does that *mean*?"

"It means," I said, "I'm not sure what it means. It means that for years I hated myself, and I was a terrible boyfriend, and I obsessed about sex, and I did things with anyone who would let me."

"*Things*?" she said.

There was a warmth in my head. "I'm in therapy now," I said. "I have a doctor, and I talk to her every week, and I'm doing better. I'm doing well."

She didn't say anything.

"It all goes back to my childhood," I said.

She exhaled. "Right. Isn't that always the case?"

"Look, I know that's simplistic," I said, "but I've never told anyone any of this shit." I reached for her hand. "I want to go with you. That's why I'm saying it."

She considered this for a second. "What does your therapist say?"

"She says if I love you, I need to put it all on the table. So there. I love you. It's all on the table."

She considered again. "I have to go," she said then, and let go of my hand, and got up and left.

The next day, I was at the dock before daybreak. I had been starved, then overfed, then starved again. Still, I dove, I walked to and from work, I didn't go beasting myself. While I shaved, I looked at my face: See what you've made? She's not coming back. Faith? Thanks, but no thanks. What sick dog of a God would have buried a spine inside the skin of your back? Four days like that.

Then, with two days to spare, Becca walks into the dive shop. She comes up to the counter. "I had an abortion," she tells me.

"I'm sorry," I say.

"That's why I left. He was my TA, and he was married, and he was an asshole. I was so stupid—"

I stopped her. "You don't need to tell me all this."

"Listen," she said. "Just listen to me."

Later, we joked that the only reason I came to Chicago was because she needed someone to carry her paintings. For years, she refused to play me at pool, and when we finally played at a dive bar in Lakeview, you could've taken her cue stick and replaced it with a torpedo, and still, she wouldn't have sunk any balls. It turned out Palau was a fluke. I kept shaking my head and saying, "How the hell did you do that?" and she said, "I was starving. And you were being a fool."

ELIANA HECHTER
Extremities

The dissector instructed us to identify the tympanic membrane, a thin connective tissue that carried vibrations into the inner ear. Daniel and his partner Julie were on the cadaver's left, and I was on the right. "Did you find it?" I asked them. I was lost, as usual, and disgusted. Each day after anatomy class, I would take a run before allowing myself to shower. I hated it, but it was a good motivator: I could look forward to the moment when I could stand under cold water, willing the oily scent of the body to wash away. Countless times I thought I'd chosen the wrong profession, but I could not bring myself to call my parents back home. I stared at the payphone in the hall each time I passed it, but I did not lift the receiver. I imagined them bragging to their friends at dinner. Some parents bought their babies mini footballs for their sons; mine had brought home a small foam model heart for me to clutch in my crib.

Julie looked up at me sympathetically. Daniel gripped the pinna with one hand and held his scalpel with the other.

"Did you find the malleus?" he asked. "It's attached."

I set my scalpel down and began to feel along the fleshy rim of the earlobe into the canal. Daniel sighed. He handed Julie the scalpel and ripped off his gloves in a fluid motion. "I'll be right back," he said. Anatomy was all about finding the right plane, just under the deep fascia, where the skin ended and the musculature began. I tried pulling back the skin over the temporal bone. I heard Daniel talking with the instructor over my shoulder.

"Dr. Fernandez?" he said. I tried to focus on cutting the tenuous threads that held the skin in place without damaging the muscle. "You've scheduled the midterm on Sukkot." Just like Daniel, I thought, to try and get special consideration. He didn't even keep kosher, I knew, even though he wore a yarmulke: I'd watched him order a cheeseburger at a food truck on Longwood Avenue a few days before. After I ordered, I met him at the ketchup counter and asked, "So you don't keep kosher?" He laughed and said, "And you're not vegetarian. What a world we live in." Although he was a small man, he exuded aggression and confidence. The confidence drew me. I'd wanted to be his dissection partner, had gravitated to this table, this cadaver, seeing Julie and Daniel together there on the far side, in need of a third.

The first day of lecture, Dr. Fernandez had asked Julie to come down to the stage so he could show us a visible jugular notch. "This weekend, I want you to go to a bar," he'd said, grinning and touching his mustache, "and find a pretty lady with a great jugular notch like this. Then I want you to say, 'I'm a medical student and I have a homework assignment. Will you help me?' Then what you do is you get her to sit down,"—he'd eased Julie into a chair and held her head back, exposing the thin muscles coursing down her neck—"And you pour a shot of tequila right in there, and you take your salt and your lime and then you suck it out." He paused to let us imagine a well of liquor in the small round space between her protruding clavicles, and then lifted her head again. "A round of applause for our volunteer," he said. Of course Daniel was the one who got her. That's just how he was.

"Are you ready to open up the temporal bone?" Daniel said. He was back with a mallet and a chisel and a pair of fresh gloves, pleased from his victory. Dr. Fernandez would allow him to take the midterm after the holiday. I took the tools from him, but I could not bring myself to hit the chisel hard enough, so Daniel took over, and expertly revealed the walls of the tympanic cavity, pearlescent in the glow of the lamps that hung over the table.

When I emerged from the changing room, Julie and Daniel were waiting for me. The hall, lined with rows of gray lockers, was empty but for the three of us.

"You didn't have to wait," I said.

"When was the last time you went out?" Daniel asked.

"I had a burrito a couple of days ago," I said. I usually ate in the dorm, and then retreated to my room, where I read and slept and tried, mostly unsuccessfully, to remember everything I'd been told during the day.

"Hans!" Julie said. "A burrito doesn't count. Come on, it's Friday."

"We were going to go out for dinner," she said. I could see her trying to wrest her fingers from Daniel's hand, but he held her tight. "Why don't you come with us?"

"I don't want to bother you," I said.

"Then don't," Daniel said. "Come on, you'll make Julie happy if you come. I think she's getting sick of me."

"I am not!" Julie said, poking him in the ribs. He smiled. "But I would be happy if you came."

"OK," I said. I regretted that I hadn't bothered to bring something other than my running clothes. We walked out of the lab and into the cool night.

"Daniel's got a car," Julie said, as we proceeded to the parking lot. There was a ticket under Daniel's windshield wiper, which he took out and threw in the backseat. I noticed there were several already there. "So how'd you get the name Hans? Isn't it German?" Julie asked.

"Also Sanskrit," I said.

There was a great deal of traffic. Daniel gripped the wheel and swore while Julie tried to keep up polite conversation. Where was I from? Bethesda. What did my parents do? My father was a lab technician, and my mother stayed home. They had moved to the States a few years before I was born, while my father was getting a degree. Did I go to that special science high school? Yes.

I learned that she was from Palo Alto, that both of her parents were academics. Her father was a famous enough economist that I'd actually heard of him, but she hadn't seen him since she was twelve; her parents were divorced. She'd been to college in Boston and then spent a year in South Africa teaching in a township school. Teaching what? I asked. "Math," she said. "It was wild. Every afternoon, a group of Buddhists would come to the school with enormous woks and cook delicious meals for all the students. But there was no running water. Occasionally, while I was teaching, a big Cadillac would drive through the township, blasting music, and all the kids would leave the classroom and run after it."

I didn't ask about Daniel. I'd heard he'd been some sort of Special Forces in the Israeli military before returning to Worcester.

Miraculously, we found a parking spot a few blocks from the restaurant. I could see huge sweat stains in Daniel's polo shirt. He took Julie's hand again and we began walking down the sidewalk. Daniel took care, as he walked, to avoid even the lightest contact with the strangers on the street, and this caused him to engage in an awkward dance. I was reminded of the games I'd played as a child, avoiding cracks in the sidewalk, or only walking along the cracks.

The crowd dissipated after a block or two, and we found a quiet, half-empty restaurant where we could eat our spaghetti in peace. After Daniel drank a few glasses of water, he seemed to return to normal. We ordered. He sat back.

"So Hans. How are you finding it so far?"

"What do you mean?"

"Medical school? Anatomy? You name it."

"Fine, I guess. It's harder than I expected."

"Just fine?"

"It's terrible. I hate it." I couldn't believe I'd said it. Daniel and Julie looked at me and didn't move. Julie's hand hovered over her bread plate, holding a piece of garlic bread but not setting it down or moving it closer to her mouth.

"Everyone feels that way, Hans," he said after a few uncomfortable seconds passed. "At the beginning. It's rough. A lot of pressure. But it'll get better, you'll see. You just need to toughen up a bit. I was miserable until Julie." I watched as he ran a hand down her hair, and thought: all of two days you were miserable.

"I'm not miserable," Julie said. "It's a lot of memorizing. That's what I hate. I mean, how are we supposed to remember all of this stuff? But aside from that, I like it. I liked college. It's not all that different. Everyone seems really nice."

"I guess I'm too shy."

"You're just young," Daniel said. "How old are you anyway?"

"Twenty."

"Twenty? You went to college at, like, fifteen?"

"Something like that."

"Well, well," Daniel said. He turned to Julie. "Told you so."

"You guys had a bet about me?"

"I told her you were the kid from the papers, but she didn't believe me."

"So I guess we shouldn't be buying you wine," Julie said. But when it came, they poured me some anyway, and from that day on I became their project.

On Sukkot, I failed the midterm. The instructors brought me into the prosection room in the middle of the foot dissection and put it to me: unless I did extremely well on the final, I would have to retake the class. They sat in a semicircle around me, on the high wooden stools they rarely used, their white coats flecked with bits of preserved flesh. I felt tears brimming in my eyes, but I was determined to hold them back.

"We know you're a good student," Dr. Fernandez began. "You ask excellent questions in lecture."

"But you need to spend more time on understanding the structures and organization."

"Do you have a study partner?" Dr. Miller asked. She had the sweet demeanor of a beloved grandmother. "How do you go over things before class?"

"I usually just read the dissector and compare it to the atlas."

"Do you have an anatomy textbook?" Dr. Fernandez said. "Do you refer to that?"

"The anatomy textbooks aren't very well written," said Dr. Miller. "You would do better by trying to really understand. Where is the muscle insertion? What does that imply about its action? You can learn a lot just by using your head."

"How about Julie and Daniel? Do you study with them? It's good to study with others," Dr. Ash added. I didn't say that most of the studying I did with Julie and Daniel involved making up for the ribald college experiences I'd missed out on as an undergraduate under the supervision of my parents: climbing to the roof of the library to look out at the view of the park; getting drunk on a dock across town; driving north to swim in the freezing water early in the morning, when you could see both the sun and the moon at once.

"Not really," I said.

"We're always here for you if you have questions," Dr. Miller said. "Hans, we don't want you to leave this room discouraged. We just want to sound the warning bell before it's too late. You understand, right?"

Dr. Fernandez nodded and stood. He seemed uncomfortable, and turned to the cadaver to pat its soleus back into place.

When I returned to the dissection, Daniel turned to our cadaver's toe and said, "He should really have done a better job of cutting his nails, don't you think?"

"Nails grow after death, don't they?" Julie said.

"So what happened in there?" Daniel said. He set his scalpel down and took off his gloves. I put on my eye goggles and looked just past his shoulder so I wouldn't have to meet his eye.

"That bad?"

I nodded.

"OK," he said. Throughout the rest of the dissection, as we probed for nerves and vessels and palpated the many tiny bones of the foot, I could not shake the anger I felt building inside me. It was manifold: anger at my parents, for pushing too early too hard; anger at Daniel and Julie, for enticing me with friendship; anger at myself, for failing.

When I emerged from the shower, they were waiting for me again. I kicked my locker closed.

"Put your scrubs back on," Daniel said.

"But we finished."

"Just do it." I noticed neither of them had changed. They waited until I changed back. On went the scrubs, and the goggles, and the apron. Finally, we went back in the room, and Julie turned on the lights.

"Get a saw," Daniel said.

"Daniel," Julie said. She touched his shoulder lightly but he shook her off.

"Come on," Daniel said.

I didn't think to disagree with him. He opened the body bag and lifted the soiled white sheet to expose the cadaver's feet.

"Choose a toe."

"What are we going to tell them?"

"We're not," he said. Daniel and Julie stood back, and I began, tentative at first, and then, when I established a groove, nearly frantic. The bone was more fragile than I'd thought. A few swift strokes and the toe fell into the bag.

One night, toward the end of the course, I couldn't sleep and decided to go back to the anatomy lab. Although we had twenty-four-hour access, no one I knew really took advantage of it, even though the dorms were just across the street. After I climbed into my scrubs, which were by then rank with the stench of formaldehyde and had an oily sheen from the fat we'd scraped from the body, I began to regret the decision. But I wasn't going to stop. I found the light switch and walked into the room.

Since the midterm, we hadn't worked below the groin, and the legs were lightly wrapped in a soiled sheet. I wanted to see my toe again. When Dr. Miller had asked me to play violin at the memorial service held at the end of the semester for the cadavers, I'd nodded assent, but ever since then I'd had insomnia. I stopped drinking coffee and increased the length of my runs, but I still couldn't sleep. So here I was, back at the lab. Perhaps I would try to sew it back on, as I imagined they might do in surgery, holding the bones together with pins. I'd brought a household sewing kit for the purpose, which included a flesh-toned length of string.

I pulled back the sheet. But my toe was not the only one missing. I was sure I had amputated the left hallucis, but the right was also gone. Daniel, I thought. You sick, sick bastard. And then, before I could stop myself, I wandered over to the other bags. There were eleven cadavers: women and men from age twenty-four to eighty-nine, who had donated their bodies to our medical education. And all of their right big toes were gone. Not, like mine, lying in the bag. Not (I checked) in the tissue buckets, among flaps of skin and wads of discarded fascia. I closed the other bags and sewed my toe back with the pink-gray thread. Then, for a moment, I held what was left of our cadaver's hand. I stroked the tendons on the dorsal surface. Dr. Fernandez had said that these bodies were our first patients. "I'm so, so sorry," I said, and my voice echoed dully off the steel tables.

It was hard to find Julie alone. She and Daniel and I took all our classes together, and they spent most of their free time in each other's rooms. But I waited patiently, hoping that some sickness would befall him before our time was up, or that he'd be distracted by an obligation. Maybe he'd have to go home one weekend. Maybe he'd skip lab one day. The days passed. I was able to sleep again, and to concentrate. I turned down Julie and Daniel's offers of further expeditions, explaining that if I didn't ace the final, I was in deep shit, and they wandered off alone. Our last dissection approached. Daniel and Julie seemed closer than ever. I walked by her room but heard the sound of his voice and kept walking. I saw her sitting at breakfast alone, but then Daniel was just at the cereal counter, only a few steps behind. And then, before the opportunity arose, the course ended and they cremated the bodies. If anyone else noticed the toes, they didn't say so.

I played violin at the memorial service, as I said I would. Julie read a poem. It had been so long since I'd really played that I developed blisters on the fingers of my left hand.

Daniel and Julie got engaged in our third year. They had a party short-ly before we began our rotations. Over pizza and wine in their small apartment, our medical school class gathered and toasted them. Julie was wearing a particularly fetching plum dress. "Hans! You came!" she said when she saw me. "I have something I want to show you." She took my hand and led me into their bedroom.

We sat on their bed among piles of coats. I was struck by the fur-nishings—a heavy cherry dresser, the bed covered in a plush down comforter. It looked like my parents' bedroom. Old-fashioned, I guess, and not how I imagined two twenty-somethings would choose to decorate.

"How have you been?" she said. "It's crazy out there."

"You should get back," I said. "It is your engagement party, after all." I was feeling warm from the wine, and realized I might have sounded caustic. Which I was, I suppose. But I didn't want Julie to think I was mad at *her*.

"Hans," she said, and when I looked at her, I realized she was on the verge of tears.

"What's wrong?" I said. I put my hand on her shoulder, and she rolled back her sleeve to reveal a bruise in the shape of a thumbprint along the inside of her wrist.

"He just gets so frustrated sometimes. You know Daniel. You know how he is."

And then, there he was, in the doorframe of the bedroom, staring at us. I took my hand off her shoulder.

"You coming back, hun?" he said to her. "Our guests are beginning to inquire."

"Of course," she said. "Just give me a minute. Hans and I are just catching up." And he left, not giving me so much as a glance.

"I'm just overreacting," Julie said, rolling down her sleeve. "It's noth-ing, really. I shouldn't have said anything." She stood and gave a little warbling laugh, and then she went back to the party.

A few minutes later, I followed. I stood in their living room and listened to what our classmates had done over their last summer of freedom, while I'd worked in a lab on a project that had gone nowhere. Internships, fellowships, travel. When I knew I'd had too much wine,

I just kept going. "I can't believe you were there too. The mountains in Aspen—stunning! Did you hike Maroon Bells?" one asked another.

"Yes! When we got to the top there was this mountain goat. Biggest fucking balls I've ever seen." I laughed with them. When asked what I'd done, I claimed to be working on getting carpal tunnel syndrome from excessive pipetting. Only one girl laughed when I said this. I didn't recognize her. She was short and pale, with dark hair and a surprisingly deep voice. It turned out she was a first year, a distant cousin of Daniel's. I offered to walk her back to the dorm, where I was still living.

I remember being shocked, as we fucked, that she seemed aroused rather than repelled by my anger. Or maybe she didn't know that's what it was. "Did Fernandez do the jugular notch demonstration yet?" I asked her afterwards.

"I was the model," she said. And, in a Pavlovian way, I was ready again. Despite all this, or perhaps because of it, she became my girlfriend.

In fourth year, I found myself on the same ER rotation as Daniel. Although we saw each other all the time at the hospital, I would hesitate to say that we renewed our friendship. He didn't make overtures, and neither did I, but occasionally, we'd eat Jell-O together in the cafeteria in the middle of the night, or work together on a case. Things were better for me than they had been since the start of medical school. My girlfriend and I were talking about moving in together. We'd gone out on a double date with Julie and Daniel once, but it had ended badly, with Daniel yelling at the waitress for bringing him cannoli instead of tiramisu. So we didn't spend much time with them after that. Of course, our plans of moving in together all hinged on my getting a residency offer in town, but I wasn't overly worried. After anatomy, my grades had improved and I thought that things would be all right.

Our ER shift started at five in the afternoon, and I'd had the whole day to catch up on sleep and read. Daniel had offered me a ride, but I'd declined, claiming it was faster to take the bus. Sure enough, Daniel was ten minutes late, and our attending growled at him. We went over the cases in the small staff room. I was assigned to a man with an enormous back cyst, and Daniel was supposed to go check out a spina bifida patient who was complaining of a possible bladder infection. Our eyes met over the round plastic table. I was eating a handful of animal crackers, and I thought Daniel looked at me with disdain, but I wasn't sure. I remember the oddest things. My mother had sent me a new pair of shoes in the mail, and I was wearing them. I remember the familiar starchy feel of the scrubs. I even remember recalling something Daniel had said to me, once, when I'd asked him why he wanted to be a doctor: "I want a job where I can wear pajamas to work every day."

I had just begun reviewing my case at the computer when I heard the sound of sirens pulling into the hospital bay. Everyone stopped what they were doing to look at the stretcher; it was the medical equivalent of rubbernecking, and I fought the urge. I felt the attending pause behind me on his way to the patient. "Hans, you should see this. Because you'll probably never see anything like it again," he said. So I stood and followed him. He wasn't a man given to hyperbole. The ER was a day job for him; his true passion was race car driving.

I noticed a police officer following shortly behind the stretcher. At first there was so much blood I couldn't tell what was wrong. Two years on the wards had still not cured my intrinsic discomfort with the gore of the human body, and in the commotion, amid the gasps of onlookers and the patient's screams, it took me a few seconds to realize that the man's right ear was dangling from a patch of skin on the side of his face.

The rest of the story everyone knows. How the patient sat up on the stretcher as the nurses tried to hold him down, one outstretched finger pointing at Daniel. How Daniel stood staring in disbelief, perhaps wondering at his bad luck. How it had unfolded: the traffic jam due to a stalled city bus. How Daniel's road rage on his way to the hospital had inspired him to cut the man's ear off before returning to his car and driving away. How, after Daniel was arrested, Julie broke off the engagement. How Daniel threatened to kill her, prompting her to go into hiding. How Daniel sat in the courtroom, touching his balding pate, perhaps wishing for a yarmulke.

VLADISLAVA KOLOSOVA
Taxidermy

Afterward, Eva turns her face to the wall and falls asleep immediately, smacking her lips like a newborn. Her husband and I are left alone, wide awake and clueless about what to do with our naked bodies. He fondles his half-limp dick underneath the blanket. His arm is thrusting mechanically, without much enthusiasm or hope.

"It's OK, really," I say.

"You think I'm pathetic," he says.

"It's normal, I guess. We're tired. It's late."

Their bed is round, and ostentatiously big, but it's still too small for three people to not have any body contact. My butt is touching Eva's, and my back feels her even breaths. I hate her for being able to sleep. My left side is pins and needles, but if I turned over, I would touch both her and Husband with my shoulders. In the glow of the dying night his body is waxy and pale, like a sweating cheese. My thong is close enough to angle it with my foot, but I wonder if that would make everything even more awkward. Nobody is naked as long as everyone is.

It's hot, and the room seems to breathe slightly, as if we were inside a great belly. I listen to the cuckoo clock on the wall. They paid for the entire night. One hour and fifty-six minutes left.

"So, how long have you been married?"

"Six years," Husband says and turns his body toward mine. His head lies on my scattered hair now. It's a little like being chained, and I think *Keep your hands to yourself.* But he, too, seems relieved that Eva is asleep and the sex is over. From atop the dresser a stuffed cat is watching us with glass eyes. I could swear it smiles, in a way animals aren't supposed to.

"Where did you meet Eva?" I ask.

"Leninsky Boulevard," he says. "Where did *you* meet her?"

"Leninsky Boulevard."

I was about to finish my shift when a redhead with a Versace bag walked up and scanned me from head to toe: "You do girls?"

I nodded: "One hundred Greens an hour."

(Her bag seemed real, plus she joggled a set of Mercedes keys around her finger, so I figured I could charge more than usually.)

"You are a seventy, my dear. I know Leninsky prices."

I was so surprised by her precise estimation I forgot to get offended.

The idea blossomed in my mind for a second. It was an easy seventy. I was tired of all the doughy family fathers with girls' asses. Occasionally, I got picked up by girls with guys' asses, but had gotten sick of them too. In bed, they all felt like bicycles. The redhead wasn't chubby, but there was plenty of her. She had skin the hue of biscuit, with freckles sprinkled all over her face and full upper arms. She seemed to be five years older than I—twenty-six, twenty-seven.

"Twelve hundred for me and my husband," she said. "The entire night."

Twelve hundred bucks was seven days worth of work. Five hours in exchange for thirty-five. I could study in bed for the next two weekends. Finish my anthropology paper. Sleep through a night. It was finals week, and I was exhausted: exams during the day, Leninsky Boulevard at night. I followed the redhead to the car.

She drove a black "gelding"—a Mercedes 600. I guessed it before, but now I was sure: she was a wife of a New Russian. Briefly, I imagined what her life was like. Waking up without an alarm. Showering for as long as she wanted to. God, she could pee whenever she wanted, just sit on the toilet bowl and pee, without using the loo time to put on makeup or call her sister. Time wasn't money for her. Time didn't exist.

"You should have asked for fifteen hundred," she said counting out the bills. "I wouldn't have given you more than twelve hundred, but one should never seem hungry to accept an offer. You are new, huh? From Podmoskovye? Ural? Siberia?"

"Omsk."

"No shit? Which school?"

"Fourteenth public school. The bilingual strand."

"I was in the Twelfth! Do you know it, the rusty four-story house next to the bus station?"

Before I could answer, she hugged me. "I'm Eva," she said and slammed her high heels against the accelerator pedal.

"Did you write down my car number?" she asked.

I shook my head and smiled: "You seem OK."

She flipped her fingers against my forehead. "Don't be stupid," she said, not without warmth. "What if I'm taking you to an apartment full of army soldiers?"

The car flew through the deserted streets of 4 a.m.–Moscow, away from the city center. Old buildings turned into high-rises, then a forest, then villas with fences higher than the villas themselves. Rublevka—the millionaire-ghetto. Geldings, Boomers, Jags parking in front of spick-and-span mansions. Here, not a trace of the Soviet Union could be seen, even though it collapsed only five years ago. No spalling paint to complain about. No overused faces proudly wearing their exhaustion, like Hero of Labor medals. New Russians were brand-new people with brand-new houses in a brand-new quarter of the town, with brand-new habits and brand-new wives. Some of them had gotten rich on oil, some on cat food, some on blood.

"Have you ever been to Paris?" I asked.

"U-hum", Eva says.

"And?"

"It was OK. Clean streets, old people with very white teeth. Very civilized. I liked the cheese. We have an apartment there."

"Will you move there? Later?"

"Why? It's boring. And when we'll be old, it will be OK here too. We will be the first generation of happy grandmothers in Russia. Like we were the first generation of rich girls."

In front of a villa with two marble bears at the entrance, Eva stood on the brakes and honked. When the security guard opened the gate, she let the car roll in, still honking. A man in a silky orange bathrobe appeared at the mansion door. "Wednesday, Eva, it's Wednesday. A weeknight," he said, rubbing his eyes. "Morning," he mumbled in my direction and disappeared in the house again.

"Andrei!" Eva called and tottered after him as fast as her high heels allowed.

I stayed at the entrance to look at the house more closely. It had four stories plus three medieval turrets, a porch supported by Greek columns and a roof of wooden lace like those from fairy tales about Ivan Tsarevich. I have never been inside a Rublevka mansion. People who live there usually didn't bother with girls from Leninsky Boulevard: not exotic, not expensive enough. But I guess even the rich like their McDonald's from time to time.

Inside, a stuffed lynx stood on its hind legs, holding the Russian flag.

I followed the music somewhere from inside the house, the furry white carpet drowning the sound of my heels. A stuffed Labrador. A stuffed gazelle. Eva and Husband were in one of the living rooms on the first floor, arguing. I stayed in the hall, pretending to admire the minimalist art in ornate, gilded frames. A giant slab of marble leaned on the wall. Engraved on it, Husband was standing with his legs apart, wearing a suit and looking all business. He wore a heavy gold chain instead of a tie, and a massive watch. Both were worked in gold. Whoever made it even took the effort to engrave "Rolex" in tiny, tiny letters. In the background: the black gelding and Eva in a short, tight dress. The thing must have weighed half a ton.

"Do you want a drink?" Eva beckoned me into the living room. The arguing quieted down.

"Nice art," I said.

"It's a tombstone", she said. "In Andrei's business, one never knows."

My mind made a connection. Those marble slabs started to appear at graveyards a couple of years ago. They were multiple times as tall as any tombstone before, with engraved life-size men, often armed. Long golden epitaphs, short lifespans.

Eva poured me a drink. I drank it. She poured me another one. I drank it as well. She turned the soapy Russian pop louder. Husband sipped on a cup of coffee. His cleanly shaven scalp and flat boxer's nose made his head seem very round. He was so muscular and broad-shouldered that he looked like a sign for a men's toilet: a circle atop an inverted triangle. Between the lapels of his bathrobe, a woolly carpet of gray was showing. He must have been in his forties or fifties. He hadn't looked at me once.

When Husband opened a little plastic bag with white powder, Eva dashed to him and blew inside it. The powder rose up in a little cloud and sedated on the glass table. "Eva," he said tiredly. She giggled, kissed him, pressed her wet lips onto the powder and danced through the room like a dervish, cheering. She swirled through the room, then sat down on my lap, clutching my waist with both of her legs, and dropped her upper body. Her cinnamon hair touched the floor and moved like sea anemones. When she came back up, laughing, her golden eyes looked animally. No thought. Only hunger and instinct. She pushed me back into the couch pillows, bent over, and pressed her white mouth on mine. Her lips were full and whippy and bitter.

The three of us went to the bedroom.

I couldn't really imagine how people coordinated twelve limbs and three genitals. I had started in the business only two weeks ago. But it was twelve hundred bucks.

I don't like my job, but I like that I can do it.

When I moved to Moscow for college, I was selling bubble gum and canned gin and tonic. The kiosk was so tiny there wasn't even space for a chair—one had to stand up for the entire twelve hours. Its walls were made of tin. In summer, one felt like a baked fish in foil. Last winter, I almost lost my ear to a cold burn.

The prettiest girl in my Human Origins class had said, Why stand on your feet all day for slave wages when you can earn money lying on your back?

One traded sex anyway, always. For a man, for a man with a car, for flowers, admiration, a white gown.

I preferred dollars.

It was easier than I thought. Educative, even. After the night in Eva's bed I was three things wiser than before.

One: It's basically like twister, only nobody tells you where to put your arms and legs—and when you decide to put them *somewhere,* the spot is already occupied.

Two: Watching naked people making out in front of you is like seeing Mount Elbrus for the first time. It doesn't even seem real at first.

Three: It's better to close your eyes anyway. When I am drunk, genitals make me giggle because they are so absurdly beautiful.

Or just absurd. Like flaccid penises. Husband's dick had the consistency of a half-filled water balloon. If I squeezed it, it became kind of hard; if I didn't, it just flopped from side to side.

With Eva, it wasn't bad, but it wasn't sex either. The powder on her lips made me grow fur on the inside of my veins and turned the whole thing into something too fluffy and warm to actually have an arc and an end. We probably would still be doing it if Eva hadn't groaned and come or maybe half-come. Or maybe she was just tired and turned her head to the wall, pretending to sleep.

Since then, I've looked at the watch hand dissecting the hour, thinking: Another minute. Poof. Gone. And I should be happy because it means

I'm closer to getting out of here. But it's so scary it makes my chest tighten. When a minute is gone—it's *gone*. Makes me crazy if I think of it too much. But the closer I watch time, the faster it spins. All clocks seem like stopwatches now.

I try to think of other things. Think of my bed. Think of an omelet. Think of how to get home.

"What are you thinking?" Husband asks.

"Nothing," I say. "Sorry for waking you up."

"I'm used to it."

"Why don't you tell Eva you prefer to sleep?"

"Have you ever had a dog?"

"My parents did. A terrier. His name was Rambo. Why?"

In the light of morning, behind Husband's left ear, I see a patch of silver hair he had forgotten to shave. His face looks lifeless, like an electronic device pulled out of the socket.

"Mine was a Labrador. Musya," he says. "Anyway, if you had a dog, you probably know this scenario: You wake up, and in front of your bed is a half-shredded bloody bird corpse. And a proud mutt looking into your eyes for approval."

"Thanks."

"I didn't mean...I'm sorry. I mean. You're beautiful. It's just...I get tired. I used to be a professional boxer. Master of sports. I need my rhythm. Regular sleeping patterns. I didn't even drink before all this," he says with a sweeping motion spanning the entire room.

"How old are you?" I ask.

"Guess."

I think fifty-two, so I say forty-three.

He looks offended. "No, forty-one."

"Oh," I say.

"Not knowing what your wife is doing is worse than not liking it."

Eva turns on her back and snorts like a wood saw. I bet she was one of those people with good sleep and digestion. Who never wonder what they are. Who never doubt if they *are* at all. Eva knows she is, because she doesn't know that she doesn't know whether she is or not.

I look around the room. This round bed, covered with white satin, like a monstrous wedding cake. The cuckoo clock. An aquarium with exotic fish—a piece of nature transplanted into the urban home, framed, domesticated. The smiling stuffed cat on the dresser.

"Did you know that when you taxidermy a small animal, you have to pull the brain through its ear?" Husband says, catching my gaze.

"Taxi-what?"

"This cat—his name is Grisha. He died when I was sixteen. He was the first pet I stuffed."

"Did you do the other animals in the house as well?"

"It was my hobby, before Eva and I got married. But she says the faintest whiff of formaldehyde makes her vomit."

"Why taxidermy?"

"I don't know. Maybe I feel like I beat death in a small way."

"What was the last animal you stuffed?"

"I don't have the time anymore, with the house, and the business, and the casinos at night."

"The casinos are a rip-off. I know a guy who works there. He says the rules are set so crassly in favor of the house it's almost impossible to win."

"Do you think it's about winning?"

I shrug my shoulders.

"It's about losing the most," he says with tired eyes. "The prostitutes, the houses…If you don't throw your money to the wind, nobody takes you seriously as a business partner."

"What business are you in?"

"Import-export."

"Of what?"

He smiles again, almost paternally. "You're not from Moscow, are you?"

"Why did you marry Eva?"

"She was the most alive person I knew. And I the most alone."

"But why did you *marry* her?"

"Men need wives."

"Not rich men. You can buy someone who cooks your food and keeps your house clean. You could buy the entire Leninsky Boulevard, if you wanted to. You have the money."

"But who will spend my money?"

I do not have an answer.

"Can I hug you?" he asks suddenly.

I wrap myself into his arms and bury my face in the wool on his chest. The clock seems to tick louder and louder. One second passes, then another, soon it will be a minute, then an hour, then twenty-four, today will be yesterday, and years will be gone, and everything will be gone, including me.

Husband strokes my back. And I find it snug and disgusting at the same time, and want it to stop, but it's as if I am somewhere outside of time, in a place where I don't have limbs that move when I order them to. I lie face down and laugh silently until his chest hair is wet and I feel as if I am lying face down in moss.

"I'm sorry," I finally say. "I am not crying. Please, please say something other than, Are you OK? OK?"

"I have a son," he says. "Last time I heard from his mother, they were in Uzbekistan."

Grisha watches from the dresser and I look in his eyes, thinking: For you the time really did stop.

But he just stares back, because he is a stuffed cat and not a metaphor.

I turn my head to Eva. In her sleep, her smile resembles the cat's, her upper lip curling upward, exposing her teeth.

Husband strokes my hair, and when he presses me tighter to his body, I realize he has a boner.

"Listen, our neighbor to the right is looking for a wife," he says stroking my hair. "He's almost impotent—should be easy. Maybe I can arrange something. Write down your number, OK?"

"I'll go get a pen," I say, and miraculously my feet obey.

Switched into vertical from the horizontal, I realize how the room smells of sex and morning breath. The morning behind the window is bleary and matte, as if it has a hangover too. From here, I can hear the horns of elektrichkas—electric commuter trains, taking pensioners to their dachas.

In the hallway, I pick up the orange bathrobe that Husband lost on the way to the bedroom three hours earlier. It's more expensive than the clothes I left in their bedroom anyway. I take my bag, recount the money and slip into my shoes. I walk past the stuffed gazelle, past the stuffed Labrador, past the tombstone, down the hallway and silently close the front door behind me.

Dad's Just a Number

Hello! I am 5 feet 11 inches and have a medium build. I have dark brown hair and blue eyes. My skin color is pale. My mother's ethnic origin is Belgian, my father's ethnic origin is Polish and French. My racial color code as established by the Chicago Bank of Life is white. I am a full-time student and barista, and on the weekends, I volunteer in the cardiac care wing of a local hospital to tenderize my guilt before gorging on it whole.

Hello. I am 5 feet 11 inches and have a medium build. I have dark brown hair and blue eyes, lagoon blue, which people have remarked on with some incredulity. My skin color is white. My mom's parents live in Oslo, though they've basically retired to their second home on the banks of the Aurlandsfjord. My dad's parents are dead, but we don't talk about that much. I am studying physics at a small graduate school because the implacable laws of the universe are of interest to me. My parents give me money, though I tell them not to. We are five kids in the family—me and four girls—and while I'm not the eldest, that doesn't mean I cannot provide for myself. Especially since the eldest, Janine, is on medication that costs $1,000 a month, except watch what happens if she misses a dose.

I make rent at a café down the block. Whatever my folks give me, I put in a jar with the grand idea of giving it back, though I am equally tempted to donate the money to the hospital where I work. Transcatheter aortic valve replacement; renal denervation; left ventricular assist devices—these innovations can be experienced at facilities nationwide. At my hospital, you'd be lucky to get an EKG. The last time we saved a patient was two years ago, and that's just because she had acid reflux, which can masquerade as a heart attack. She was twenty-three and manning a local fish-and-chips truck, which paid her in fish and chips. Now she eats salads and tofu, which I credit to my influence, me being a vegan and also her boyfriend, though if you ask Violet, I haven't been boyfriend enough for several months. She is unstoppably carnal; I am easily turned off. When I am donating to the Chicago Bank of Life, I do not think of her.

*

Hello. I am 5 feet 11. My build is average, though by this I just mean I'm not winning the World's Strongest anytime soon. My hair is brown, my eyes are blue. My mom likes to say it's a miracle my eyes are blue because I am the first to have them in the family. But when I tease her and say maybe I'm adopted, it's as if all the travesties being executed worldwide find a showing on her face. She'll say, "Don't let your father hear you say that kind of thing," and, like that, there's the war in Syria coalesced in the cleft between her eyes. My mother used to be a human rights activist. Growing up, I thought jail was where everyone went at the end of the day. As the story goes, she met my father in jail, though he was there for something else. Something stupid, like riding his bike on the sidewalk and resisting arrest when told to stop.

My father does not like the police. He does not like people in uniform. Sometimes I'm not sure if he even likes me. He is stern and dour and weirdly tyrannical given that he mistrusts authority, though my mom says he means well. His name used to be Moishe, which sounds fine when you're in Poland but ridiculous in New Haven, where he was brought as a boy by Jewish philanthropists in '45. Problem was, they didn't have time to raise a boy who spoke no English, so they pawned him off to some other family that also didn't have the time, so that my dad, at age thirteen, ended up in an orphanage. When he got out, he changed his name to Mike, moved to New York, and landed a job at the zoo, which he kept for most of my childhood. Nights he'd come home bleached in the humiliation of his day and be so tired he'd fall into his chair and say, "Lila, you married a shit shoveler," before serving himself a ladle of stew.

I never spoke much at those dinners, though I don't think anyone noticed. I was always spindly and short for my age—unimpressive, Janine used to say—and easily overlooked in the presence of my sisters and my older brother, Ben, whose charisma obliterated whatever affect I might have been trying to cultivate for myself. Ben died about ten years ago in a lake by our house, jumping off a tire swing that'd been there since before any of us was born. He never came up out of the water. Turned out he had a heart condition no one knew about. We were eight years apart, so I was always able to worship him openly and without shame. Janine, though—they were twins, something that runs in the family—she took his death hard. She fell into a hole and the doctors said she was bipolar, and my mom, who had no patience for luxury problems like mental illness when half the world was starving, delegated the problem to my dad, who delegated it right back. Mental illness made no sense to him either.

My father dealt better with Ben's death because it sustained theories he'd had about the world ever since he was a child—that it was glib and sinful, which was, to him, a terrible combination. If I've thought about challenging him on this topic, I've also understood the futility of trying to counter an ethos bedrocked in grief, lest I end up challenging that grief by accident. Hence, physics: a discipline in which caprice and cruelty have no standing simply for being human qualities. *People* are cruel. The universe feels nothing.

Sometimes Violet says my orthodoxies are every bit as austere as my father's. That I need to be more flexible. She might say this while we're sharing a Coke float at the fifties throwback diner near her place. She'd say, If I were your dad and been tortured with my twin at Auschwitz, I'd definitely want to petition the universe for answers and accountability. Because, she'd say, if the universe is indifferent to our suffering, then tragedy can never amount to more than the sorrow that proceeds from it. We have these talks, which sometimes mitigate the distance I feel between myself and other people, though it doesn't last. After, I pay our bill and then we go back to her place to watch movies. Or get drunk and have sex, which is when I am most likely to yearn for more than what has been afforded me in the ways and means of love.

Hello. The main thing is: I am tall enough to handle myself at some distance from my computer camera and still conceal my identity. Mostly I've been using an online roulette service, which makes it an equal opportunity experience, though I do have predilections that have begun to assert themselves, though *begun* is, of course, inaccurate. When I was thirteen, my lab partner was James Kirkpatrick, who dyed his hair black and straightened it with an iron every morning. He'd come to school with it parted in the middle and fanned out down the length of his back, looking like Ian Astbury, lead singer of The Cult, who modeled a life for James that seemed ideal, if unattainable. Acne came early to James, which made his hair an asset the rest of us would covet years later, but which at the time seemed prognostic of suicidal ideation, which it was. James overdosed on morphine prescribed for his terminally ill grandfather. He didn't have many friends, but we all showed up at his funeral. And that night, after having the same dream I'd been having for months, I awoke to a wetness in my pajamas and an understanding that the raven-haired seducer who'd been featured in this dream had always been James.

After, there was Peter and Alex, Teddy and Neil, though my feelings for them were circumscribed by notions of decorum and rectitude. Even in my dreams, at most we ended up on a beach talking Algebra I. And then not talking at all, because my brother's death awakened me to obligations that would have never passed on to me had he lived. So I went out with Christina and Deirdre and Caroline Moon. But I'm sure my indifference showed as badly as if I'd had dirt under my nails.

Violet has been my only serious girlfriend, owing to the timing of her stagger into the hospital just days after my father had a mini-stroke that thrust his mortality into the foreground of all our thoughts, especially his. Still, it's the seriousness and duration of our relationship that's driven me to seek other sources of gratification. Some nights, I've brought her to my parents' place for dinner and then gone home to have video congress with a Guatemalan prostitute named Modesto. Sometimes I've made the mistake of trying to talk to him, but he doesn't speak English. Sometimes I cannot climax for feeling so lonely. But I keep coming back because here is the answer to at least some of the questions I have had about myself, though it would be nice if answers were also solutions.

Hello, I am 5 feet 11 inches, though Violet recently informed me that I am 5 feet 10 inches, which, she said, makes perfect sense, since I keep lying about everything else. We were at her apartment. She'd gotten a hold of these recordings and been appalled by what she's decided is my attempt to defraud people who want children. My donor profile is a fake, is what she said, and then she left the room. In other words, we've had another fight. Though *fighting* presumes two people at odds with each other, when, in fact, I have no defense against her accusations. I *am* unattentive. I am distracted. And while I'm not exactly a liar, I am also not serving up for display or consumption parts of my inner life that recoil even from me.

"Oh, come on," I said, and went after her. "What's an inch? Kids always outgrow their parents anyway. 5 feet 11 inches is just a better sell!"

She snorted and reached for her jacket.

"Don't leave, Vi. I'll change it, OK? It's just, I need to look good to these people."

She laughed. One thing I've always liked about Violet is her laugh. It is rich and throaty and tender, whether she's being scornful or not. She said, "Right, by being a big old liar."

"Can you stop saying that?"

We ended up sitting on the floor with our backs to her stove, which we'd turned on for heat. I was supposed to have confronted her landlord about this weeks ago. But when I tried, he talked me into having a beer instead, and by the time it was 4 a.m. and I hadn't so much as mentioned Violet's name, even I had to concede my priorities were askew.

After a while, I said, "I'm not a liar. I've never lied about anything." I went on to say I had no secrets. And that I'd even been up front with her about sperm donation, which I could imagine a lesser guy being cagey about.

"Wow," she said. "Good for you."

"Vi. Come on." I took her hand. She wore multiple rings on multiple fingers, but the one that counted was bare. I told her I loved her, and this was true.

She began to unbutton my shirt and kiss my neck. I did not pull away, but I didn't encourage her either.

"Exactly," she said. And then she asked me to leave. And to return her key.

Hello. I am 5 feet 10 but didn't have my growth spurt until tenth grade. *Shorty, Shrimpy, Half-Pint, Girl.* Know what it's like when Sam Shalako and his crew pin you down and ink GIRL into your forehead right before a schoolwide assembly convened to celebrate, among others, yours truly for excellence in poetry writing? It was a permanent marker, so I had to get up there and accept my prize with hand pressed to my forehead like a Southern belle, which only grew my roster of epithets by one. I was *Belle* for the rest of the year.

It didn't help that whenever I got cut up horsing around with Ben, everyone seemed appalled, like here were skid marks across the face of Venus. After a while, it got so Ben wouldn't come near me unless I pleaded with him, which often meant crying, which never helped my case much. The day we went to the lake, I'd decided on a different tactic. I said I was going and he could come or not, what did I care, knowing full well he couldn't let me go alone, the tire swing being old and unreliable and me rather Belle-ish in terms of the fortitude it might take to survive a broken tire swing. So we went. Of course, Ben didn't even want to swim or use the tire, but I goaded him on. Called him a sissy, which was like calling the sun black, even though it felt great. I hammed up the good time I was having in the water, and tried to push that tire to the max. How high could I go? Something about putting my brother down while sailing through the air exalted my self-worth to include notions of infallibility and certainties of greatness, which I remember because that was the last time I felt either.

Soon, my brother was in the water with me. It seems now that I heard the splash before I saw him on the tire, though this cannot be the case. I swam for where he'd landed, and when he didn't come up for air, I waited. And when he still didn't come up, I imagined him breathing through a reed with head submerged, so I skirted the banks. And then I went back out, though by then it seemed he could be anywhere. I was sixteen. Past puberty. Past at least some of the growing pains and big questions that confront us as we transition from adolescence to adulthood. Are people good? Am *I* good? I had ideas about who I wanted to be in the world, and though they were vague, they still were not built to sustain the profundity of what was happening to me right then in a lake just two miles from my home, where my father was living his last moments under the impression of being a man who had survived the Holocaust and bred a firstborn son.

Panic came as an adrenaline rush that outfitted me with skills I didn't otherwise have, like swimming under water with my eyes open or swimming several feet below the surface. But it didn't matter. The lake was dark and dense and finally inhospitable to anyone who'd come to profile her secret life. After fifteen minutes, I went back to shore and sat on the bank with head hung between my legs. I watched beads of water roll down my calves and puddle at my feet. I studied the pruned effect of so much time in the lake on my fingers. I might have been in shock, though it's possible I was just being pragmatic about what was in store for me. My brother had drowned. Running home screaming would not change that. And maybe I wanted just one more chance to be borne up by the conviction that this wasn't my fault.

Hello again. I am—well, let's look at it this way: My father has no pictures of his parents or any real memories of them from which to draw new ones, but it's safe to presume their features were ranged within ours, or at least his, and that any child of mine can inherit the same: a longish face, as if in the putty phase of development, someone pulled my chin a little too hard, and a narrow mouth as a result. Violet says I look like Alan Ruck in *Ferris Bueller's Day Off,* and I guess that's right. My father does not talk about Auschwitz, but he does talk about extending our bloodline, which amounts to the same thing. In the years since Ben died, I've caught him appraising me like a farmer might his stock. Before Violet, these appraisals were often followed by whispered exchanges with my mother in the kitchen and one of them asking me if everything was OK at school.

Violet's been over for dinner many times. My dad likes to ensure he's there for these occasions. More than once, he's asked about her plans and if she'd like to have children and how many and is she Jewish because with a name like Violet, you never know.

Per my dad's wishes, I took Violet to Norway last summer, where we spent a weekend with my mom's parents who are taxed with problems that had them mistaking Violet for Janine and me for Ben until the whole thing bespoke the virtue of a retirement home and the horror of Alzheimer's Disease. Genetically speaking, the good news is that they both got it late in life. The bad news is self-evident. I have thought about testing myself for APOE e4 but then figured I probably don't want to know. My dad, in any case, seems to be doing fine, though he is frequently depressed under the guise of fatigue, lest he, too, have to concede feelings he cannot control.

My dad's number is A-7064. Once, for the holidays, my mom bought him laser treatment, thinking he'd want that tattoo removed now that there was a way to do it. But in the end, the treatment went to Janine, who was more than happy to blot out a Mt. Rushmore-type homage to the Nixon administration she'd gotten on her shoulder to spoof the integrity of our politics, though no one read it that way, and Janine had to stop wearing tank tops. I visited her last week. She's in an assisted-living facility because while the meds keep her stable, she still can't keep a job. I bought her babka, which she loves, and pictures from Dad's birthday, because she hadn't been up to going. Since Ben died, our relationship has evolved into a source of relief for us both, she trampling me with blame and me heaving underfoot. In general, though, discretion tends to characterize our arrangement. But sometimes not. I hadn't been in her room more than five minutes before she asked why Ben wasn't in any of the photos.

I relaxed into an armchair she'd gotten off the street and reupholstered in neckties. "Because, J., I made him come to the lake and he died."

"Everyone knows that," she said, and rolled her eyes.

It's true that being mentally ill has not reformed Janine's cant toward drollery, but I don't always remember this when it counts.

"Then what do you mean?" I said. "I don't understand."

"Me either. That's just what I'm saying. Why wasn't Ben there? Why wasn't I there? Can you explain any of that?"

Now it was my turn to roll my eyes. "Why am I me and you you? Oh, please, J., let's not have this conversation again."

Sometimes it felt as if we'd been having this conversation all our lives.

"You're gross," she said. "Your whole attitude. How can you stand to think we live in a morally indifferent universe? That everything's just chance?"

Janine looked middle-aged, though she was only thirty-four. Her hair was short gray curls cauliflowered about her head. Her neck was already pleated with skin because she'd lost a lot of weight, and about her eyes were the telltale crimps of time gone by, like hash marks on the prison walls of your life. So being queried by her on this stuff was like watching an old man who'd missed the boat on wisdom flounder in its wake.

I told her I had somewhere to be. But that, yeah, I was comfortable with my opinions and that I didn't want to live in a cosmos accountable to logic of my devising. Which was just as well, because it wasn't. Character is fate? I don't think so. But then she laughed, though I'm not sure why, and said the kind of thing that sounds right just for having been put into words, something about how dogma is always forged in dread of its being untrue.

"How's Dad?" she said. "He have fun?"

"He's not talking to me," I said.

"Why?"

"I gotta go," I said. "Places to be, people to see."

Hello. My dad is swarthy and squat, which is why, in the photos from his birthday, I look like a beanpole in contrast. I clear him by about four inches now, though I don't think I've been growing. Even so, I never seem to exist for him until Violet shows up. She and I were on the outs, it's true, but I had begged her to come because her absence would ruin his birthday. He'd get ideas about our relationship being over and even though it was almost over, my plan was never to let him know.

On the phone, it went like this: "Vi, there's a lot of pressure on me. Just do this one thing, OK?"

"Why? Just say it. If you say it out loud, I'll do it."

I heard the faucet turn on and the toilet flush, which should give you a sense of how discrepant were our investments in this conversation's outcome.

"Because my dad loves you, that's why."

She hung up before I could say anything else, so I was surprised when she showed up anyway, with cupcakes that said *Happy Birthday, Moishe,* which seemed like a bold move, but which dislodged something in my dad so that he patted her cheek and raised his glass to make a toast, even though we were gathered there to toast him. He is seventy and has taken to using a cane. I think he's done this to appear distinguished, though when he held up his champagne flute, I had to accept the cane's rollback on his chances of falling down in that distinguished moment. He still has all his hair, which he slicks back with water. He was wearing a pinstripe gray suit that was too big for him and black Velcro sneakers. He asked for quiet and then said wonderful things about my mom. And my sisters. About family and lineage and something confused about a kind of flower he used to see through the gates at Auschwitz, though he didn't say the place by name, just that he'd been a boy when this beautiful flower caught his eye and that he'd derived courage from knowing its species was immortal, if not the flower itself.

My dad and I have never been close. He'd lavished a good deal of his energy on Ben, and when he died, I suspect my dad's grief closed shop on whatever feelings he'd had left for the rest of us. But guilt has a way of making you absolve everyone who does you wrong, and anyway, it was impossible to resent a man who'd survived as he had done. And so, despite the subtext of his speech albatrossed around my neck, I was touched. At least until looking at my mom, who had the Holocaust and its burden troughed into her face, and then tracking that look as it landed on my dad, who was talking to Violet.

"What's this?" he said, and took me by the sleeve. "You two are breaking up?"

I shook my head immediately and looked at Violet with what I hoped would pass for shock in the moment.

"We're just not...compatible," Violet said.

"Compatible?" my dad said. "What's compatible?" He was looking at me now, but I'd had enough. I ushered Violet out of there and said, "Who do you think you're helping?"

"You," she said, and walked out.

I tried to tell my dad we were just having a fight, but that it'd be fine. That I was even going to propose. And when that failed, I tried to tell him there were plenty of other women out there. But he just slumped into the nearest chair and tapped his heart. "I'm old," he said, and seemed to age twenty years just for saying it.

Hello. I am 5 feet 10 and of medium build, but cannot hold my liquor. After the party, I went to a bar and got drunk and met someone named Wyatt. Forgive me if my timeline seems compressed or hasty, but I don't want to pretend to remember more than I do, or that my experience with this man was distended for being the first of its kind or racked on the magic that makes the turning points in our lives feel any bigger than the moments right before or after. I met Wyatt and two minutes later, he asked me to join him in the bathroom. I didn't think stuff like that actually happened, but apparently it does. He was from the South. He was unshaven and wore a plaid shirt. He wasn't pretty. But he still knew his reach. I followed him through the bathroom door, which he locked behind us. And then instinct took over. How did I know to drop my pants and brace my hands on the urinal? I'm not sure how long he had at me, but that it was long enough to agonize into consciousness the knowledge that I had made a choice that would cast my father, irretrievably, into an indifference about his life that was like snapping an astronaut from his tether.

Wyatt left me as I was, bleeding, panting, and wondering how to contrive seeing him again. But I have not seen him again, even though I've spent nearly every hour in that bar since.

Hello. I am donor number 13115. I am 5 feet 10 inches, with a medium build, brown hair, and blue eyes. My skin color is egg. My parents are from Europe. The Chicago Bank of Life says I am white. I am a student, but also work at a café and a hospital. I hope my sperm is motile and copious. I hope many families will profit from my contribution to their lives. I hope to bear at least ten children, ten being a minyan, which isn't so important to me in terms of my Jewish identity, but which will matter to my father when he sees that I am committed to furthering our genetic line even as I cannot do it the way he would have liked. I know you all have hundreds of options. I have seen the competition and realize it's fierce. And even though I have mental illness in my family and a touch of Alzheimer's, I'd ask that you not hold this against me. Janine's problems are circumstantial. And she's still smarter than most people I know. Sometimes, when I've been hoping to see Wyatt and levying self-disgust against notions that I was just "born this way," I've even thought that Janine is right: that the universe does redress our crimes. That because Ben is dead, I have grown into a man who cannot keep us alive.

Which is why I need you. Because if the universe is cruel, *people* are good. People survive their fate. People keep each other going. And so I'm asking you to do the same for me. Donor number 13115. In the name of kindness and all those other humane qualities that are abundant among us, I ask you to save me.

REBECCA MAKKAI
The Miracle Years of Little Fork

In the fourth week of drought, at the third and final performance of the Roundabout Traveling Circus, the elephant keeled over dead. Instead of stepping on the tasseled stool, she gave a thick, descending trumpet, lowered one knee, and fell sideways. The girl in the white spangled leotard screamed and backed away. The trainer dropped his stick and dashed forward with a sound to match the elephant's. The show could not continue.

The young Reverend Hewlett was the first to stand, the first to signal toward the exits. As if he'd just sung the benediction, parents ushered their children out into the park. The Reverend stayed behind, thinking he'd be more useful here, in the thick of the panic and despair, than out at the duck pond with the dispersing families.

The trainer lifted his head from the elephant's haunch to stare at the Reverend. He said, "Your town has no water. That's why this happened."

The elephant was a small one, an Asiatic one, but still the largest animal the Reverend had ever seen this close. Her skin seemed to move, and her leg, but the Reverend had watched enough deaths to know these were the shudders of a soulless body. The clowns and acrobats and musicians had circled around, but only Reverend Hewlett and the trainer were near enough to touch the leathery epidermis, the short, sharp hairs—which the Reverend did now, steadying one thin hand long enough to run it down the knobs of the creature's spine.

The Reverend said, "There's no water in the whole state." He wondered at his own defensiveness, until he saw the trainer's blue eyes, accusatory slits. He said, "I'm not in charge of the weather."

The trainer nodded and returned his cheek to the elephant's deflated leg. "But aren't you in charge of the praying?"

At home in the small study, surrounded by the books the previous Reverend had left behind two years prior, Hewlett began writing out the sermon. *Here we are,* he planned to say, *praying every week for the drought to end. And yet who among us brought an umbrella today?* He would let them absorb the silence. He'd say, *Who wore a raincoat?*

But no, that was too sharp, too much. He began again.

*

The Roundabout was meant to move on to Shearerville, but now there was the matter of elephant disposal. The trainer refused to leave town till she'd been buried, which was immaterial, since the rings and tent couldn't be properly disassembled around the elephant—and even if they could, their removal would leave her exposed to the scorching sun, the birds, the coyotes and raccoons. The obvious solution was to dig a hole, a very large hole, quickly. A farmer offered his lettuce field, barren anyway. But the ground was baked hard by a month of ceaseless sun, horses couldn't pull the diggers without water, and although the men made a start with pickaxes and shovels, they calculated that at the rate they were digging, it would take five full weeks to get an elephant-size grave. These were the men who weren't away at war, the lame or too-old, the too-young or asthmatic.

The elephant was six days dead. Reverend Hewlett called a meeting in the sanctuary after Sunday services, which a few of the circus folk had attended—the bearded lady, the illustrated man, the trainer himself—and now more filed in, joining the congregation. A group of dwarfs who might have been a family, some lithe women who looked like acrobats. Reverend Hewlett removed his robe and stood at the pulpit to address the crowd. He was only thirty years old, still in love with the girl he'd left in Chicago, still anxious to toss a ball on Saturdays with whoever was willing.

He looked at them, his flock. Mayor Blunt sat in the second row—the farthest forward anyone sat, except, once a year, those taking first Communion—with his wife on one side, his daughter, Stella, on the other. The mayor had decided that the burial of the dead was more a religious matter than a governmental one, and had asked Reverend Hewlett to work things out.

The Reverend said, "I've been charged with funeral arrangements for the elephant. For—I understand her name was Belle. We ask today for ideas and able hands. And we extend our warmest welcome to the members of the Roundabout." In the days since the disaster, his parishioners had already opened their homes, providing food and beds. (The circus trailers were too hot, too waterless, too close to the dead elephant. And the people of Little Fork had big hearts.) The performers, in turn, had started helping in the gas station and the library and the dried-out gardens, even doing tricks for the children on the brown grass of the park. They were drinking a fair amount of alcohol, was the rumor by way of the ladies at the general store, more in this past week than the whole town of Little Fork consumed in a month.

Adolph Pitt, of Pitt's Funeral Home, stood. "I called on my fellow at the crematorium, and he says it's nothing doing. Not even piecemeal, even if the beast were—forgive me—even if it were dismembered."

"*She*," the elephant trainer said from the back. "Not *it*." The trainer still carried with him, at all times, the thin stick he'd used to guide the elephant, nudging it under her trunk, gently turning her head in the right direction. No one had yet seen him without it. Reverend Hewlett imagined he slept with it under his arm. The man slept alone in his scorching trailer, having refused all offers for a couch and plumbing. Hewlett was an expert now in grief—they hadn't told him, at seminary, the ways his life would be soaked in grief—and it wasn't the first time he'd seen a man cling to an object. Usually, he could talk to the bereaved about heaven, about the warm breast of God, about the promise of reunion. But what could he say about an elephant? The Lord loveth the beasts of the field? His eye is on the sparrow? Surely the burial would help.

Reverend Hewlett saw it as his duty to raise an unpopular option the men had been mulling over the past few days. The mayor couldn't bring it up, because he had an election to win in the fall. But Reverend Hewlett was not elected. And so he said it: "The swimming pool was never filled this summer. It's sitting empty."

Some of the men and women nodded, and a few of the children, catching his meaning, made sharp little noises and looked at their parents. The circus folks didn't much respond.

"It's an old pool," the Reverend said, "and we can't dig a hole this summer. We can dig a hole *next* summer, and that can be the new pool. This one's too small, I've heard everyone say since the day I got here."

"There's no dirt to bury him with!" Mrs. Pipsky called.

"Maybe a tarp," someone said.

"Or cement. Pour cement in there."

"Cement's half water."

The mayor stood. "This town needs that pool," he said. The youngest Garrett boy clapped. "We'll find another solution."

And before the meeting could devolve into argument, Reverend Hewlett offered up a prayer for the elephant (the Lord loveth the beasts of the field), and a prayer that a solution could be found. He invited everyone to the narthex, where the women of the Welcoming Committee had laid out a sheet cake.

The Reverend made a point of greeting each visitor in turn, asking how they were enjoying their stay in Little Fork. "Not much," the illustrated man said.

The Reverend thought, with awe, how God had a plan for everyone. Some of these people were deformed—a man with ears like saucers, a boy with lobster-claw hands—and yet God had led them to the circus, to the place where they could find friendship and money and even love. And now He had led these people to Hewlett's flock, and there must be a purpose for this too.

In the corner, the fire eater chatted with the mayor's daughter. Stella Blunt was sixteen and lovely, hair in brown waves, and he was not much older, with a small, dark beard that Hewlett figured was a liability for a fire eater. Stella leaned toward him, fascinated.

The following Sunday, most of them returned. They sang along with the hymns and closed their eyes to pray, and one of them put poker chips in the communion plate. The fire eater sat in the rear next to Stella. They looked down at something below the pew back, giggling, passing whatever it was back and forth.

Over the past week, the smell of the elephant had crept from the tent and over the center of town. It was a strangely sweet smell, at least at first, more like rotting strawberries than rotting meat. Reverend Hewlett had planned a sermon on the beatitudes, but when the time came for prayer requests, Larry Beedleman asked everyone to pray for enough food to last his guests (all five trapeze artists were living in the Beedlemans' attic), and Mrs. Thoms asked them to pray for the Lord to take away the stench of the elephant. Gwendolyn Lake wanted them all to beg forgiveness for the sins that had brought this trial upon them. So Reverend Hewlett preached instead about patience and forbearance.

After the service, he caught Mayor Blunt's arm. He said, "Isn't it time we used the pool?"

Blunt was a large man who tucked his chin into his neck when he spoke. He said, "I'll lose the vote of every child's mother."

"Have you seen," Hewlett said slowly, "the way your daughter looks at that boy?"

"We've taken him into our home," the mayor said. As if that were definitive and precluded the possibility of teenage love.

"Joe," the Reverend said. "You'll lose more votes to scandal than to a hole in the ground."

And so on Tuesday fifty men and women dragged the elephant to the town pool on waxed tarps and lowered her until she rolled in with a thud and a sudden release of the smell they'd all been gagging against to begin with. They covered her with cartloads of hay—everyone had a lot of hay that summer whether they wanted it or not—and they covered the hay with the gravel Tom Garrett had donated, and they covered that all with fresh tarps, held down by bricks.

Reverend Hewlett gave the funeral service right there, with the locals and circus folk in a ring around the pool. The elephant trainer sobbed into his small, calloused hands. He did not have the stick with him, for once.

Afterward, when the other circus workers went to take apart the tent, to fold up the benches and load things into their trailers, the elephant trainer stayed behind. He put his hand on Reverend Hewlett's arm, then drew it back. And, as if it choked him, he said, "I can't leave her here."

"Will you pray with me?"

"I'm saying I don't think I can leave this town."

"My son, I won't let anything happen to the grave."

"I'm saying that my parents were drifters, and I'm a drifter, and I've never had a part of myself in the soil of a place before. And now I do, and I think I ought to stay here for the rest of my life."

Hewlett marveled at the ways he'd misread this man. Perhaps it hadn't been grief he'd seen in the man's face, but thirst.

He said, "Then it must be God's will."

The tarp stayed put through the dry fall and the dry winter, and the smell subsided.

Before Christmas, Stella Blunt came to Reverend Hewlett for help. The fire eater was long gone, but her stomach had begun swelling and she was panicked.

The Reverend arranged, to her parents' naive delight, for Stella to spend the spring semester doing work at the VA hospital downstate. Only she didn't really go there; he set her up in the vestry with a bed and a little library. She wrote her parents postcards, which Reverend Hewlett would mail in an envelope to Reverend Adams down in Landry, just so Adams could drop them in the postbox and send them back to Little Fork.

Hewlett visited her three times a day, and Sheila Pipsky, who used to be a nurse and could keep a secret like a statue, stopped by twice a week. The Reverend would sit on the floor while Stella sat on the bed, legs folded. If he had time, he ate with her. They spoke French together, so she wouldn't grow rusty. When the church was locked up for the night, he'd turn out the lights and let her know she was safe—and she'd walk around and around the pews, up to the little choir loft, down the hall to the Sunday school classrooms. As she grew bigger, less steady on her feet, he'd hold her arm so she wouldn't trip in the dark. If he closed his eyes—which he let himself do only for a second at a time—he could believe he was walking down a Chicago street with Annette, the breeze on their chests, her hair in a clip.

"It's funny," Stella said to him once. They were standing in the nursery, the rocking horses and dollhouse lit with moonlight. "I thought I loved him. But if I loved him, I'd remember him better. Wouldn't I?"

Hewlett had the utterly inappropriate urge to touch Stella's cheek, the top of her white ear. He slowed his breath.

Stella giggled.

"What is it?" he said.

"Your shoes. They're untied, like a little kid's."

In May, the doctor came in the middle of the night and delivered a healthy baby girl, and Reverend Hewlett called the Millers, who had come to him praying for a child that fall, and they were given the baby and told she came from Shearerville. They named her Eloise. Hewlett had looked away when Stella said good-bye to the baby. He muttered a prayer, but it was a pretense—he couldn't absorb her pain just then. He chose, instead, to think of the Millers. He chose to thank the Lord. Stella stayed two more weeks in the vestry, and then she went home. Hewlett continued his nighttime circuits of the church, though. They'd become habit.

The elephant trainer worked on one of the farms, tending the cows and horses, until he decided to open a restaurant in the space left empty when Herman Burns had gone to war. He used to cook for the circus folk, after all, and he missed it. He served sandwiches and soup and meatloaf. Soon they were calling him by his name, Stanley Tack, and by June he had fallen in love with the Beedleman girl, and she with him.

It made Reverend Hewlett think, briefly, of writing home to Chicago, to Annette. He worried she was waiting for him, the way her girlfriends were waiting for their boys to return, battle-scarred and strong and ready to settle down. But the war abroad would eventually end; Hewlett's war never would. And Annette would not join him on this particular battlefield. She'd made that clear. She would stay in Chicago, in her brownstone, and type for a firm, until he came to his senses and moved home to teach history. That she never doubted this would happen broke his heart doubly: once for himself, and once for her. She hadn't written in three months. And he did not write to her. To do so would be to punch a hole in his own armor.

As soon as summer hit, there was torrential rain—as if all the town's prayers from the previous year got to heaven at once, far too late. The bridge flooded out, and Stanley Tack's restaurant flooded, and nearly everyone you passed, if you asked how things were, would respond, "I'm building an ark!"

There were drowned sheep and missing fences at one farm, where the river now came to the barn door. An oak toppled in the park, roots exposed, like a loosened weed. Stella Blunt, lining up with the choir and looking through the stained glass, said, "It's like someone's trying to tear apart the world."

They sang "our shelter from the stormy blast" as thunder shook the roof. They sang "There Shall be Showers of Blessings," and some of them laughed.

Stanley Tack had come every Sunday that whole year, but always sat quizzical and silent through the prayers, the hymns. He never carried the stick anymore. He was always alone; the Beedleman girl worked the Sunday shift at the hospital. He never put anything in the offertory and he never took Communion. Reverend Hewlett started to see this as a personal challenge: Someday, he would give the sermon that would bring Stanley to his feet, that would open his blue eyes to the light shining through above the altar, that would make him pause on his way out of church and say, "Do you have a minute to talk?"

They planned, as soon as the rain let up, to pour cement into the old pool and dig the hole for the new one. But the rain never let up. On the fortieth day of rain, folks stopped Reverend Hewlett at the pharmacy and the gas pump to joke: "Tomorrow we're due our rainbow, right? Tomorrow we get our dove?" At least no one much minded not having a pool that summer.

The Millers brought little Eloise to church, and she was baptized as Stella Blunt looked on from the choir. Reverend Hewlett poured water on the baby's head and marveled at her angry little eyes. The daughter of a fire eater, born into a land of water.

Despite the tarp, the pool had filled around the elephant and the hay and the gravel, and if you walked by and peered through the chain-link fence, you'd see how the tarp was now sort of floating on top, how the whole pool deck was covered in an inch of water that connected with the water in the pool. The children dared each other to reach through the fence and touch the dirty elephant juice. Mrs. Thoms wondered aloud if the elephant water would go through the pool drains and into the town supply.

One day, Reverend Hewlett braved the rain to visit Stanley Tack's restaurant. After the downstairs had flooded, Stanley had taken over the vacant apartment upstairs, cooking out of its small kitchen and serving food in what used to be the living room. On an average Saturday, you'd find three or four families huddled around the tables, eating soup and listening to the rain hit the windows, but today the Reverend was the only one in the place. It seemed people were leaving their houses less. The spokes of their umbrellas were broken, and their rain boots were moldy, and they realized there wasn't much they truly needed from out in the world. A lot of sweaters were knit that summer, a lot of books read.

The Reverend sat, and when Stanley brought his cheese sandwich and potato soup, he sat across from him. He said, "I believe this is my fault."

The only "this" anyone in town was talking about was the rain.

Reverend Hewlett said, "My child. This weather is the will of God."

"You preached—you gave a sermon, right after I chose to stay. And I couldn't help thinking it was intended for me. The story of Jonah trying to sail away from Nineveh. Of God sending the storm and the whale."

The Reverend tried his potato soup, and nodded at Stanley. The soup was good, as always. Never great, but always good. He said, "I was thinking of many things, but yes, one of them was you. The way the Lord sends us where we need to be, regardless of our plans. I was reflecting on my own life, as well. I ended up in Little Fork by chance, and in my first year, when I felt doubt, I'd think of Jonah in the belly of that fish. It was preaching, you know, that he was meant to do in Nineveh. That's what he was running from."

"Yes. But"—Stanley looked out the window, where the rain was slicing sideways—"what if this isn't my Nineveh? What if this is the place I've run away *to*, and all this, all the rain, is God trying to wash me out and send me on my way? Just as he sent that storm for Jonah."

This troubled the Reverend. He bought some time by biting into his sandwich, but then it troubled him even more. Stanley had reminded him of Annette, on the day he left Chicago, fixing him with dry eyes: "I don't see how you're so *sure*," she'd said. And he'd said, "There's no other way to be." And whether or not he was truly sure back then, he'd grown sure these past three years. Or at least he'd been too busy counseling others to foster his own concerns. He'd broken down in doubt a few times—not in God so much as in his plan—when he'd had to bury a child or when soldiers came home in boxes, but he'd always returned to a place of faith. Look at little Eloise, for instance, growing plump at the Millers' house. Exactly as it was meant to be. But somehow the elephant trainer's question had hit a sore spot in his own soul, a bruise he hadn't known was there.

He said, "All we can do is pray, and ask that God make clear the path."

"And how, exactly, would He make it clear?"

"If you listen, God will speak."

Most always, when he said something like this, his parishioners smiled, as if assured they'd hear the voice of God that very night. Sometimes he even had to clarify: "This is not the age of miracles, you realize. His voice won't boom from the clouds. You'll have to listen. You'll have to look." And they'd leave to await the message.

What Stanley said was, "God doesn't talk." It wasn't something Reverend Hewlett was used to hearing in this town. And then, all seriousness, he said, "I think I've broken the universe."

Reverend Hewlett looked at his own hands, the veins and creases. He imagined they might crack open like the parched earth had last summer.

Or at least, he felt a small crack somewhere inside, one that didn't hurt but was letting in a bit of air. All he could think to say was, "It's raining in the next town over too. And in the next town beyond that."

Reverend Hewlett's name was Jack. This was increasingly easy for him to forget. He'd become John, and then—in the bulletins and on the sign outside the church—Rev. J. Hewlett, and since there was no one in Little Fork who didn't know him as the Reverend, since even the few Catholics who drove to services in Shearerville greeted him as "Rev" or sometimes, slipping, as "Father," he hadn't heard his own name in three years. Annette no longer wrote to him at all, no longer extended the tail of the J down like the first letter of a chapter.

And why had he left her? And why had he come here? Because he was needed. Because his mentor at seminary had said, "God is calling you there. God is calling me to send you there."

And that man, with his great beard, his walls of books, his faith in the hand of God, could not have been wrong.

That night there was a dance at the Garden Club, on the east end of town. It was Little Fork's version of a debutante ball, the same youngsters debuting themselves each year, in the same white dresses, until they were too old for these things, or married. Only tonight they were soaked through. Reverend Hewlett stood against the wall watching—his mere presence, everyone agreed, was salubrious—and observed the boys in their sopping bowties, hair plastered to their heads, and the girls wrapped against their will in their mothers' shawls. No boy would see through a wet dress tonight. Heaps of galoshes and umbrellas by the door.

They coupled and uncoupled in patterns that seemed casual, chaotic, but of course were not. Every move, every flick of the eyes, was finely orchestrated. There were hearts being broken tonight. You just couldn't tell whose.

Gordon Pipsky sidled up and offered a sip from his flask. Gordon's son was out there dancing, a girl on each arm. When Hewlett accepted, Gordon winked and grinned. "I'll never tell," he said. Even though he saw the Reverend take the Eucharist every Sunday. Perhaps what he meant was, "I'll never tell that you're just a man like me."

Was it a secret, really? He'd never been anything else.

He had felt like an impostor when he first put on his robe—but then everyone felt like an impostor, he'd learned in seminary. And now, after all this time, he rarely considered himself a fraud. But nothing had changed, really. Except that he had grown used to that robe, that second skin, just as he'd grown used to God's silent ways.

There was Stella Blunt, dancing in white. A debutante still.

The next morning, the rain stopped. Not the kind of pause that makes you worry the sky is just gathering more water, but a true, clear stop, the air bright and clean and dry.

And then the wind started.

For the first few hours, it just shook the windows and door hinges and made people sneeze—all that new mold now flying through the air—but by nightfall, it was bringing down tree branches and shingles. By morning, it had knocked down phone lines and garden fences and was tearing at the awnings on Center Street.

And worse: By late afternoon, with most of the surface water gone (blown to Shearerville, everyone said), the tarp blew off the old pool. No one was outside to see that part, but a fair number were witness to it flying smack up against the library, five blocks south, before continuing on its way. It took folks a while to realize what it was—and by that point, there was gravel skittering down the streets nearest the pool. There was moldy hay in everyone's yard.

Gwendolyn Lake came banging on the parsonage door to tell Reverend Hewlett. His first thought was to run and see if the elephant was uncovered, but his second thought was of Stanley, who should be kept from the pool. Stanley, who would want to run there but would regret it later. Who might take it all as some sort of sign.

Hewlett told Gwendolyn to get her brothers. "Use sheets," he said, "and bricks." He himself ran in the opposite direction, toward Center Street. The wind wasn't constant but came in great lumps: Every three or four seconds, a pocket of air would hit him, would lift him from beneath. If he'd had an open umbrella, he'd have left the ground. Trees were down, garbage blew through the streets, the bench in front of the barbershop was overturned.

Sally Thoms ran crying down the other side of the road, blond hair sucked straight up like a sail. "My cat blew away!" she cried. "He was in a tree and he just blew away!"

"I'll pray for you!" the Reverend called, but the wind ate his words.

He pulled with his full weight on the door beside the one that read STANLEY'S DINER, the door that everyone knew led up to the real place. Stanley stood in the kitchen, peeling carrots. He said, "You're early for lunch, Rev."

For some reason—even later he couldn't figure out what had possessed him—the Reverend said, "I'd be happy if you called me Jack."

"Sure," Stanley said, and laughed. "Jack. You want to peel me some carrots, Jack?"

They stood side by side at the counter, working.

"What do you make of this apocalypse, Jack?"

He began to answer as he always did of late—something about God wanting to test us now and then, maybe something about Job—but instead he found himself telling a joke. "You hear about the man who couldn't see what the weather was like, because it was too foggy?"

"Ha!" He wasn't sure he'd ever heard Stanley laugh before. It was more a word than a laugh. Stanley said, "I know an old circus one. Why'd the sword swallower swallow an umbrella?"

"I—I don't know."

"Wanted to put something away for a rainy day."

It was a terrible joke, but Hewlett started laughing and couldn't stop—perhaps because he was picturing Stella Blunt's bearded fire eater, an umbrella blossoming in his throat, just as the baby had stretched Stella's figure. This wasn't funny either, but the laughter came anyway.

He went to the sink for a glass of water, to cure his laugh and the cough that followed it. As he drank, he looked out the back window, over the yards behind Fifth Street and the abutting yards behind Sixth Street. Down below, on the other side of the block-long stockade fence, the Miller family had ventured out into the yard with baby Eloise. In the time between gusts, they were examining the damage to the old well, the top of which had tumbled into a pile of stones. A summer of baking and a summer of rain must have loosened everything, and all it took was a day of wind to knock things about. There was Ed Miller, peering down the hole, and there was Alice Miller, holding the baby, when a blast of wind—up here Jack Hewlett could see and hear but not feel it—tore limbs from trees and tore shutters from houses and tore Eloise from her mother's arms and into the air and across the yard. He must have made a noise, because Stanley rushed to peer over his shoulder just in time to see the baby, her pink face and her white dress, go flying over the garden and over the next yard and finally into the Blunts' yard, where, just as she arced down, there he was, Mayor Blunt, running toward the child. He caught her in his arms.

Hewlett heard Stanley inhale sharply. Neither man moved.

The mayor had been outside alone—presumably inspecting the maple that had fallen across his yard, the one that, were it still standing, the baby would have blown straight into—but now his wife ran out, and his son, and Stella. The two men watched from above as Stella leaned over the baby, covering her own mouth. Her mother's hand was on her back, and Hewlett wondered if she was crying, and—if she was—how she'd explain it. Well, who wouldn't cry at a baby landing in their yard?

The wind took a break, and Mayor Blunt handed the baby to Stella and wrapped his coat around her front, covering them both. Hewlett imagined what the man would have said: something about "You know I can never hold a baby right." Or "This should be good practice for you!" And the mayor led a procession around the front of the house and down the street to the Millers'. Hewlett hadn't thought to look back to the Millers for a while—they weren't in their yard. Ed Miller had scaled the fence to the lawn between his and the Blunts' and was running through the bushes, around the trees, behind the shed. Alice Miller stood out front, hands to her head, shouting for help. She ran toward the Blunts when she saw them, but she couldn't have known what was under Stella's coat until the mayor pulled it back, chest puffed out, proud of his miracle. He handed the baby back himself. Alice Miller covered the infant with kisses and raced her into the house, Mayor and Mrs. Blunt following. Stella stayed out on the walk a minute, looking at the sky. What she was thinking, Hewlett couldn't even guess.

"Well," Stanley said. "Pardon the expression, but Jesus Christ." The carrot and peeler, still in his hands, were shaking.

Hewlett wanted to run down, to see if Stella was all right, to make sure the baby wasn't hurt. But he wasn't a doctor. And he couldn't leave Stanley alone, couldn't let him think of checking on the pool. So he just said, "I think we've seen the hand of God." He wasn't at all sure this was true. Part of him wondered if he hadn't seen a miracle at all but its precise and brutal opposite—a failure of some kind, or the evidence of chaos. Whatever he'd just seen, it troubled him deeply. Was God in the wind, blowing that baby back to Stella where she belonged? Or was God in the catch, in the impossible coincidence of the mayor being in the right spot, in the return of the child to the Millers? Or—and this was the thing about a crack in faith, he knew, the way one small fissure could spread and crumble the whole thing into a pile of rocks—was God in neither place?

Stanley put his carrot down and turned. His face was soft and astonished, blue eyes open wider than Hewlett had ever seen them. He looked like a man who'd just survived an auto crash, a man who'd taken part in something bizarre and terrifying, not just witnessed it from above. "It's not true, is it?" Stanley spoke slowly, working something out. "What I said before, about Nineveh. We're—we're all where we're supposed to be. I was supposed to wind up here." He braced himself on the counter, as if he expected God to blow him across town next. "A beast brought Jonah to Nineveh, and a beast brought me here."

Hewlett said what he'd said so many times before. "The thing is to be listening when God speaks."

By the time Reverend Hewlett walked home that night by way of the old pool, Davis Thoms and Bernie Lake were down there mixing batch after batch of cement and pouring it into the hole. For the first time in more than a year, there was both enough water to mix the stuff and not so much water falling from the sky that it would turn to soup.

He continued toward the parsonage. The wind was done. It had simply left town.

It was so strange to be outside without the roar of wind or rain, without the feel of air or water ripping at his skin, that Reverend Hewlett stood awhile on his own porch feeling that he was floating in the midst of vast and empty space. Everywhere he turned, there was nothing. No baking sun, no drenching storm, no raging wind. There were people coming out of houses, and people going into houses, and people walking from one store to the next. And people picking up branches, and people sweeping up glass. As if they'd been directed to do these things.

All this happened a very long time ago. And it's hard now to argue that what happened so far back *wasn't* inevitable. If the elephant hadn't died, there wouldn't be, on top of the old swimming pool, the playground that originally had some other name but quickly became known as Elephant Park; and the Little Fork High School football team would not be the Mammoths; and Stanley Tack wouldn't have stayed in town, and the son he had with the Beedleman girl (she was expecting already that day of the windstorm, she just hadn't told him yet) wouldn't have married Eloise Miller, and today the town of Little Fork wouldn't be half full of Tacks of various generations, all descended (though none of them know it) from a fire eater.

Jack Hewlett might not have given up the cloth and returned home to be with his girl, with Annette, who'd waited for him even after her letters stopped—only to be drafted two months later, no longer clergy, no longer exempt from war. He might not have died in France, a bullet through his lung. But who's to say that the outcome of that battle—even of the entire war—hadn't hinged, in one way or another, on the bravery of one man? He was, after all, an exceptional soldier. He took orders well.

Or at least it can be said: this world is the one made by the death of that elephant.

The Sunday following the storm, Reverend Hewlett looked out from the pulpit at his battered congregation. There were black eyes and broken arms from the wind, and the women with husbands stationed overseas were exhausted from cleaning up their own yards and their elderly neighbors' besides. It was a good town that way. These people believed in things. Eloise Miller, unhurt and pink, slept in her mother's arms through the service. A green bonnet framed her face.

Hewlett, under his robe, was thin. He'd lost five pounds that week. His stomach felt empty even when it was full, so why bother to fill it?

Stanley Tack held hands with the Beedleman girl. For the first time, he joined the hymns. He opened the book of prayer.

Stella Blunt looked pale and tired. Hewlett tried to catch her eye. He felt he owed her at least a look, one she'd be able to interpret later, the next morning, or whenever it was that the citizens of Little Fork would find the parsonage deserted.

If he owed anything to Stanley Tack, he'd already given it. Hadn't he handed the man his own faith? It was in safer hands now than his own.

He said, "Let us read from Paul's letter to the Romans: *Whom he did predestinate, them he also called: and whom he called, them he also justified: and whom he justified, them he also glorified.*"

He said, "Let us lift up our hearts."

ANDER MONSON
Some of Us Are Gone

None of us are gone.

You may call us gone. You may moan. You may dash from the places where you would sit and you thought we wouldn't find you. You mourn our loss, we know. You walk on the floorboards of the house as if you were alone, eyeing every corner. Your habits stay mostly the same. Mornings when you wake you turn and look for us. We used to be where you are. We don't know how to say it better. You thought of us only rarely, at night, in dreams when you got aroused, or when you felt we failed you. When we were not home when we said we'd be. When we didn't make it in until late. When we failed to return your calls. When you saw us out with someone else. When you passed a parked car that looked like ours and you thought what if it was us. When you believed we had a secret life. When you questioned us. When you were embarrassed about it, after.

When you moved in the darkness, not used to the empty bed and the lack of breath beside you. When you looked out the window after something had woken you and all that was there was the empty neighbor's house beside you and you stood, awake but not entirely, staring into the darkness, wondering whether you were the only one awake.

You were not.

When after minutes had passed and nothing changed that you could see in the world outside, you adjusted yourself and thought of us and got all melancholy as you do, because you are a sentimental being, and then you let the moment pass or so you thought, and then you could hear an animal singing—or maybe dying—somewhere in the distance, and then it wasn't an animal but a couple, a handful, a dozen. All of them, you thought, howled or moaned and it was as if they were singing out our names.

It is hard to forget us. We know this. Our names come across the radio waves in passing and you catch a riff from a song we used to love.

You know this, and you know that no one else knows this, and it is in the look in your eyes that we see you are still there and that you still think of us. A moment catches. Then another. Something pulls you. You don't know why you thought that thing, what brought back that trace of memory that almost had receded into the synapse wash.

If you are not careful those moments will add up. You could spend your life like this, we tell you while you're sleeping, our breath a haze along your face, as if you were a window and we were fogging you up and tracing messages on the glass. Some of us trace our fingers on your face, now or at other times when you're not wary.

We are here in the walls of the Victorian we helped you to refinish, that you were so proud of that you wrote our names on a thousand sheets of paper and stuffed them in a wall cavity for the future before you dry-walled it up. You never told us this. We didn't know it then.

We know it now as we know many things that were kept from us. The outlines of your pornography. The fact that you only like it sweet and innocent and never told us this, and we never understood until our time was past. That you wanted us in white, like now, like childhood, like nothing else. That you wanted us in mornings. That you wanted us with other girls but not really. That you wouldn't open yourself up that way. That you never told us the full details of your former loves.

Now we know them too. It broke our hearts at first. The revelations continued. And continued. The lies you'd told. The lives you'd switched out of and never wanted us to know about. The hundred thousand latent sadnesses and the selective revelations that, en masse, we guess, compose a life.

We know what you said. We remember what you said. With time our hearts have grown. They are stronger. They hold more without filling, without tiring.

We know the slip of silk across the skin, the ways in which we debased ourselves thinking that was what you wanted. We know how our leaving freed you. How it paralyzed you. How it broke you. How you

Ander Monson 87

bet everything in your life on us, and what that meant, and what else slipped away.

We don't, we can't know everything, of course. But we contain more than you could possibly contain. We connect to others and we share capacities. We remember everything, our last moments, how you seized up when you knew we were almost gone, that you would be alone, how your heart was filled almost to bursting in that moment and you still couldn't tell us everything.

What we can't know is what that loss is like. We can't know how you might get past it, if anyone gets past anything. To us the world is a million times a million minus signs. We wade through. We know subtraction, don't we, well. But we cannot accrue, even if we understand.

We were surprised at first.

When we came here and were new, we still believed in such a thing as now. We thought we could know everything there was to know about the world and our diminished place in it. What was this place and its relation to the old, how could we shadow you but never touch?

Well. We could touch, but touch is not the same as before. Our touch is more like trace, our fingers' memories of lace. We can push ourselves against, along the boundaries that separate thing from thing. We can get inside the house, into the slightest crack. We can press ourselves through cheesecloth, sieve, or wicker.

We cannot walk on the scuffed-up floor that we refinished, insisting that we could do it, that you could grant us this. You did. We cannot feel wood under our feet, even if we are here and if we now hear almost everything. If we try exceptionally hard, if we give what remains of our lives over to ether, we have been told that we could make something happen. We could throw a book across your room and stun you into silence and wonderment. We could make your whole world change in a moment.

If we did this we'd give up what remains. These are the rules. We don't know why things happen. *Why* is not for us. *What* is ours, however.

How is ours. *When* is ours, even if *when* makes less and less sense the longer we stay here. Was it a year ago that we had left you at the altar? That you spoke those words to the dearly assembled and we could not reply? What was in our hearts that kept us from saying yes as we had meant to do? Was it a year later you'd forgiven us? Was it another month after that when our heart stopped for the final time? It seemed so close and now it's not. It's moved away. We can feel those moments diminishing. Is this what we used to call time?

HELEN OYEYEMI
"Sorry" Doesn't Sweeten Her Tea

> *To you who eat a lot of rice because you are lonely*
> *To you who sleep a lot because you are bored*
> *To you who cry a lot because you are sad*
> *I write this down.*
> *Chew on your feelings that are cornered*
> *Like you would chew on rice.*
> *Anyway life is something that you need to digest.*
> —*Chun Yang Hee*

"Be good to Boudicca and Boudicca will be good to you," Chedor-laomer said. Boudicca and I eyed each other through the blue-tinted glass of Ched's fish tank, and I said: "Tell me what she is again?"

To the naked eye Boudicca is a haze of noxious green that lurks among fronds of seaweed looking exactly like the aftermath of a chemical spill. But Ched's got this certificate that states Boudicca's species is *Betta splendens,* colloquially known as Siamese fighting fish because fish of this kind have a way of instigating all-out brawls with their tank mates. It's almost admirable. Boudicca doesn't care how big or pretty her fellow fish are; if they come to her manor she will obliterate them, whether that means waiting until the other fish is asleep before she launches her attack or, in the case of a fish that simply refused to engage with her, eating the eggs that the other fish had spawned and then dancing around in the water while the bereaved mother was slain by grief.

So now Boudicca lives alone, which is exactly what she wanted all along.

I get this vibe that Ched the eternal bachelor sees Boudicca as a fish version of himself, but he's never said that out loud, at least not to me. We don't have those kinds of talks. Even if Ched and Boudicca are on some level the same person, the fact remains that the man is able to feed himself and the fish needs someone to see to her nutrition a couple times a week.

Ched called me over to tell me he was going away for two years and he expected me to take care of Boudicca. Twice a week for two years! Plus, Ched's house is spooky. The House of Locks, it's called. That's the actual address—House of Locks, Ipswich, Suffolk. He travels a lot and I have his spare set of keys for use while on best-friend duty, watering his house plants when he used to have house plants, collecting post, etc., but when I'm in there, I don't linger. Nothing has actually happened to me in there. Not yet, anyway. But every time I go into that bloody house, there's the risk of coming out crazy. Because of the doors. They don't stay closed unless they're locked. Once you've done that, you hear sounds behind them: sounds that convince you you've locked someone in. But when you leave these doors unlocked, they swing halfway out of the doorframe so that you can't see all the way into the next room, and it's just as if somebody's standing behind the door and holding it like that on purpose. The windows behave similarly—they won't fully open unless you push them up slowly, with more firm intent than actual pressure. Only Ched really has the knack of it. Apparently, the house's first owner took a particular pleasure in fastening and releasing locks—the feel and the sound of the key turning until it finds the point at which the lock must yield. So for her the house was a lifetime's worth of erotic titillation.

It's a nice house for Ched too, in that it's big and he got it on the cheap, and anyway, he's not really comfortable in overly normal situations. As it is he hears voices. Nobody else hears these voices, but they're not just in Ched's head, you know? In this world there are voices without form; they sing and sing, as they have from the beginning and will continue until the end. Ched borrows their melodies: that's the music part of the songs he writes. For words, Ched uses rhymes from our village, the kind that nobody pays attention to anymore because they advocate living by a code that will surely make you one of life's losers. A lot of stuff about living honestly and trying your best. Even if you only have one tiny job to do, do it well, do it well, do it well...

These songs of Ched's turned out to be a hit with a lot of people outside our country. Ched got Internet famous and then magazine famous and all the other kinds of famous after that. It was fun to see. His mother still says to me: "But don't you think people overreact to our Chedorlaomer? These girls screaming and fainting just because he looked at them or whatever. He's just some boy from Bezin."

That's the power of those true voices, man.

And now that you know that Ched and I are from a small village that might make you say, "Oh, OK, so that's why this guy believes in voices he's never heard." But trust, living in a small village in a country that's not even sure it's really a country you see a lot of shit that's stranger than a shaman (which is what Ched is, or was, before he started making money from the voices). Every day, there was news that made you say, "Oh really." Some new tax that only people with no money had to pay. Or yet another member of the county police force was found to have been an undercover gangster. If not that, then a gang member was found to have been an undercover police officer. An Ottoman-style restaurant opened in a town nearby; it served no food but had a mineral-water menu tens of pages long, and fashion models came to drink their way through it while we played football with their bodyguards. Oh, and speaking even more locally, there was this one boy at our school who had quite a common first name and decided to fight every other boy in our postal code area for the right to be the sole bearer of that name–can you imagine? I was one of the boys on his hit list, and I was already getting picked on because I didn't have a father. But what a ridiculous place we were born into, that fatherlessness was a reason people would flick a boy's forehead and say insulting things to him, then pile on four against one when he took offense…it's not our fault we're ridiculous people, Ched and me. How could we be anything else?

Ched was the absurd-looking boy who suddenly grew into his features and became really good-looking overnight. That didn't seem right, so he got picked on too. But Ched had been thinking, and the result of that was his going around offering assistance to the other boys who had the same name as me, arguing that if our little problem fought us individually, he would easily beat us, but if we stood up to him together, none of us would have to change our name. The others feared duplicity more than anything else (this was wise, since duplicity was all we knew) and decided it was better to take their chances as individuals. I believed Ched though. With the solemnity of a couple exchanging vows, we slipped knuckle-dusters onto each other's fingers, four for each hand. Then I walked over to the boy who didn't think he should have to share his name with anybody, and without saying a word to this boy, I smacked the pot of chocolate pudding he was eating right out of his hand. He was so astounded he just stood there pointing at me as his friends came loping over like bloodthirsty gazelles. I didn't even check whether this Chedorlaomer boy really had my back, but I trusted that he did, and he really did. What a great day, a day that a modest plan worked. That guy changed his own name in the end. And it's been like that ever since with Ched and me. He was lucky enough to be a year older than me, and when he graduated from our school, it was like being the only sane person left in an asylum. There was more and more bullshit every day. But Ched waited for me at the school gates, and he had a lot of good pep talks.

That's why it's pretty odd that Chedorlaomer went back for mandatory military service. Only passport holders have to do that, and I thought he'd given up his passport, like I had.

"No, I never told you that," Ched said.

"But why would you keep it? Haven't you seen the stuff they write about you over there? You've sold out, you're scum, blah blah blah. So what, now you're trying to change people's minds? Why those minds in particular? I thought we—"

"Yeah, I know what you thought," Ched said. He laughed and ruffled my hair. All of his was gone; he'd just come back from the barber's. Baldness made him look younger than I'd ever seen him, and toothier too. Like a stray, but a dangerous stray; you could take him home if you wanted to, but he'd tear the walls down. "It's time for me to be part of something impersonal," he said. "Duty is as big as it gets. Do these people like me? Do I like them? Am I one of them? All irrelevant. I'll be directing all of each day's effort toward one priority: defend the perimeter."

Other things my best friend said to me: Two years was but a short span. And in the meantime, he hoped his house of locks would become a kind of sanctuary for me. It would've been a really nice speech if Boudicca hadn't been blinking balefully at me the whole time. *You there... forget to feed me once, just one time, and you're dead.* I mumbled that I had a lot on at work but I'd see what I could do.

I don't tell Ched how often the things he says come true. That's for his own good, of course, so that he stays humble. But here's an example: this past couple of weeks alone I've come to the House of Locks seven times. Four times to feed Boudicca and walk the length of her tank—

the first time, she raced me to the farthest corner, and all the other times, she's turned her back. The rest of my visits have been for sanctuary, I suppose. Just like Ched said. All I've seen or heard of him since his departure are blurry photographs of his arrival at barracks, these posted on various fan sites. He hasn't called or replied to emails, so I walk through the wing of the house that he favors, passing the windows with various views of his fountain. A girl of pewter stands knee deep in the water, her hands cupped, collecting streams and letting them pour away. Her eyes are blissfully closed. In the room I'm watching her from, the curtains hang so still that breathing isn't quite enough to make me believe there's air in here. The front door is the only one I lock behind me, so as I go through the house all the doors behind me are ajar. It's still hair-raising, but it's reassuring too. The house is wonderfully, blessedly empty—nobody else will appear in the gap between the doors—that gap is a safe passage across all those thresholds I crossed without thinking.

About work: I run a clinic for my Aunt Thomasina's company. A "Swiss Style Weight Loss Clinic," to quote the promotional materials. This basically means that people come here for three days of drug-induced and -maintained deep sleep, during which they're fed vitamins through a drip. This is a job I jumped at when it was my non-Ched-dependent ticket out of Bezin. It's not as peaceful as I expected; most of the sleeping done here is the troubled kind. A lot of sleep-talking and plaintive bleating. None of the sleepers are OK, not really. On the bright side the results are visually impressive: most clients drop a clothing size over those 72 hours. Aunt Thomasina experienced this herself before she ever tried it out on anybody else. Something awful happened to her when she was young—she's never even hinted at what that might be—and she took what she thought was a lethal dose of valerian and went to bed, only to wake up gorgeously slender three days later. *This will be popular,* she said to herself. And she was right. Most days the waiting room is full of clients happily shopping on their tablet devices; the whole new wardrobe they just ordered will be waiting for them at home after their beauty sleep. Of course, weight loss that drastic is unsustainable, which makes the clinic a great business model. We send our monthly customers Christmas and birthday cards; they're part of the family.

We have doctors who make sure that we're not admitting anyone likely to suffer serious complications from our treatment, so my job is mainly monitoring and addressing complaints and unrealistic expectations. I can fake sympathy for days: Aunt Thomasina says I am a psychopath and that it's a good thing I came under the right influences at a young age. I also do night shifts, since we can't lock anybody into their rooms and I'm good with sleepwalkers. Last week we had two. One guy rose up pulling tubes out of his skin because he's not used to sleeping indoors in summer. He grew up in an earthquake-prone region, and his family hit upon the strategy of sleeping in a nearby field so as to avoid having their house fall down on them. My shift partner got him back into bed with warm assurances of safety, but when it was my turn, I merely whispered: "You are interrupting the process, my friend. Do you want her to regret or not?" He sleep-ran back down the corridor and had to be restrained from re-attaching himself to the vitamin machine. That was what he'd written in his questionnaire beside "objective": TO BE SEXY SO THAT SHE REGRETS.

Our other sleepwalker was just really, really hungry. You can't coax someone out of that. This client got up and searched for food with such determination that she had to have her drug dose significantly elevated. For a couple of hours, it seemed her hunger was stronger than the drugs. I sat out the third intervention and stayed in the monitor room watching the camera feed: it was fascinating to watch her returning to the surface of sleep, crying, "Chips... chips..." but eventually she went down hard and stayed under. Ultimately, she was happy with her results, but apart from the usual disorientation she also looked really thoughtful, as if asking herself: *Worth it?* She probably won't be back.

The sleepwalkers upset my shift partner Tyche. Her being upset helps her get through to them, I think. They can tell that she cares about them and isn't judging them like I am. Tyche is someone that I think Ched should meet. She's only a part-timer at the clinic; her business card states that the rest of the time she does PUPPETEERING-ODD JOBS-INVOCATIONS. Invocations. Something she learned while trying to do something else, she says. So she can relate to Aunt Thomasina's weight loss discovery.

Tyche's beauty is interestingly kinetic; it comes and goes and comes back again. Or maybe it's more that you observe it in the first second of seeing her and then she makes you shelve that exquisite first impression for a while so she can get on with things. Then, in some moment when she's not talking or when she suddenly turns her head, it hits you all over again. There's a four-star constellation on her wrist that isn't always there either. When it is, its appearance goes through various degrees of permanence, from drawn-on-with-kohl to full tattoo. I mentioned this to her, but she laughed it off: "But don't you stare at me too much? Everything OK with your boyfriend?" In my matchmaking capacity I've paid closer attention to her visuals than I would pay to anybody on my own behalf. On to inner qualities: She's powerful. Not just in doing whatever she does to make people listen to her instead of watch her, but…I think she heals herself. She wears a wedding ring, so I made reference to her partner, but she held her hand up and said: "Oh, this? I found it." Then she told me about it. A while ago she'd been in a relationship with someone who was adamant about keeping her a secret, to the extent that they didn't acknowledge each other if there was even one other person in sight. Her superpower was picking emotionally unavailable partners, and she doubted she'd get a better offer. She also assumed that the relationship would gradually get less secret. Nothing changed, and while she continued to profess her commitment to her secret boyfriend, her body disagreed and tried to get her out of it. She got sick. Her hair started falling out and her skin went scaly; she was cold all the time, and could only fall asleep by reciting words of summoning.

Nobody came, but one evening at the pub down the road from her house, she found a ring at the bottom of a pint of lager she was drinking. The ring was heavier than it looked, and she recognized it without remembering exactly where she'd seen it before. Since no one at the pub seemed to know anything about the ring, she took it to the police station, only to return there to collect it at the end of the month: there had been no inquiries related to the item, so it was hers. And when she wore it, she felt that a love existed, and for her…her, of all people. And it was on all the time. Of this love there would be no photographs, no handwritten declarations, no token at all save the ring. If this was the only way that what she'd called could come to her, then it sufficed; she was content. The hand that wore the ring grew smooth, and she recouped her losses.

"Didn't some nuns used to wear wedding rings?" I asked her.

She nodded and said that that was something she thought about a lot.

I'd best introduce her to Ched before the nuns get her. Ched's voices are bullies: they won't let him play unless it's for keeps. Tyche might have an answer for them.

But why am I treating Ched's celibacy as something to be fixed? Maybe because I am so much in his debt for so many things and I can't think of any other way to settle up; maybe I've become evangelical ever since I got a little family of my own. The scene at the homestead is different every day. My boyfriend has joint custody of his two daughters with his ex-wife, whose schedule is ever-changing, so the girls might be at home or they might not. Dayang is the elder at sixteen; Aisha's eighteen months behind her. Day is studious and earnest, a worrier like her father—she carries a full first aid kit around in her school bag and tells me off for calling her boyfriend by a different name every time I see him. In my defense, the boy genuinely looks different every time he comes over, but Day's concerned that he'll think she has other boyfriends. This would be catastrophic because Mr. Face-Shifting Boyfriend is The One. And how can she tell he's the one, I ask. Well, how did I know that her dad is my One, she asks. Some things are just completely obvious, GOSH.

Day is great, but Aisha is my darling and my meddlesome girl. She's the one who gets the question "But why are you like this?" at least once a day from her father. If she isn't growing something (she is the reason Noor finds toadstools in his shoes) or brewing something (she's the reason it's best not to leave any cup or drinking glass unattended when she's at home), she'll pass by singing and swishing her tail around (she put her sewing machine to work making a set of tails that she attaches to her dresses). A fox tail, a dragon's tail, a tiger's tail, a peacock's. On a special occasion she'll wear all of them at once. Last month, Matyas Füst released a new album and Aisha hosted a listening party for five bosom friends. The bosom friends wore all their tails too…

Those were the good old days, when Aisha's love for Matyas Füst was straightforward idol worship. Her wall was covered with posters of him; she sometimes got angry with him for being more attractive than she thought anyone was allowed to be and would punch a poster right in the face before whispering frantic apologies and covering it with kisses. She had Noor or me buy certain items because she'd read an interview in which he mentioned he loved this or that particular scent or color on a woman. All of Aisha's online IDs were some variation on her official motto: "Matyas Füst Is Love, Matyas Füst Is Life."

Ched had met Füst a few times and said he wouldn't want any daughter of his going anywhere near "that dickhead," but the first time he said that, I took it with more than a pinch of salt. For starters Aisha's polite refusal to have a crush on her friendly neighborhood pop star was something of an ego bruiser. There were a few other small but influential factors: Füst's being ten years younger than Ched, and its being well known that Füst composes, arranges, and writes the lyrics for all his (mostly successful) songs himself...no voices. It just wasn't really possible for Ched to like him. Füst was forever being photographed wearing dark gray turtlenecks, was engaged to be married to a soloist at the Bolshoi Ballet, didn't seem to go to nightclubs, and reportedly enjoyed arthouse films, the occasional dinner party, and the company of his cat, Kleinzach. A clean-shaven man with a vocal tone reminiscent of postcoital whispers, that was Matyas Füst. The way he sings "Twinkle Twinkle Little Star" is no joke.

Ched had been away for about a month when I got home to find "love to hatred turn'd."

Noor was making dinner, checking his recipe board after each step, even though he knew it just as well as if he'd written it himself. The not-so-hidden charms of a man who takes his time over every detail... especially once you distract him for just long enough to turn all his attention onto you. It didn't occur to me to ask about the kids until halfway through our very late dinner. Bad stepfather.

"Er...have the kids already eaten?"

Noor shook his head. "They promised they'd have something later."

"Hmmm. Why?"

"Not sure. Heartbreak, I think."

"Ah, so the face shifter isn't The One after all?"

"No, it's not Day—well, it is Day, but only because she can't let Aisha go through it all on her own."

The sisters were huddled together on Aisha's bed with a laptop between them. They closed the laptop when I came into the room, leaving me to look around at the bare walls and wonder what had happened. Both girls were red-eyed and strenuously denied being upset. When I left the room, I clearly heard Day say: "You've got to stop watching it," and Aisha answered: "I know, but I can't." Then she said, "Maybe it isn't true, Day? It probably isn't true." and Day said, "Oh, Aisha."

Minutes later Noor and I watched the video ourselves downstairs. It was called "A Question about Matyas Füst." Noor found it hard to watch in one go; he kept pausing it. This cowardly pacing would normally have been grounds for a dispute; I agreed with him just that once, though. The video opened with a woman sitting on the floor in her underwear, showing us marks all over her body. A lot of the marks were needle track marks, but they were outnumbered by marks I hadn't wanted Day and Aisha to ever become acquainted with: bruises left by fists and boots. I dreaded the end of the camera's journey up to the woman's face and didn't know what to think when I saw that it was untouched, even a subdued kind of pretty. No makeup, clean, mousy-looking hair, age absolutely anywhere between twenty-five and forty-five. I'd seen girls who resembled her waitressing in seedy bars across the continent, removing customers' hands from their backsides without turning to see who the hand belonged to, their gestures as automatic and unemotional as swatting midges.

She pulled a T-shirt on and looked at the camera for a little while before she started talking. You could tell from her eyes that she was out of her head on something and probably couldn't have told you her own name if you'd asked her. Her English was far below fluency, but since she was in her happy place, she didn't bother struggling with pronunciation, just said what she had to say and left us to figure it out. She wanted us to know that "the entertainer" Matyas Füst had picked her up on a street corner a few hours after he'd played a sold-out concert in Greenwich. She'd spent the rest of the night with him, and he hadn't proved very entertaining at all. *Tell us a bit more about yourself,* the person holding the camera said—a woman, I think, trying to sound gentle, but her voice was thick with anger. The woman on camera obediently stated that she was often on street corners trying to get money, and that she didn't often get lucky: the men she signaled to could usually tell just by looking at the backs of her hands that she'd gone too far into whatever she was doing. But Matyas Füst didn't care about that: he'd had a fight with his controlling bitch of a girlfriend, and it had taken all he had not to hit the girlfriend. Taking your fists to a prima ballerina with an adoring host of family and friends would be a very messy and expensive blunder. So he went looking for someone nobody cared about. *And he found…me…*the woman on-screen said, and giggled. Noor pressed pause again and left the room, went upstairs, and knocked on Aisha's bedroom door. "Come and eat," he said, and Aisha and Day said they'd come in a minute.

Hours later they still hadn't come downstairs. We'd watched the rest of the clip by then. The whole thing was only three minutes and thirty seconds long, but we kept trying to watch it through Aisha and Day's eyes, this woman telling us that after they'd had sex, Füst had insulted her, so she slapped him, and once he'd received the slap, he'd smiled (her fingers plucked at the corners of her mouth until we could see just how he'd smiled), told her she'd "started it," and proceeded to beat her until she couldn't stand up. She'd hit back, she said, even from her place at his feet she'd hit back, but every time he hit harder. Then he stood over her in all his wealth and fame and arrogance and shrugged when she said she wasn't going to keep quiet about this. Matyas Füst had shrugged and asked her if she thought anybody was going to give a shit that someone like her had got hurt. A nameless junkie with seriously crazy English. *Look at you,* he said. *And look at me.* He threw a handful of money at her and told her it was better for her to keep her mouth shut and spend that, or save it for a rainy day. Then he went back to his girlfriend. They must have made up, because she'd seen photos of them having a romantic dinner in a restaurant, and hints had been dropped about their wedding plans. *Every day I look him up on Google.* The woman on camera seemed proud of her diligence. Then she asked us her question about Matyas Füst: *Did* anybody care that he'd hurt her, someone like her? She was just wondering. She laughed and gave us a perky little wave at the end. *Thank you. Nice day to you.*

Aisha came downstairs cradling her laptop in her arms. Day followed, hands helplessly rising and falling. "It's not just the clip, it's the *comments,*" she said, when she saw us.

Ah, yes, the comments.

Noor couldn't make himself look, so Aisha and I read some of them aloud. There was a lot of *LOL cool allegations junkie, maybe it was all a dream?* and *LMAO people will say anything to ruin a good man's reputation stay strong Matyas!*

If only that was the worst of it. Aisha's haggard face as she read: *Oh boohoo. What's this one complaining about? He paid her, didn't he? She hit him, didn't she? Admitted all this herself. Does she think you can hit someone and just walk away?* I read: *She should count herself lucky: men probably treat broken-down old whores worse than that in her country. And she got to bang Matyas! Matyas Füst can beat me up any time baby LOL.*

Then the apologists came out to play: *Even if this is true is it the full story? We know that Matyas wouldn't just lash out like that so we need to be asking what she did...*

Day showed us a screenshot she'd saved. She'd posted a comment of her own: *Guys, are you being serious? I'm appalled and really scared by this and all the reactions I'm seeing...this isn't the world I want to live in.* She'd received so many replies telling her to kill herself that she'd decided to delete her account.

"I still don't think it's true," Aisha said. "He couldn't have done something like this." When Noor put on his solicitor voice to point out that the video had been up for half a day, had a view count of half a million, and would have had Matyas Füst's team of lawyers swinging left and right if the content hadn't had any basis in fact, Aisha said through gritted teeth: "But he hasn't said anything at all."

"He'll probably make a statement in the morning," Noor said. We were failing as the men in Day and Aisha's life. We weren't doing what we were supposed to do. This came through very clearly in the way that Day and Aisha were looking at us, or more not looking at us, really.

The morning brought no statement from Füst, and Noor sounded relieved (and ashamed of his relief) when he said: "Looks like she hasn't got any proof and he's going to ignore or deny it." In the afternoon there were reports of an eyewitness to the beating coming forward, and about an hour after that Füst's legal team announced that he'd voluntarily made himself available to the police for questioning.

At the clinic, my concentration was poor and I mixed up checkout forms so that departing clients got to read details of each other's low self-esteem and experience the outrage of not being unique. Tyche Shaw and I were on the same shift again and got authorization to offer free secondary sleep sessions all around so we wouldn't be sued. But like Aisha, Tyche was addicted to the YouTube clip. She spent her break time watching it over and over on her phone and ran the battery right down.

"I found that one tough to watch," I told her.

"Really?" She said. "But it's just someone talking about this time she got beaten up. No bullets or gore or bombs or anything. This is nothing compared with other things you can see on this site."

"I don't know what to say. I can't explain it."

"Well, I hope she sees the view count and accepts that as an answer to her question about whether people care. These numbers are up there with the numbers for footage of the world's most brilliant strikers scoring the decade's most brilliant goals. So it's not that we're indifferent... We care...just in a really really really fucked up way..."

Matyas Füst's fiancé released a statement as we were leaving work: She was shocked and upset to hear of "the events described in the video" and would be paying the victim a visit to see if there was anything she could do for her. She had never seen a violent side to Matyas' character, but it was now clear that he'd been struggling with some issues, and they'd be spending some time apart while he completed a course of anger management therapy.

"No jail time for Füst...just a fine and some therapy," Tyche predicted, even as she admired the photo of the prima ballerina, who was elfin and ethereal and all the rest of it.

"Yeah, well, I beg to differ," I said.

Tyche stuck her hand out. "Bet you a hundred pounds."

"I suppose this is all just a joke to you, but I know a girl who's pretty badly shaken up by all this."

Tyche sighed. "She was a fan?"

"She's still trying to be one, I think. Clinging to every possible delusion."

Tyche's sigh deepened. "Let me know if there's anything I can do for her."

"OK, thanks..." I had it in my mind to ask Tyche what she thought she might be able to do for a girl she'd never met—in a spirit of curiosity, not hostility—but had to hurry over to the House of Locks. Terry, the man who maintained Boudicca's fish tank, was waiting for me to let him in. After Terry left, I stayed a few more hours, reading Matyas Füst updates aloud to Boudicca, who looked suitably incredulous. YouTube woman was glad she'd had the chance to meet the woman she'd found herself taken a beating for and wouldn't be pressing charges. She'd hit Füst first—that was an excessive response to some words he'd said, and his response in turn had been excessive; all she asked was acknowledg-ment of that. A sincere apology. So Matyas Füst was preparing a sincere apology.

Has she read any of the comments? That's what I wondered. Did the woman from the YouTube video understand that the public wasn't on her side? She made her requests with such placid mirth, as if talking into a seashell or a shattered telephone, as if Matyas Füst fans weren't actively looking for her, probably in order to finish her off. Even those who'd begun to condemn Füst believed his apologies should be direct-ed elsewhere ("It's his fiancé I feel sorry for in all this...") Those who claimed they *wanted* to feel concern for YouTube woman didn't like that she'd filmed her allegations while high. And yet she might not have been able to talk about it sober.

Noor texted that he was considering taking Aisha's laptop away until the Füst case died down. She seemed to have spent the entire evening engaged in a long and rambling argument with her friends via six-way video call. She attacked Füst's reputation, defended it, then attacked again, berated the friends who'd gone off him for their faith-lessness, cursed the infinite stupidity of his unchanged fans, and threat-ened to put on a Füst mask and beat them up to see how they liked it. She'd skipped dinner again and was running a temperature. When was I coming home?

Two firsts: Being reluctant to leave Ched's house and being reluctant to enter my own. I said I'd been at the gym. Ched does have a home gymnasium; he works out a lot, his body being his backup plan in case he gets ugly again. But I don't know why I lied.

Aisha will get over this. But what of her tails and her plant-growing projects and the remarkably potent gin she was perfecting? "That gin was going to make us richer than an entire network of 1920s bootleg-gers," I said, to see if that wouldn't rouse her. She likes money. Now it seems she liked it because she could exchange it for Matyas Füst–re-lated items. What worries Noor is that three of Aisha's graven images fell off their pedestals at once: him, me, and Matyas Füst. The girls seemed to pity our weakness. Noor's brusque talk of judicial process and media treatment. My awkward, awkward silence. Is it really bad that the girls have found us out, though? I never projected strength. Not on purpose anyway.

"What are you really worrying about, Noor?"

He shuffled papers into his briefcase, rearranged his pens, straightened his tie. "It just…I think I've lost them. Just like that, overnight. Their mother says they're fine with her…"

I loosened the knot of his tie a little, just a little. It still looked neat, so he couldn't complain.

"Nah. I don't even know them as well as you do and I can tell they're just thinking." A casual overview of all their main emotional attachments reveals that Noor and his ex have been better parents than they realize; while Day and Aisha appreciate strength, lack of it isn't a deal breaker in the matter of whether they respect a person or not.

All was quiet on the Matyas Füst front for a few months; I kept an eye on that situation (among others) and read that the reporters who managed to get a sound bite out of Füst all got the same one. He was completing his anger management therapy and was still preparing his apology. This sound bite was paired with another obtained from the YouTube woman: *Looking forward to it.*

It was around that time Ched and I started talking again—not often, but enough. I'd be entering or leaving the House of Locks, the phone would ring and it would be Ched. He described his current existence as a cycle of drills and chores, and was so tired he'd fall asleep mid-sentence. It was good to speak to him, not just because it was him but because he didn't know the first thing about the incident that had rocked my household. When I gave him a brief outline he said: "Oh, you know the apology Füst's preparing is going to be a song, right? And that song is going to become an anthem of repentance. It's probably going to be called 'Dress Made of Needles.'"

"Nice—I'll go down to the betting shop tomorrow."

There was something else I wanted to talk about while I had him on the line. When I answered his phone calls, he needed half a second to adjust his greeting, and it sounded as if he was disappointed that I was the one who'd answered. Well, disappointed is too strong a word. It was more as if I wasn't his first preference. Which was fine, except that I'm the only other person who has keys to his house. His mum's been trying to get a set for years without success.

"So what's going on? You met someone?"

"Not sure," he said. "I...think so."

"And this person has keys?"

After a lot more questioning, he eventually confessed that he hadn't given a set of keys to anybody else and had never actually met this woman in person, but was fairly sure that she had keys because she sometimes answered the phone when he called. When he said that I adjusted my position so that I was able to watch all the open doors and I said: "That's wonderful, Ched. I'm really happy for you."

"Don't overreact," he said. "She's a nice voice at the moment, nothing more. Like one of the ones that sing. Except that she just talks."

"Did you ask her how she got in?"

"Of course."

"Well, what did she say?"

"She encouraged me to think of a better question."

I glared at Boudicca; no wonder she'd been filling out lately. "Maybe she feeds your fish too."

"Haha, maybe. But while we're talking about this, could you do me a favor? I don't think she wants to be seen, so if you let yourself in and happen to notice that she's around, just leave immediately, OK?"

"OK, Ched. No problem."

Just another day in the lives of two boys from Bezin. Still, I checked every room in Ched's wing of the house before I left. His alarm system's in working order and none of his valuables have moved. For now.

Ched's phone girlfriend earned me the first direct smile I'd got from Aisha in weeks. "You stupid boys," she said, lovingly. A string of text messages appeared on her phone and her smile vanished as if it had never been.

"Brace yourself," Noor shouted from the next room. "It's Matyas Füst's apology."

Day wasn't ready to leave her bubble bath—"Oh, no, no apology for me, thank you," so Aisha grabbed a couple of foam stress balls, jumped onto Noor's lap and said, "Go." We watched and listened to Matyas Füst singing a song about a girl who walked the earth in a dress made of needles that she couldn't remove without maiming herself. People with good intentions kept trying to pull the needles out and give her something soft and warm to wear instead, but the needles pricked their fingers so much that they gave up. Then the girl met a bad man who drove the needles in deeper. Not with a hammer, but with his hands, for the thrill of joining his own torture to hers. Luckily, luckily the bad man managed to bleed out before he could kill her—it turned out his bones were magnetic(?). I might have misunderstood that part of the song, but whatever it was about his bones, they drew the needles from her and into him, he died in the utmost agony, the end. I kept waiting for Füst to wink, but he didn't.

"My favorite thing about this song is the way it starts out all about her and ends up all about him," Noor said, as we refreshed the page and fat red love hearts accumulated in the comments beneath the video.

Matyas understands
This is exactly how I'm feeling today
Thank you Matyas
Think we can all agree he shouldn't have done it in the first place but now he's done the decent thing
We forgive u

All I could say was "Amazing."

How did it go from "Füst should apologize to the woman he beat up" to "Füst should apologize to his fiancé" to "Füst should apologize to us"?

Aisha spoke through the stress ball she'd stuffed into her mouth, removed it, and started again: "Maybe this is a piece of conceptual art? Like something out of one of Matyas' favorite films. Couldn't YouTube woman be an artist who's worked out a concept that uses the media to show us something about fame and its...its magic touch. So what if that touch is a punch? She's famous now. Maybe she's trying to get us thinking about the different ways people get famous. By excelling at something, or by suffering publicly. Maybe what that eyewitness saw was a performance? What if she already had an agreement with Matyas that he would beat her up for the concept? Doesn't it seem like there's no way to avoid getting punched by someone or other? Doesn't matter who you are, it's just a fact of life. So isn't it a little better if you get to choose who punches you? You know, I think if I could pick, I would have chosen him too."

She was doing well until Noor, who'd stopped me from countering every single one of her speculations, said: "Ah, darling. Would you?"

Then she buried her head in her dad's jumper and howled. We couldn't tell if it was heartbreak, rage, mirth, or simply the difficulty she was having unimagining Mr. Matyas Füst.

The rehabilitation of Matyas Füst was in full swing. His compulsory course of therapy was over, but he was continuing of his own accord. His fiancé quietly moved back into his house, and he was doing a fuck-load of charity work. The charity work was the last straw for me. Before I explain the part I may or not have played in another man's complete mental and physical breakdown, I just have to quickly praise myself here. Yes, I have to be the one to do it; nobody else even understood how patient I was being with Aisha's mourning process in the midst of every other event worthy of grief going on in the world. Aisha herself was in a hurry to attain indifference to "the Füst matter" but you can't rush these things. The cackling with which Aisha greeted YouTube woman's simple and dignified acceptance of Matyas Füst's apology, that cackling was not ideal. Words were better, a little less opaque, so I was patient with her outbursts. More patient than Jesus himself!

The first I knew of my contribution to the charity of Matyas Füst's choice was an email that arrived while I was pursuing quotes from satisfied customers. The email thanked me for my £10000 auction bid—the winning bid!—and expressed hope that my daughter Aisha would enjoy the private concert that Matyas Füst would accordingly be putting on for her. Ten thousand of my strong and painstakingly saved pounds, Matyas Füst, that was all I was able to compute. Oh, and I saw red arrows between the two. Ten thousand pounds to Matyas Füst. I had some sort of interlude after that, running between my keyboard and the nearest wall flapping my hands and choking. Tyche came into my office, glanced at my computer screen, threw a glass of water in my face and left. That got me to sit back down, at least. Five minutes later, Aisha Skyped me from her school computer lab. I accepted the call, put my face right up to the camera, and bellowed her name until she resorted to typing:

OMG PLS CALM DOWN
YOU'VE GOT TO CALM
I'M CASHING THE VOUCHER
I SAID I'M CASHING THE VOUCHER!
"What voucher?" I asked the camera.

Aisha held up a finger, rummaged in her schoolbag, and held up a voucher I'd given her her last birthday, the last of a booklet of six. There in my own handwriting were the words: *This voucher entitles you to one completely fair and wrath-free hearing.*

"Ahhhhhh," I said, banging my chest, trying to open up some space in there. "OK, OK, I'm ready."

"I used your emergency debit card," Aisha said. "You know Dad always wants to know why I'm like this, and all I can say is I'm sorry I am. But I think—no, I'm sure, I'm sure, that if I just look him in the eye...I know it's a lot of money. I didn't really think the bid would go through. I didn't know you had that much on there! But please understand. I will pay you back. I'm going to get a job, and I'm going to make some stuff and sell a lot of it."

"It's OK," I said. "It's OK." My heartbeat was returning to normal. Aisha had been operating on the principle that I wouldn't want to be that guy who embarrasses himself by withdrawing a ten thousand pound donation he made to an enormously deserving cause. But I am that guy, so it's fine for me to do that.

Noor's ex-wife came over for coffee and spoke of seeking psychiatric assistance for Aisha, particularly in the light of Day's discovery that Aisha had made a purchase from her laptop: a liter of almost pure sulfuric acid—96 percent. The three of us sat silently with our coffee cups, picturing Aisha and Füst alone in some garland-bedecked bower, Füst singing his heart out, maybe even singing his latest hit "Dress Made of Needles"...then as the last notes of the song died out, Aisha uncapped the bottle of acid hidden beneath her dress and let fly. For about a week, Noor couldn't look at Aisha without shouting "What are you?"

All we'd hear from Aisha was the bitter laugh, and I tried to soothe her by saying "He's been forgiven, Aish. Everyone else has forgiven him," but I stopped that because there was a look that replaced her laughter, and that look haunted me.

It was Ched's opinion that it might have been all right if the apology had been something that Aisha could consider real, but now this thing wouldn't end unless she was able to take or witness vengeance upon Matyas Füst. Tyche agreed, but with a slight modification: Aisha would be able to move on if Matyas Füst was able to deliver a sincere apology for what he'd done. "At least…that's how it would be for me," Tyche added, twirling her wedding ring around her finger. "I mean, the galling thing about 'Dress Made of Needles' is that as a piece of music it's fine, but as an apology it takes the piss. But you know what, at least we got a meaningful song out of it, at least he wrote this good song because of her…"

The constellation on Tyche's wrist was definitely a tattoo that day and her breeziness was macabre. I thought for a long time, or what felt like a long time anyway, before I asked her if there was anything she could do for Aisha.

"Let me talk to her," Tyche said.

I wasn't allowed to listen to their conversation, but I know that it concerned the invocation of a goddess, and Tyche was very well prepared for it, arrived at our house wearing an elegant black suit and carrying a portfolio full of images and diagrams that she and Aisha pored over at length.

"Just FYI, we decided on Hecate," Tyche said on her way out.

"Yeah? Who's she?"

"Oh, nobody you need to worry about…"

"Come on, let me have the basics."

"Well…she keeps an eye on big journeys from the interior to the exterior, or vice versa. She's there for the step that takes you from one state to another. She's someone you see at crossroads, for instance. Well, you sort of see her but don't register what you've seen until it's too late to go back. She holds three keys…some say they're keys to the underworld, others that they're access to the past, present, and future. And—ah, you're zoning out on me…"

Tyche struck and held a warlike pose in the doorway.

"Picture the image of me fixed in this doorway, and also in every other doorway you pass, sometimes three dimensional and sometimes vaporous, whatever I feel like being at the moment you try to get past me," she said. "Imagine not being able to stop me from coming in, imagine not being able to cast me out because I own all thresholds. As an additional bonus, imagine me with three faces. That's who we're sending to have a little chat with Matyas Füst."

"Oh! Why didn't you just lead with that instead of the benevolent stuff? But listen, hang on, Tyche, is that not a bit much—"

She was already gone.

*

Summer has come back around, and with only a week until Ched returns from military service, I write this from a bench beside Ched's water fountain at the House of Locks. The woman with the voice he likes came in while I was feeding Boudicca, so I left.

Anyway, events of recent months, presented without comment, for who am I to comment after all?

- The day after Tyche and Aisha had their meeting, a black bordered notice appeared in one of the national newspapers:

  R.I.P. Matyas Füst,
  Happy Birthday Matyas Füst
  And good luck. Your rebirth will be a difficult one.

  Naturally, a lot of questions were asked, since Matyas Füst was alive and, at that time, well. It proved impossible to discover who was responsible for the notice.

- The day after the notice appeared, Matyas Füst phoned into a 5 p.m. radio show that was popular with commuters all over the country and announced that he'd like to apologize for his apology, which had come more from his head than his heart. He also asked that his fans cease their verbal abuse of the victim of his attack, since she had "been through a lot" and hadn't asked for a penny in compensation beyond their original transaction. The hosts of the radio show had to ask him to repeat his declarations of remorse several times because his weeping made them unintelligible.

- About a week after that, Füst interrupted his performance on the live taping of a variety show to state that he was being "hounded" and that he feared for his life, that "they" pricked him with needles and slammed his hands in doors. When members of the audience pointed out that he was uninjured, he appeared confused and said that it had only happened "inside where no one could see." Before the broadcast was halted, he also managed to say that he believed that in attacking the woman he'd met on the street he'd been following a bad example set by his father, who had frequently beaten his mother in front of him. His parents issued a joint denial that basically boiled down to *We have no idea why he's saying these things but it's making* us sad. Füst's fiancé moved out of his house again with talk of plans to "focus on her career"…that was funny, and rather sweet…if there was ever anybody focused on her career it was this prima ballerina, but her statement suggested she thought it didn't show. As for her ex-fiancé, a few close members of his family moved into his home, "to look after him." The close family members were unable to prevent him from phoning into radio shows and appearing on breakfast TV to apologize for his previous apologies and make further apologies. He ended his most recent TV appearance with the reflection that quality was probably better than quantity and that he'd take his time to find a genuine expression of his thoughts. He'd been told that the key to a real apology was the identification of one's real mistake. He hoped to be able to do that soon.

- Healthcare professionals were reported to have joined the close family members surrounding Füst at his home, but he escaped them all and was reported missing for six months.

- Füst was found to have been sleeping rough all winter—a very hard winter, so much surprise was expressed that he'd lived through it. He gave one interview, to a reputable chronicle of paranormal phenomena. I think he intended for the interview to dispel the rumors of his insanity, but it had the opposite effect. Especially when he spoke about "them." "They" demanded that he apologize and then called his apologies glib. He said that "they" were three women and yet "they" were one, and that one of them took his pain away so that the others could return it to him, and so it went on. He said he should have died during the winter, but it pleased "them" to keep him alive in order for him to learn what he could say or do to keep them off. If there was anybody who knew how to convince this woman that he was sorry, Matyas Füst begged to know that secret at any price.

- Aisha may have abandoned tails for good, but all-heal plants are flowering in her window box, she's working on reducing the aphrodisiac effect of an otherwise very convenient headache cure, and she's looking forward to Matyas Füst's forthcoming book, *An Outcast's Apology*. She reckons Füst is getting closer to identifying his mistake, and says he should keep trying.

Safe Home

Cuauh always greases the landings. If the winds are strong, he lands in the desert north of Obregon, on a sand strip outlined by burning tar barrels, desert oak, and split saguaro cut lengthwise to catch the neon sun. But if the winds are calm, Cuauh lumbers his aircraft, an aging M20J, onto a neighborhood street in Lomas de Poleo just inside Ciudad Juarez. All of the homes abandoned. Everyone gone from the drug wars.

The neighborhood landing always warrants thirty degrees of flaps, the elevators popped low with the shimmy damper extended full to the hook and bolt, no further slack to give. The flexing tension of the wire pings up and down the length of the aircraft as it descends. You can hear it ringing like a bell in the sky from both sides of the border: From one hill the Ejército—the Mexican military—gazing up with silent admiration for the pilot who can grease such a landing. From the other hill, the Americans looking down into the city with a fixed gaze, as if willing the cartel plane to crash.

Cuauh dives in at an angle, on a slipstream, with his left rudder pushed full to the carpet and his ailerons turned fist-over-lap so the plane falls fast and loud, the up-gush of wind roaring high through the idled propellers, the plane like a screaming vulture descending crooked into the remnants of the neighborhood. Five hundred feet, four hundred feet, and he'll kick out the rudder to right the plane just before impact. He'll land it clean and free onto a street named Nahual where the crumbling tar-gravel and rock splatter up against the nickel-plated underbelly of the plane behind the thrust of the cooling twin flat-eight Lycoming piston engines still revved to a thousand RPM.

The wingtips, forty-eight feet from one tip to the other, scrape along the thresholds of the houses on either side of Nahual Street. The power lines roll up and stretch over the bump of the cockpit. All the birds move to either end of the line, unimpressed by the smoking four hundred and fifty horsepower engine threatening to suck them in. The driver, too, waits unimpressed at the end of the road.

The driver is always the one asking questions. The driver is both

Cuauh's ride home and his interrogator, his friend and his enemy. *How was the flight? Any messages to be relayed? Any peculiarities along the way? Are you sure? Are you sure?* he'll ask. Cuauh knows the routine, and he knows better than to incriminate himself on what he did or did not see from the skies.

The driver is always different but more or less a variation of the same man. Mid-thirties, severely overweight, reeking of Delicados and cheap sex and Tommy Hilfiger cologne. Probably named Chuy, which is short for something. Cuauh can never remember.

From his cockpit, Cuauh can see the driver sitting back in his pleather-covered seat, drumming his nicotine-stained fingers on the steering wheel of the truck. He listens to the American radio pouring in from the station atop the hill. He hates Ke$ha. He loves Katy Perry. He checks his watch and waits for the engines to cut. He checks his hair in the mirror, perfectly lacquered with Tres Flores pomade. He cracks his spearmint gum. His breath smells like Swiss cheese.

Cuauh purges it all from his mind before his boot even touches the ground. He forgets the bloody road leading up to San Miguel. He forgets the private strip in Sweetwater, Texas, called Fraley, where he made his drop, cocaine by the smell of it—it had no smell. He purges his memory of looking down on Interstate 20 running east of El Paso. Those burning cars. Hot, greasy, diesel smoke pouring black up into a plume that screened out the sun and painted the whole scene wispy in shadows of smoke. That familiar burnt-orange Ford Lobo—the one he'd ridden in so many times before from the airstrip—gushing from the undercarriage. Blood and oil and gasoline in the sand. A body pouring out from the driver's side wearing purple boots. Cuauh knew, even from the sky, who those boots belonged to. He purges that name from his mind too.

He plants his foot on the running boards of the white Dodge Durango at the end of Nahual street and climbs into the passenger seat.

"Any peculiarities?" the driver asks him, cracking his spearmint gum. Cuauh glasses him over. They've never met before. "No," he says. Cuauh keeps a stolid face, but his hands give him away, his finger pulling at the long, puckered scar on his left arm where it was cut the night he was deported from Texas, the night he was kidnapped and forced to fly cartel planes.

Cuauh says nothing as he eases his body into the passenger seat of the car. He turns down the radio and clicks it to the AM band. Texas High School Football. Westlake vs. Copperas Cove. He takes the driver's Stetson from the dash and drapes it over his sun-wearied eyes.

"I can't understand English," the driver says.

"I know," says Cuauh softly and lowers the brim.

The engine turns over and the driver pulls out onto a side road. The driver expertly weaves through the boulders strewn pell-mell about the streets that keep the police from navigating the neighborhood and keep the military out too.

Cuauh closes his eyes and feels his neck fuse with sweat to the hot pleather headrest. His mouth is dry. His bones are aching. The driver takes Cuauh the long way to the safe house, which looks like all the other safe houses in Juarez. A squat, pale-brown one story. Bad foundation. Meandering cracks in the walls that split jagged in the cold months like sweeping bolts of lightning.

Desert wasps make their home in the seams where the warmth escapes. They breed and die. They shred up the adobe with their lives until the house takes on the fragile look of a cracked egg, or like tempered glass about to shatter.

Cuauh eases his aching body from the comfort of the pleather. He moves to turn off the radio but it's already off. He walks around the fender and slaps the numbers tacked on the wall of the house just for kicks. 410. All the safe houses end in 10—2810, 510, 4510. Cuauh commits every safe house address he's tried to bring down with the slap of his palm to memory.

The door opens. Darkness pours out from the threshold. A wiry little man with ropy muscles lays out the flat of his hand. Cuauh and the driver hand over their chirping Nextel phones like they do every time.

The little man puts them in an oversize Ziploc bag and says, "I hope all is well." Cuauh's eyes adjust to the musty darkness inside so he's nearly blind. He can only feel the little man's words on his neck now, a plume of smoke that cools just above the shirt collar and hangs there at the volume of a whisper. The driver follows behind.

"All is well," says Cuauh to no one in particular and the door shuts behind him.

Inside, there's the too-sweet smell of perfume and sweat. There's the honeyed sound of women's voices, soft, like heather—the lilt of beauty queens or beautiful liars who say they're beauty queens. There's the knock-knock-knock of their heels against the tile, tiny women who seem almost weightless as they glide.

They appear to Cuauh behind the iridescent patches of light that burn away from the center of his gaze, his pupils fully dilating in the dark. All the women look the same to him. He wonders if he's met any of them before.

On the long table in the living room are silver bowls of cocaine, an RCA universal television remote, a polished pistol reeking of Hoppes 9 oil, a sweating beer, a half-finished ham torta sandwich with a bag of Sabrita potato chips.

"All is well?" asks the little man again. Cuauh takes a bite of the sandwich and a swig of the beer and repeats, "All is well."

The man with purple boots lies unconscious in the safe house tub, his hair still tinged with the sulfury smoke of burnt diesel. His hands are smoked black and his eyes are two fiery coals peering out with a thousand-yard stare. His name is Lalo and he's barely breathing. He's soaking wet in his clothes: a blue pearl-snap shirt, a pair of Wranglers, a pair of purple Larry Mahans that have all but cracked the fiberglass wide open. Along the inside of the tub are long, black arcs where the heels have scuffed in the struggle. The leather of his boots bloats about the same time his skin does. His fingers turn white and slough off their outer layer into the water.

Cuauh's face turns ashen at the sight of Lalo—this man he'd purged from his mind only thirty minutes ago. A million thoughts course through Cuauh's brain just then but none louder than the questions.

"What happened? What's going on?" says Cuauh. He acts just as surprised as he should be, though of course he'd seen this coming from way down the pike.

There's a doctor sitting on the toilet in a white coat, R.M.P. embroidered on his lapel. Across from him there's a boy with blue tattoos up and down his arm, these beautiful Chinese dragons with red eyes. The boy is wearing jeans rolled up to his calves and a plastic green rosary that dips in and out of the pink water of the fiberglass tub. He seems to be holding Lalo down or at least guarding him.

The doctor checks Lalo's pulse, consults his watch, and then produces a capped needle from his breast pocket. He plunges the needle through the denim into the fleshy part of Lalo's thigh. Lalo's eyes spring open, the black of his pupil spreading like ink to chase the green of his iris away.

"I only fly planes," says Cuauh to the little man staring up at him. The little man rubs his eyes and says, "We need to know who else. We know you were close. We need to know who."

"I only fly planes," says Cuauh. He says it again and again. He keeps repeating it as if it might change something.

Of course, Cuauh knew these things happened, but he never dreamed he'd ever be part of it. He knows what's coming and Lalo knows too. Everyone looks down on Lalo in the tub. The air is static. Lalo refuses to look anyone in the eye or speak for that matter.

"I need you to tell me where it's at," says the boy with blue tattoos into Lalo's ringing ears. He grabs Lalo by the neck. Lalo coughs deep and raspy from the diaphragm. He looks at Cuauh finally. Cuauh looks away.

"Where's the money?" the boy asks Lalo, tired and aggressive as if he's asked him a thousand times before. Lalo swallows his own voice. "Where's the money? Where is it? Who has it? Tell me," says the boy with a cool, unnerving calmness. A whisper. A plea. "Tell me. Where is it? Where is it?"

Lalo's eyes stay open even beneath the water. They only close right before a giant, pink glug escapes his lungs and clouds the tub with a rolling boil. Lalo's hands grasp the sides of the tub. His index finger points at the boy, then the ground, then Cuauh standing by the doctor.

The doctor waits a beat or two and then raises his hand. "That's enough," he says. The body is still.

The doctor rubs his eyes and puts a plastic device over Lalo's mouth that makes him puke up water until his teeth chatter, until the color returns to his lips.

"You'll get us those names," says the little man. He leaves the bathroom and Cuauh and Lalo are left alone. Everyone knows what Cuauh knows already.

Lalo's eyes are still dilated wide, the adrenaline in his veins faster than the cortisol.

"Don't say anything," says Cuauh to Lalo, and Lalo nods his chattering head. Lalo points his index finger to the mirror over the sink, and Cuauh looks up at it. Presses his thumb to the glass to check if there's a space between his thumb and its reflection. It's flush. It's a two-way mirror.

Cuauh turns off the lights and lights the votive candle over the toilet with the single match left in his ruddy matchbook. Saint Rita. Cuauh places the candle between him and Lalo.

He produces two crushed Faro cigarettes from a soft pack in his breast pocket and puts one behind his ear, puts the other at the corner of Lalo's face, the bent cigarette jumping up and down, up and down with Lalo's chattering jaw. Little flecks of tobacco fall from the end of the cigarette and rest on the surface tension of the water.

"How long has it been since you ate?" Cuauh asks.

"Long," says Lalo.

"What do you want?" Cuauh says. He rubs his eyes.

"Please," says Lalo.

"Chinese food?"

"Please."

"That's good," says Cuauh lighting his own cigarette from the flame of Saint Rita's candle. The smoke casts shadows on the wall. "That's good," he says again and takes Lalo's cigarette by the filter to light it with the cherry of his own.

He places the cigarette back into the corner of Lalo's face. It's wet, so it burns better at the top than it does at the bottom. Lalo takes quick puffs to keep the fire from going out. His mouth fills with hot smoke. He coughs and coughs, unable to get a breath.

To Cuauh, it's the saddest thing he's ever seen.

Some people said Lalo was a queer, but others said he was just like that—purple boots, those games he used to play. That one he used to do with a ten-dollar bill.

He'd stick it in a urinal, a cantina urinal, and then go back to the bar and drink with Cuauh and watch, observe, take note of everyone who stepped inside to take a leak.

He liked to take bets with the bartender: who'd be the one to reach in and fish it out? The thought of it amused Lalo to no end, his little giddy chuckle amplified by the half-emptied cantina glass at his lip that made him look retarded.

Every so often a patron—a nice elderly woman or a vaquero or someone—might pat Cuauh on the shoulder and say, "So nice of you to take your brother out. He looks better every day," or "Lucky him to have a brother like you. How is he doing as of late?" to which Cuauh would say, "fine, fine," and end it at that. Lalo would take little swigs and then laugh again to himself. He taught Cuauh to laugh in those days. Cuauh would laugh only when Lalo was right about who'd take the bill from the urinal.

Almost always, somebody would pay the bar with the piss bill and the bartender would know (Lalo would smell just for proof) and the matter would be settled. If the bartender won, Lalo would cover 5 percent of whatever the cantina was paying the cartel that month in collections. But if Lalo was right, the bartender would pay 5 percent to Lalo on top of the standard fee. It was usually a wash, the odds favoring the bartender if anything, which is why the bartender kept betting with Lalo.

For Lalo, the kicks were enough, and when he won, he'd always split the earnings with Cuauh, which is how they got talking about money in the first place.

This was in the beginning, when Cuauh was freshly deported. The new pilot from Texas who'd once been a crop duster. He was kidnapped in Nuevo Laredo, right after he'd walked the bridge, and ever since, he'd been lonesome in that briny way—sulking, scared, stone hopeless. For all the lore he'd heard growing up in Texas about the Zetas and Sinaloa and El Golfo, with all their evil ideas and all their evil ways, he'd never expected a narco to look like Lalo, who was more silly than scary and a little bit stupid too.

But Lalo, like Cuauh, was also an outcast within the cartel—one of those men who were kidnapped and not recruited—and that made them brothers in a way. They were both paralyzed by their circumstances. Their loneliness hurt and throbbed like a bruise. It was only when Cuauh thought of escape, of going home, that his body felt at ease. Cuauh could sleep when he dreamed of escape. He ate, he breathed, he laughed knowing that everything he did, every cent he made in this line of work, would all be put to use someday—not too far from now—when he'd leave Mexico and go back home to Harlingen. He decided, from the day he was kidnapped, to dedicate his life to returning, and he and Lalo mostly talked about that. How Cuauh planned to go back to his old farm in the orange groves and dust the crops until he bled black in the nose. He told Lalo about June bugs and cicadas that come every so many years and the smell of all that chlorpyrifos raining down from under his plane like the tang of urine. He told him of other smells too. The smell of his mother's posole stew boiling hot on the kitchen stove. The smell of tobacco drifting in off the breeze from the grove master's cigarillo, wet like rain but sweet like autumn.

"Work on a farm like a fucking slave?" Lalo would say to Cuauh. His lecture was always the same. "That's your big dream?"

"Maybe," said Cuauh to Lalo.

"That's the problem with paisanos, Cuauh. We're still slaves. Even in Texas, Tucson, wherever. We make El Norte run and we bring this country to its knees. But at least there's some dignity to destruction. Some dignity in living here. It's nice for a little while, don't you think? But eventually, I'll leave this too. We'll both leave it, you and me."

"How?" he asked Lalo one time. And Lalo looked at Cuauh almost surprised, as if he didn't expect that question or at least the audacity of it. It was only one word—*how*—but between them both it was the most dangerous word. It was the bridge between dreaming and doing. *How* connected them at the brain. *How* was the end but also the beginning of everything. And suddenly, it was out that they were both planning, scheming against their captors. They would both leave their cartel, escape it, which, of course, carried its own dangers, especially for those who were kidnapped. The cell chiefs kept names and addresses of relatives. Even if they couldn't find you they would find your brother or your parents. It was the thing that kept Cuauh from simply taking his plane and flying off into the north. It was the fear of it that kept him coming back, day after day, to the desert strip or the little road in Lomas de Poleo.

"Out with it, then," said Cuauh, as excited as ever. "How? How?"

Lalo's answer was simple. "A lot of cash."

"How much?"

"A lot."

"From where?" asked Cuauh.

"From everywhere," said Lalo, and he explained how he kept his money in one place but never on him. He kept it in the base of the aluminum-lined false steering column in that burnt-orange Ford Lobo he'd drive across the border into Texas, that hollow space where drugs were kept and stored. Safe from the prying eyes of X-rays, gamma rays, whatever rays reflected off the aluminum sheet inside the steering column. Other drivers drove that pickup too, but the money was still safe. Everyone knew that to steal from the cartel was a death sentence. And of course, everyone talked about the stash in that steering column, but nobody knew who it belonged to, so nobody dared take it. The other drivers assumed it was a test of sorts, of loyalty or something. And Lalo got a kick out of that.

He loved the idea of his money traveling to all the places drugs went, the places he might go some day after this—Houston, Wichita Falls, Oklahoma City, Tuscaloosa, Raleigh, New York, Montreal.

"Come with me," Lalo would say, and they'd make plans together. They dreamed of fancy hotels, fancy dinners, Buchanan's Single Malt Scotch, never having to work again.

Lalo told him that when it was his turn to drive the Lobo, he always checked on his money and it was always there, packed against the back of the column down by where the Freon hit the A/C vent. The bills were always cold and he liked to fan them in his face. The smell, like plastic.

Cuauh remembers Lalo telling him all of this. And he remembers asking again, "But how? So, you have a lot of cash. But what do you do with it?" Cuauh remembers that crooked index finger on Lalo's hand and how it waved the bartender over with just the tiniest motion that night in the bar, the cold of the January wind slapping hard against the window panes.

Lalo took a hundred-peso bill from his wallet, looked off toward the Cantina bathroom, and said to Cuauh, "Let me show you what honest men will do for money."

In the bathroom, Lalo busts his chin on his way toward the porcelain lip of the toilet. He hurls and hurls, his voice splattering echoes inside the toilet bowl that rattle out at the tiled corners of the ceiling and ping with a long whang like the tight, coiled racket of a kicked doorstop. Nothing comes up. A beaded string of spit arcs from the fleshy part of his lip to the clear water below.

Cuauh hooks his arms under Lalo's and pulls him up so he's kneeling. His chin sluices bright red. It meanders in streaks like jagged lines that dry maroon, brown, black, and then stops at his collarbone. He looks as fragile as an egg and just as pale. That incredible voice, that incredible noise.

"Don't talk," says Cuauh, "don't speak," and he takes the Chinese food from the ledge of the bathtub and places it on the floor. "Don't eat," he tells Lalo, who tries his best to be a good sport about the whole thing.

They look at the mirror and then look at each other. They see themselves. Lalo, the boy he used to be. Cuauh, the man he might become—the bloody mess, that pulp of a person. He looks at Lalo the way you might look at a car wreck, the way you might observe it and rubberneck because you don't want it to happen to you. He observes Lalo begging. Cuauh swears when it's his time that he won't beg.

"Please," says Lalo shivering in his cold clothes. "Please," he says reaching for the food, and Cuauh lets him have it.

He nibbles at the breaded chicken. He can't keep anything down.

Inside the tub the ashy cigarette from Lalo's lips, snuffed and bloated at the filter. It spins slow under the drippy faucet.

Cuauh takes off his shirt and ties it like a scarf around Lalo's neck. He pats him dry with the tail of it. He grabs him by the shoulders and blows out the candle.

The sodium lamps pour in through the window and light up half the tub orange. In the dark the other half is blue. Lalo's skin is yellow, his torso cut in half. The water is green, the same shade of green Cuauh remembers so well from his childhood.

He eases Lalo's head into the water and closes his eyes. Lalo wraps his legs around Cuauh, and Cuauh lets his mind drift back in time. The warmness of Lalo's escaping breath. Like Texas heat in the summertime.

Cuauh lets his mind go elsewhere. He imagines walking barefoot in his old backyard or what he considered his backyard at one time. It's where he played anyway, him and his little brother. It's still teeming with sounds. The tick of the heat in his ears, the tick of the insects flapping pell-mell from one tree to the other, ruining everything he's ever worked for.

Behind his closed eyes are the cicadas too, seventeen-year-old cicadas humming pitch perfect in the shade of the orange-tree branches. You can't see them but they're there. And they'll die eventually, like all the other critters and crawlers and men and women in the grove—all poisoned by the pesticides.

Lalo moans and Cuauh brings his toes to a point. He's flexing his calves, he's bringing his body up two or three inches to the tree. He pulls down a switch and plucks a cicada from the branch. He pinches its humming legs between his fingers and dangles it away from his face, as far as his arm can reach, staring at its molting body. The cicada feels the same way it did when he was seven—the last time he handled a cicada—like a sliver of metal but undeniably alive.

He remembers how they'd make them fight, him and his brother. How he'd clip their wings and set them off against each other in a dirt ring like oversize ants. Being flightless made them hostile. They circled for a long time before they attacked one another. They made them carnivores, him and his brother.

It was always a quick death. He remembers how placidly his little brother watched as one cicada would split the other open, the broken one's exoskeleton sloughing off like flaking bits of fish food. And they'd talk over it just like teenage boys might talk over cigarettes or old men might talk over dialysis at the Harlingen Scott & White down the road—what is the worst way someone can die?

His little brother would always come up with the funny deaths: ants, getting killed by a hooker, getting killed by ants and a fire and a hooker at the same time.

When it was Cuauh's turn, all he could think about was shriveling to death, sloughing away like that bug—molting, beautiful and iridescent like that cicada drying in the dirt.

What a slow death, he thinks. How cruel children can be.

He thinks of the cicada and thinks of the drivers and thinks of Lalo and thinks of himself. Disposable, just like everything else. He'll molt under hot dirt eventually, somewhere in the world. In his mind he can see their skin sloughed off by zip ties or bullets or fire. He's suddenly conscious of his own scars all over his body: the puckered red blips of skin around his wrists from when he was zip-tied and kidnapped in Piedras Negras; the pink laceration over his arm when he was made to fight gladiator-style at midnight; the serrated bead sutures across his clavicle from when he crashed a plane for the first time with his brother.

He opens his eyes and sees that face underwater. Perfectly still. Perfectly at peace. He imagines plucking each scar from his body to lay them over himself. He thinks he can remember what it felt like to be flawless at one time.

ALEX SHAKAR

In the Flesh, We Shone

They met at a dinner party. She was young and blond. He, tall, dark, and dead. Seated beside him, she found it hard to stop watching his pale, veined fingers stroke the fabric of his placemat. She only knew her aunt here whereas he seemed a friend to most. Across the table, a mousy guy with a mustache was talking about a long-ago boat trip, in which the dead man, not then dead, had been swung out over the sea by a sail in a storm, before swinging back to calmly tie it down and save the day.

—He looked about as ruffled then as he does now, the mousy man said, to chuckles.

—We had him reanimated, the hip middle-aged hostess leaned in to tell Jill, because our gatherings just wouldn't have been the same.

—Oh? He must have a mordant wit, the young woman said.

She'd felt bold at the outset, but by the time she'd spoken, she doubted herself, wondered if as a stranger she didn't have the right, and almost added the terrible mistake of not looking at him and including him in the joke.

—I'm afraid I've never been the life of the party, he said.

The women laughed. His voice, low and gentle, made her skin charge. Maybe it was only her mind that for a second heard in it an otherworldly harmonic.

—It was mainly for those eyes, the hostess stage-whispered.

Those eyes, blue-green, recessed, with which the corpse modestly beheld his empty plate, seemed then geological, the heart of some million-year stone just opened to daylight. But as part of his overall expression, she soon saw, they could look amused, appreciative, if just a bit wistfully detached, as if he were watching old home movies. After some small talk about the unpredictable weather (she was new to Chicago winters), he drew her out and she told him about her life, what little there was to tell. To get away from her sleepy central Illinois town, she'd gone to college in California, then found a marketing job at a tech startup, where she worked for three years until the company imploded. She was here now for grad school, anthropology, pursuing a kind of vision she'd had one day. In the cafeteria of the building where her startup had been based, she'd watched a guy play checkers against a Muppet-eyed robot, the machine craning and dropping the pieces from square to square. Then, heading home on the train, she'd noticed a half-dozen people moving little colored jewels around on their phones. It had struck her that society was a kind of dream. And that maybe her own life had amounted to nothing more than moving jewels around. An image had flashed in her mind: she'd seen herself working in the dirt, unearthing cookware shards and bones.

—Of course, that's probably just moving jewels around too, she said. Probably there's no escaping it.

Around the table, silverware clattered, people exclaimed, reacted, belaboring more appropriate subjects, she assumed. She felt silly for airing her vague disgruntlement with life to a dead man.

—And if this dinner party woke up from its dream, he said, what would happen then?

—I don't know, she said. Maybe we'd dance on the tables.

—Or the whole thing would be a dance. He flipped a pill into his white wine and watched it fizz to orange.

Games, dances, there seemed little difference—she supposed the dead had no direct line to wisdom. But as she looked around the overcrowded dining room, for a moment the pink meat hopped into people's mouths, the watches and bracelets flipped their captive arms to display themselves, Jessica the hostess turned back and forth to wind up the men to either side, and she herself, Jill Vale, set against it all a little less, was executing her head-tilt-lip-purse maneuver, was flirting, in other words, with a goner.

—I guess I'm dancing with death, then.

—You're a live one, aren't you?

—Is that your only criteria?

The blanket lost to the floor, Jill nestled under his arm along the length of his side.

—Rigor mortis has its uses, he said.

—You've been saving that one up, haven't you?

He wasn't cold—his skin was warmer than room temperature; she'd ascertained that much on the night of the party when he'd taken her hands and said goodbye. And now that she was flushed and sweaty, his

skin felt pleasant, like wax cooling from a candle and still slightly mal-
leable. On their first night out, she'd been surprised to see him shiver
in an outdoor Christmas market for German crafts downtown. They'd
drunk mulled wine, his spiked with his neon orange pills, in a tem-
porary beer hall of folding tables under a billowing tarpaulin. She'd
talked mostly about herself again, and as she'd expected, he seemed not
to mind. For some time she'd needed to talk things out with someone
more impartial than her sister Cindy (her usual confidante), someone
sympathetic but not to the point of taking on her own worry and reflecting it back at her. It was a lonely, uprooted time. She'd left a non-
committal boyfriend who seemed always on the verge of leaving her, as
well as what could have been a lucrative career, to come to school in a
place she barely knew anyone. She'd done it hastily and maybe stupidly,
and the classes were interesting but slow and she didn't know if she had
the patience. He asked good questions, listened intelligently, if that was
a thing. She scanned the air in front of him when he spoke; seeing no
steam, she felt a ticklish chill, then a luscious warmth at the sight of her
own voluminous puffs as she went on talking. As for his life—his ex-
life—he'd been an engineer or something, the kind that makes buildings, a bachelor, no kids, though he'd had his heart broken if she had to
guess. She didn't ask much. It could have been impolite. After all, what
did any of that matter now?

Tonight, she'd asked him to tell her more, but not too much more.

—Not too much more?

—No. Just one fact.

They were in a hotel bar—he was developing an affinity, he said,
for transient places. She'd gotten drunk, and he'd at least pretended to,
alcohol mainly a preservative for him, plunking pills into his martinis,
waiting for them to fluoresce and effervesce.

He said he'd worked on some of the tallest buildings in the world.

—Why is it every chance you give him, a man will try to talk about
his penis?

She'd shocked him, she saw. Leave it to her to shock a corpse. Then
a few yellow-chalk teeth peeked from his ashen lips.

—Oh? Am I the one talking about it?

An enormous mirror ran the length of the wall over the bar, reflecting the whole low-lit, tourist-filled room around them, but of themselves, all she could make out over the bottles were the tops of their

heads. She wanted more, wanted to see how they looked together. As they walked to the river through a soft snowfall, he told her about the buildings around them, about a roaring-twenties jewelry building with an elevator for armored cars, about a building whose marble façade had crumbled from the winters and had to be replaced with granite. He talked about one he'd wanted to make, if he could have only persuaded an architect to design it, a developer to finance it. It would have been shaped like an hourglass, with beams twisting in the middle like Mobius strips, so slender there it would seem to defy gravity. If not in Chicago, then in Dubai or Bahrain. He liked to envision it surrounded by sand.

—What's a Mobius strip again?

He was skewing his joined fingertips, talking about countertwisting cores and equilibriated tubes, something like that, but she barely listened, instead thrilling to the touch of his broad, dead hand on her lower back—the dead feel mostly due to his gloves and her coat, she knew, but so what—and sneaking glances at their ghostly images in storefront glass.

Back in her bathroom, while he sat being sniffed at uncertainly by her cat on the couch, she posed in the mirror under the dressing room bulbs, admiring her full, rosy cheeks, the curves within her jeans and top, her breathily parted lips juicy as a starlet's. It wasn't like her—she wasn't normally vain, usually the opposite; she knew herself as anxious, time-haunted, feeling in her twenties as if her prime had already passed, and what use had she made of it? But with the dead man (his name was Felix, but to her friends and in her mind he was still the dead man) she saw herself as she felt he must have—mouthwateringly vital. She didn't know what her deal was. She'd never even liked vampire movies as a teen. In the bedroom, though the light was out, she made sure the door was cracked, the streetlight sufficient to show their naked forms in her full-length mirror. She let him look first, kissing him, feeling for his tongue with her own, giving it a little lick, pretending every new place she touched she was bringing to life, and every place he touched he was bringing to death. She turned and pressed against him, running the backs of her arms up over his shoulders, clasping his neck. He was only slightly paler than she in the mirror, but in her imagination he crested around her like a glowing moon.

—It's only our second date, she whispered afterward.

—Do you think I'm a whore?

She'd have felt mocked if his tone weren't a little earnest.

—Yes. Who do I call about a dead hooker in my room?

He laughed, the first time she'd heard him do so, and she felt a surge of accomplishment. It had been her wildness more than her easiness that had made her ask for reassurance. *Act fast,* her sister Cindy had advised over video chat. *I heard they can decay after a couple weeks.* Not remotely true, Jill had argued. A few of the first ones were still going after a year. Though, true enough, it wouldn't be long, and this more than the necrophilic thrill was what Jill had wanted—part of the satisfaction, she'd imagined, would come from quite possibly being the dead man's last, no woman to follow her; and peace of mind would come from the certainty that tonight couldn't go anywhere. It wouldn't matter, and this wouldn't feel bad, because she'd know going in that it couldn't. Dude's already gone. Which was why it had been fine just now to wrap him a little too tightly, to run her lips on his bluish nipple, to inhale the sweetish, faintly naphthalene smell of his skin. Yet her second-date remark surprised her for another reason. She hadn't intended a third.

—Just my luck, he said, running two fingers ever so slowly down the side of her face. Maybe it was just the dead thing, but maybe it had been so too in his life: he had this way of looking at her. She felt she was being beheld by quasars, black holes, the milk of the Milky Way.

—What's just your luck? And something in her leaped and plunged even before he replied.

—That I never once met you, in all my life.

For a dead man, he wasn't that old, she told Cindy. Older than her, sure. *And deader,* inserted Cindy, who was starting to worry. Still, though. It wasn't like dating a senior citizen. Before his time and all that. And from such an interesting life, his stories full of travel to subtropical cities, conniving competitors, bureaucrats with their hands out, colleagues unraveling from mad business schemes.

—It must have been nice, making those huge buildings, she said. Knowing they're still there. With all these people making other things inside them. Making money, making love, making friends.

—Watching cat videos, mostly.

They were in a huge building just then, the Macy's downtown. He'd wanted to show her the old vaulted Tiffany ceiling. Beside a rack of leopard-print blouses at a third-floor railing, they gazed up at the tile work, sky-blue ovals wrapped in golden braids, then watched the shoppers below for a minute, then turned to find a woman wearing leopard-print pants browsing the rack. They'd just been to the natural history museum, where they'd lingered on the hominoid skeleton displays. She'd been teaching Felix some of the stuff she'd been learning about their evolution into anatomically modern humans. She pressed her fingers and thumbs to his face and head to show him his braincase shape and lack of occipital bun, opened his mouth to trace his receded dental arcade. She showed him her own, had him touch the third-eye point where her supraorbital foramen separated her brows; and they stood like that, molding each other like clay, families making wide paths around them, until finally they freaked even themselves out and took off for the ice rink.

It wasn't like dating a younger man either, full of himself and insecure, or a middle-aged man, for whom she'd risk being a kind of trophy. For Felix, she wasn't a possession, for what could he really possess at this point? She was precious, and strange, and soon to be lost. She was a fucking miracle, and really, all of it was, and when with him, she could see it this way, as if through his eyes.

—You think she'll wear the top with the pants?

—It's the cat videos, Felix whispered.

—What is it with these breathers?

—No, no. He took a blouse and held it to her. They're all the rage in the afterlife too.

He'd died in such a random, trifling way—a live wire in a sub-basement of a construction site, no fault of his own, so meaningless—that it only seemed right to his friends to give him a bit of a do-over.

—How did it feel? Jill asked, one night at his place, a small but swank panty-dropper of a high-rise. They sat at his granite island counter, one end piled with bereavement cards—*So Sorry for Your Passing* above photos of candle flames and calla lilies. Going? she said. Then coming back?

She was curious about those very last and first moments, whether he'd seen his own body, or a light, whether the air had been sweet as he'd gasped and risen from the mummifying goop. But he didn't recall any of that. It was just one moment he was himself, doing his job, checking the concrete fill, the ring beams and water lines, directing contractors, everything he'd been trained and habituated for by life, wanting to get it done quickly because he had to take a piss; the next he was in a cheap chair in a drab room somewhere with a bunch of pale and slightly greasy old cadavers watching a video on proper flesh maintenance. When he found himself out in the brightly colored streets, fall in Chicago, it seemed as if not he but everything else had surreptitiously ended, and in its place now, cranked on a spindle, some shimmery hologram.

—It's like winning the lottery, he said, and getting paid out in Monopoly money.

—Is that what I am to you, then? Monopoly money?

—Baby, you're the real Atlantic City. But I'm a tiny top hat made of lead.

This was still early in their friendship, when she could bear to bring the whole deceased thing up. At first, she'd kept up the jokes, while he'd been the sensitive one. *You're so dead,* she'd said with an eye roll when he'd failed to get some pop culture reference, and he'd smarted. *Waiter, there's a corpse in my cruller,* she'd texted back at his selfie from a hip coffee shop. *A handsome corpse* ☺, she'd amended a few minutes later, but he hadn't replied for hours until she'd videoed an apology. Yet in just a few weeks, the poles had switched, and now she was the one hurt when he was inconsiderate enough to bring the thing up. *Brains,* he'd say, lifting mesmerized arms toward her. Or: *I could lose myself in you,* and just as she'd start to melt, *literally.*

—Why don't you run with me, she said.

—The dead don't run. By definition.

But it killed her to see him by the window with his nuclear orange tea, eyes to the cityscape, farther and farther adrift. He could sit so horribly still at times, silent for minutes on end, until she'd panic, fly over and drop on his lap, wriggle until his hands were active, cupping her, sliding the length of her over her shorts and down and up her leg, as if she were the one who needed to be warmed—maybe she was. The almighty Internet was of two minds, of many minds, really, on the issue of what best kept a dead body going; some counseled rest, others activity, others proprietary oils. Jill thought it had to be exercise.

He fished a tracksuit from a bottom drawer, and soon they were running in the brisk spring mornings without major mishap. Other joggers on the lakefront stared at first, the older ones seeming the most put out, probably fearing not even death would release them. Felix's legs were paler than the rest of him, a milky white, but as the weather warmed they tanned just a little, and when she noticed this, Jill was giddy with hope. *It's just something new with the pills,* said Cindy, whose husband, a geriatric doctor, though not trained for it, had been getting the odd walk-in cadaver. *They're still deteriorating. You can't keep seeing him, Jill. Don't you want one of these?* She pulled her bubble-headed four-year-old into the frame, had him wave and kiss the screen. There was a guy she wanted to set her sister up with, a med student her husband's family knew, good-looking, good prospects, *not to mention a pulse.*

Felix himself was just as unhelpful, told her more or less the same— she shouldn't stay, there was only so much time, only so much he could do even to hide the changes. His skin, though tanner, was more like the tan of a hide, sunk around his ribs and the bones of his face. It only made him look to her more chiseled, jawline more masculine, eyes more lucent, as though he was being pared to his essence, flesh made soul. Living men, those bags of jelly and breath—how could they compete? The exercise was working, she was sure, contributing to his glow. Yes, there were the microlesions, the scrapes and shaving cuts that would neither bleed nor heal and could only be glued. And the audible creaking of his joints, and the dryness of his eyes and mouth he had to slake with day-glo drinks. But it wasn't rot (she could barely think the word), wasn't anything like that. Maybe it *was* purification. And anyway, she snapped at Cindy, weren't we all dying? Dust to dust? Wasn't everybody else just fooling themselves? At least she, Jill, wasn't fooling herself.

Except that she was. Or trying as hard as she could.

—We should take a trip, she told Felix as he made her a green smoothie, his own former go-to breakfast. Like, a road trip.

At first, she didn't think he'd heard her. He seemed caught in some inner loop, running his finger gently over the edge of a halved peach.

—Sounds fun, he at last replied. And sounded like he meant it. But maybe like he meant it in the abstract, as if it was one of those many things he'd done in the past and others would go on doing without him for the next million years. He'd been slowing down, going out less, and mostly only when she made it happen. But what bothered her more was watching him toy with a flinty indifference, turning his eyes from the news, from passersby, anything moving—from her—rejecting it all before it could him, the way she'd preemptively left her dithering boyfriend. It was a pose, she knew. She could see this in the way he couldn't help but stroke the skin of a fruit, or delight in watching her eat it.

Still, bit by bit, he was clearing out his apartment. She'd caught him yesterday stuffing another garbage bag full of clothes. He brought them to Goodwill, didn't bother filling out donation receipts for taxes. Most of his dress shirts had vanished, even ones he'd worn a couple weeks back. Dispensing possessions was commonly approved of, regarded as one of the nice ways those brought back from an unexpected departure could tie up their own loose ends, along with making out post-living wills (though these were still often contested in the courts) and arranging their own incinerations and services. But Jill herself couldn't imagine going back out like that, with a whisper, as it were, erasing all traces of herself and submissively bowing out the door. If she came back, she'd be one of those death-defiers with a bucket list from hell. The "go-goers," she'd heard them called. Dropping out of airplanes in hang-gliding suits. Rocketing over the atmosphere, strapped to the bulkhead, feeling the suction of space as the bay doors opened. Some sad breathers had started spending more time planning for their hedonistic post-lives than they did for their actual ones. So maybe not the orgy stuff, maybe not the self-started-funeral-pyre bash when the jig was up. But she'd want at least something out of the ordinary.

It wasn't a round-the-world jetfoil cruise, a road trip. But it was at least a change of pace.

—Like right now. We'll pick a direction. How about counterclockwise? She smiled. All around the lake. I hear it's beautiful up north.

—You've got your classes—

—I took incompletes—it's done. She hadn't, not yet, but if she'd framed it any other way, he'd have said no. Even as it was, he seemed so upset for her sake she didn't think he'd agree. But she impressed on him with the fierceness of her stare that this was not just for him, and he softened.

—How about Detroit?

—*Detroit?*

Why the hell not Detroit? She got some Motown music going on her laptop and he started to pack, with actual enthusiasm now that it wasn't just to give his erstwhile life away. He booked a rental car online, calling out the possible upgrades—luxury! moonroof! leather! check, check, check!—while she threw his pills and some wine and snacks into a cooler. She'd started to dance, and was heartened to see him bound over. Then she was being twirled, dipped, pulled in close. She stood on tiptoes and nuzzled his neck, smelling the melon and sandalwood cologne he'd started using. He lifted her, spun. Then came a cracking sound.

—Sorry to fall apart on you, baby. He assembled a smile.

The only thing keeping her from doing so on him was how afraid he'd looked the moment it had happened, more than a hint of which dread now lingered as he watched the clinic tech, a slouching man in a grease-stained white coat and tool belt, drill a hole through his shot anklebone. A pungent, mushroom-sweet plume escaped the puncture. *Dry rot,* she might have heard the guy say over the drill's whine in the midst of a meandering narrative about the various joints he'd been see- ing disintegrate of late. The tech sank a bolt into the bloodless orifice and snapped on a jointed brace while Felix just watched, blinking once. He was feeling less pain, these days. Maybe that was a silver lining. Jill summoned the courage to ask the tech what he'd said while drilling, but he just *well*ed and *aah*ed and patted the brace, a good one, he said proudly, carbon fiber, lighter than steel and four times as strong, would outlast its owner, would outlast us all.

At the rental place, the clerk wouldn't let Felix list himself as a driver, but as soon as they stopped for to-go coffee a few blocks away, Jill in- sisted.

—My reflexes…Felix began.

—Shut up. You hit on me at that party. You asked me out. You drive.

They rode in an uncomfortable silence until well outside the city. How could he have done that, she was thinking, put on nice clothes and gone to a party and acted all charming with a living woman and ask to see her again. How callous. Or desperate. How self-deluding. But what would she have done in his place? He hadn't asked to be reanimated. At least he claimed he hadn't. He'd handled the state in which he'd awoken with more grace than many others, than she would have for sure. And she certainly hadn't stopped him. What was with her anyway? Was it some kind of death wish?

She didn't think so. If anything, the opposite. She'd just wanted to feel alive.

Felix drove with care, his good foot on the gas, his thumbs lightly caressing the leather of the wheel.

—Say something, she said. What's happening in there? Is your brain starting to embalm?

Why did she want to hurt this man, in his last days?

—Good chance, he said. It's hard to know. For a minute it was like everything had the same texture. The sunlight, the air, your voice, me. All the same material. And I've felt it before.

He seemed to be waiting for her to ask what it was all made of.

—Well, stop doing that. You're creepin' me out.

Though she wondered what he would have said.

They didn't get as far as they'd planned. They did have an oddly not-so-bad day in Detroit, driving around the potholed, weed-grown streets, the burned-out houses. Felix had programmed a list of ruins mentioned on urban explorer sites into his phone, and they'd navigated from one to the next—the old Packard plant, husks of warehouses that stretched for nearly as far as they could see; the Metropolitan train station, a grand old towering skeleton for which the most the city could do was to cordon it off with a chain link fence and keep up the flowerbeds on the surrounding parkway. It was less sad than Jill had feared, the emptiness of the place more peaceful and powerful. She snapped dozens of pictures of turreted houses sagging inward like fallen cakes, crumbling schools sprouting trees amid moldering books, church naves bleaching like bones under the open sky. Felix only lifted his phone to get one or two of her. They took in some of the city's fledgling renaissance as well. At an outdoor market, he bought her a jar of locally made probiotics from a hippie chick, giving it a little shake, as if he might see the billions of microbes darting around. The next day, they managed a short hike in a state park, the mosquitoes harassing them both, but falling from him, poisoned by the orange fluid in his veins.

—Ah, he'd said. Sweet revenge.

On the way to the quaint lakeside town where they'd booked a bed and breakfast, he began to weave on the road.

—Keep going. She grabbed the wheel. He slowed and kept to the right lane, but it didn't prevent a state trooper from pulling them over.

—Sorry, Jill called to him in the window. My bad. I'm such a back-seat driver.

—I'm driving from farther than that, Felix said, almost too softly to hear.

The cop deliberated, sitting stark still in his front seat, either having an existential moment or thinking through the paperwork involved. In the end, he issued a warning, and watched them get out and switch places, Jill helping Felix, an arm around his waist. He walked as if he were made of wood, but as he leaned into her, he seemed so light she wondered if in the end he'd just implode in a puff of dust.

At the B&B, the proprietress, a woman with a wall-eye and a Cookie Monster sweatshirt, leveled a dire stare at Felix as he handed her his credit card. Jill wondered if she'd turn them away.

—Do you have a turn-up service? he asked, and mimicked raising a sheet over his face.

It took the woman a few seconds to get it, but when she did, she guffawed.

They left their bags and walked over a drawbridge, through the placid streets of town, and along the marina to its end, where a slip of land extended past a small beach toward a distant lighthouse. Couples and families made their way to and from it, but here was a bench, and this was probably the best view anyway, of the lighthouse itself against the dark silver lake and the sun behind the low clouds coming through in embers. Seagulls squawked, waves burst on the sand, a flag flapped continuously. A passing couple agreed to take their picture. Their eyes caught the flash in a spectacular way; in the years to follow, Jill would think how right they looked together on that bench, her head on his shoulder, his tilted over hers.

He unslung his briefcase and handed it to her: a beautiful old thing, its scuffed and worn leather only looking better from use. She bet it had been around the world with him.

—What's in it? she asked.

—Two clues. It's lucky and stiff.

—Stop it! She hit him, laughing, her eyes flooding.

She took the leather fob and pulled the large zipper, which opened with an oily smoothness. The dark, sleek interior held a sketchbook. She turned the pages. Buildings. He pointed out the ones he'd helped make, the ones he'd just imagined. She paused on the hourglass one he'd described, its outer beams twisting strangely at the center, its top half floating dreamily above the bottom. In the crosshatches of the pencil lines, she imagined she could see the curved glass windows, the mite-size people looking out, and up, and down, the whole thing trying to get a view of itself.

—Are you sad you didn't live to see it made? she said, lifting her head from the page.

He just twined her fingers in his, and smiled.

SJÓN

"Alda" Means "A Wave"—An Exercise in Hope

Translated from the Icelandic by the author

during a multinational, musical theater performance about a sea journey, a plainly dressed woman in her sixties gets up from her seat in the
center of the third row, and holding her purse tight in her hands she starts
making her way to the steps to her right. the actors continue with their
play, pretending to be out in the middle of the atlantic, supposing that she
is on her way to the restrooms.

the woman walks calmly down the steps, onto the floor by the first row,
where instead of turning to the right for the exit, she steps onto the stage.
the actors continue with the scene they are playing out: in the second decade of the twentieth century a young danish woman and her daughter
are stepping aboard a three-masted barque for an arduous journey to the
icy shores of greenland. the actors and musicians throw her side glances
of wonder.

the woman nods to the actors and musicians, and her polite way of
being makes them fall silent one by one and slowly step out of their roles
to become her audience.

she starts talking:

Dearest audience, dearest actors, musicians, please, excuse my sudden
intrusion. Please, believe that I would not interrupt this show without
a good reason. I am by nature shy and unobtrusive but the facts of the
matter that propels me from my seat onto the stage are too powerful a
force for a mere woman to fight against.

So, here I stand and there you sit.

When I read in an article in the weekly newspaper for the southeast-
ern Horn of Iceland that you were bringing your show to Reykjavík, I
instantly knew I had to leave my home village to go and see it, that here
I would find myself in the company of like-minded souls, people who
shared my lifelong passion—some would say obsession—with the sea,
pardon, the ocean. I was drawn toward it as forcefully as Sinbad's ship

was drawn toward the famous Magnetic Mountain in the tales of that fearless seafarer. Yes, I was drawn from my home county, Hornafjörður, to be here with you today, to be close to fellow men who might have a better understanding of my call for help than most others...

The wide, endless, unfathomable, colorful, mysterious "Hafið," "la Mer," "das Weltmeer," "the Ocean," the O-cean. It is easy to get carried away by the mere thought of it, by simply rolling its many names on the tongue—yes, just as easy as it is being carried away by it in reality...

the gravity of her last words silences the woman, and for a moment it looks as if this will be the end of her sudden "performance." but then, just as one of the actors is about to put a friendly hand on her shoulder to escort her off the stage, she finds her bearing and continues with determination:

Which brings me to why I, Alda Eiríksdóttir, a 62-year-old seaman's daughter from Höfn í Hornafirði, happen to find myself standing here in front of total strangers...On a stage...

she allows herself a dramatic pause before the next sentence:

My father, Captain Eiríkur Björnsson, is lost at sea with his ten sons, my brothers. The same sea that laps at the shoreline of the city where we find ourselves tonight, the Atlantic Ocean, that endless body of water...

On the second Friday of the month of May, in the year 1954, the eleven of them set out to sea from our home town, Höfn í Hornafirði...

she turns to the multinational group of actors and musicians:

Höfn means "harbor"...

she returns to the audience:

My father's new fishing boat was a vessel so brand new that it still hadn't had its name painted on the bow, and neither was it painted on the wheelhouse. My mother said to my father that he was tempting fate by going out to sea on an unnamed vessel and begged him to wait until it had been properly blessed. But the pastor was away and had promised to do so after mass the coming Sunday.

My father kissed my mother on the forehead and said everything would be fine. They would only go a mile out on the fjord to have the boat photographed for the annual *Fishermen's Day Journal,* that it was not as if they were going to be crossing the Atlantic. Then he laughed and pinched my cheek...

I was too young to go sailing with them, as I was only 16 months old and still in the arms of my poor mother. So, as she waved after her husband's boat, carrying him and the ten sons she had borne him, I also waved my little hand...

It turned out that my mother's fears were justified. And it was all the more painful for her as the boat was going to be named after her: "Anna"—her full name being Kristín Anna Jónsdóttir.

the woman falls silent again. but now actors, musicians, and audience wait patiently for her to come back to her story:

Sveinn Axelsson, the town's photographer, had gone out into the bay ahead of them, on his own little skiff, powered by a single outboard motor. And there he waited for the unblessed and nameless boat to come sailing toward him. He readied his camera, it was a calm day, the boat was steady on the still sea—and just as the boat with my father and ten brothers passed him by he managed to snap a single image...

she puts her hand inside her purse and messes about in it before bringing out a stack of postcards:

I have had postcards made with that picture, the color photograph of them and the boat they got lost on...that fateful day...

she steps off the stage and hands out the postcards to the audience in the first two rows of the theater:

Please, please accept them, pass them around, take a good look, memorize the faces of the men, the make of the boat, its shape and colors...

she makes sure the audience is distributing the postcards:

As you can see in the photo, my brothers' faces show nothing but excitement, the happiness of being together on a boat that sails smoothly under a clear blue sky. My father's face shines in celebration of the independence a boat of one's own brings its captain. They are unaware that it is going to be impossible for them to turn the boat back...

On the harbor my mother and I, the baby girl at her bosom, and all the other townspeople who had come to witness the photographing, waited for the boat to gracefully turn in the bay and make its way back to us...

But instead of returning, it kept sailing, sailing ever faster, sailing on and on, ever faster...until it disappeared over the horizon...

The poor photographer tried to follow them, but his small skiff only took him so far. The last thing he saw before he was forced to return to the harbor was my poor father running down into the engine room, obviously hoping to kill the machine and stop the boat's mad rush to nowhere...

tears well up in her eyes, she takes her time to hold them back before she continues.

This was 61 years ago. But it still feels like yesterday.

And now I will tell you the reason for my trespassing of the stage, my disruption of this play about an Atlantic Crossing and all the fine artists who were entertaining us all so well with music and spectacle—an act I sincerely hope you will forgive me when my tale is told, my motive is clear...

the tone of her speech changes from the emotional to a more obviously rehearsed one:

I know that many of you have come to this show tonight in order to prepare for your own Atlantic voyages, hoping that by listening to tales of seafarers and songs about the salty seas you will be better equipped for your journey over that vast ocean with its mysterious, dark depths and unpredictable, moving surface...

And it is because of YOU that I am here. You see, my only hope is that someone who looks out over the Atlantic's vastness for the first time in their lives can find my father and my brothers. Only those with fresh eyes can spot a small fishing boat lost in its infinite kaleidoscopic mirror-play of blues, grays, reds, greens, blacks, yellows, reds…

After talking to many, I have come to believe that those who have already crossed the Atlantic Ocean have made a pact with it and therefore will not help people like me who are trying to get it to return what it has taken from them.

It happens at the end of the first crossing, in return for allowing you passage to your destination, it makes you swear allegiance to itself, for life, all eternity…In a dream, maybe, with a salty farewell whisper in the ear as the travelers' feet touch land, perhaps…

No one has been able to explain it to me. So, I am sorry to say, even those who cross it for the second time have become its mates, its unwitting accomplices…

the woman puts a hand over her brow to shield her eyes from the stage lights, scrutinizing the audience, as if waiting for a response to her speech, continuing all the while:

I am not unrealistic; I know my father might have passed away by now. But as many of our relatives have become very old, I keep my hopes up and believe it is possible that he is still alive. My aunt, Hallfrídur Katrín Björnsdóttir, a former fish factory worker, is 103 years old and living in the old people's home in our town of Höfn. She is sound of mind and trusts she will live long enough to witness her brother's return. Aunt Fríða helps me in my campaign in many ways, mostly financially, and we have her to thank that I am here tonight, as she generously offered to pay for my trip, both the flight and the accommodation, taking the money from her meager pensioner's allowance…

But it is not only on her behalf that I plead for your help. My mother is also alive at the age of 109, but she is quite ill and heavily medicated. Still, each time I tell her I will not give up the search for her husband and sons, I notice a faint smile on her wrinkled face…

she sighs at the thought.

My father would be 112 years old today. You should recognize him as the sturdy man in the middle of the group. He is wearing the gray suit, made of local tweed, that my mother tailored for him with her own hands. I have been told his laughter is gentle, and even though I don't expect his pipe to have seen a grain of tobacco for five decades, it should still be lodged between his teeth, on the left side of his mouth.

It is very important that you know my father's name and the names of my brothers so you can properly greet them when you find them. It should make the shock of finally having been rescued a little less severe.

I list them by age, starting with my father:

Eiríkur Ragnar Björnsson (born 1903),
Ólafur Björn (born 1928),
Andrés Trausti (born 1931),
Einar Sveinn (born 1934),
Alexander (born 1936),
Helgi Rúnar and Rúnar Helgi, twins, (born 1939),
Jón Jón (born 1941),
Karl Nói (born 1942),
Egill (born 1945)
and Leifur Thór (born 1948).

My father and my eldest brother are experienced seamen and know how to provide for themselves out on the open seas. Neither hunger nor scurvy will have taken them, as they know many means to battle those two enemies of the drifting sailor: chewing seaweed that might come floating their way, snaring seagulls, or sending a good man down to scrape the barnacle off the keel, for therein is a chewy bit.

Still, I must confess that I fear for Rúnar Helgi and Jón Jón. From what my mother told me while of better health, and my aunt has confirmed, these two brothers of mine were of a somewhat weak spirit and might have crumbled under the mental hardship of being lost at sea...

she looks at the audience with tearful eyes:

So, dear audience, seafarers to be, I ask you to look for the unnamed fishing boat and the men in the picture while you cross the waters of the Atlantic Ocean for the first time. They do not belong there. They belong at home in Höfn í Hornafirði with my mother, my aunt, and myself.

The photograph on the postcard should serve as a measuring tool for all the boats you meet on your first crossing. If you feel the need to photocopy or scan it and distribute it more widely by hand or on the Internet, please, feel free to do so. The rights to the photograph are in the public domain, as they were given to me and the cause by Sveinn, the photographer, before he died last year at the age of 117.

Since I reached maturity, I have been on the lookout for people who are about to cross the waters of the Atlantic for the first time in their lives. I ask for their help, sometimes by writing, sometimes by telephoning, sometimes by seeking them out in person, but most often by showing up at gatherings like this one. I have dedicated my life to finding my father and ten brothers. I have neither married nor borne children and will not do so until they are found.

she steps down from the stage, takes a step toward the exit.

Dear people, audience, actors and musicians, I thank you for your patience, for being good listeners, and with all my heart I trust that my tale has moved you to compassion. I greatly value your help and hope to hear from you at your journey's end. And should you fail to notice anything during your transatlantic crossing that you would want to report to me, you can still choose to support my campaign to bring back my father and ten brothers with a financial donation.

My banking details are listed on the back of the postcard:

> Ms. Alda Eiríksdóttir
> Social number: 020152-3469
> The National Bank of Iceland
> Austurstræti 11, 101 Reykjavik,
> Iceland SWIFT: NBIIISRE
> IBAN: IS19 0172 3271 8428 0201 5234 69

The note with transaction should read:

> Re/Lost at Sea–1954.

she bids her farewell in a rather hurried speech:

I thank you for your compassion, your listening to my tale, and bid you good night.

the woman clutches her purse in her hands, takes a small bow, and leaves the theater.

XUAN JULIANA WANG

Algorithmic Problem Solving for Father-Daughter Relationships

To be a good computer scientist, a man needs first to understand the basics. Back away from the computer itself and into the concepts. After all, a computer is just a general-purpose machine; its purpose is to perform algorithms.

It is due to the fact that algorithms are unambiguous that they are effective and executable. However, algorithms aren't only for machines. In designing an algorithm, a person can execute a complex task through observation and analysis. To be a good father, it would be a logical assumption that these same acquired skills should apply.

As I used to say during my lectures at Dalian University of Technology some thirty years ago—Everything in life, every exploit of the mind is really just the result of an algorithm being executed.

For example: To peel garlic

- Obtain a bulb of garlic and a small baggy

As long as there is still-wrapped garlic, continue to execute the following steps:

- Break the garlic petal from the garlic bulb
- Peel off the outer skin
- Put the smooth garlic into the baggy
- Throw the skin into the wastebasket

To my students and colleagues I famously said the same can be applied to something as complicated as getting married. As long as an adult male is still without a wife, continue to execute the following steps:

- Ask librarians, family members, and coworkers if they know any single girls

- Invite girls to watch movies

Assess compatibility facts as follows:

- Beauty
- Family
- Education

If compatibility measures up to previously set standard, move to step e, if not, start from beginning

- Ask the girl to be wife

A coworker introduced me to my ex-wife. Her nose was too small for her face, her hairline too high. However, she came from a family with good Communist party standing and we attended similarly ranked universities.

One day on the way to see a play, she lost the tickets and I yelled at her for her carelessness. I thought that was the end of us. Then on the way back, I stopped along the street and tied an old man's shoes for him. She agreed to marry me after that.

There was a miscalculation in this equation, which I see now of course. I liked the girl I married very much, but not the woman she became after we immigrated to America. This woman never respected me. All the data was there to be sorted, I just didn't decode it until it was too late. She had this way of making me feel spectacularly incompetent. She was a literature major in college, she had what people said was a nice sense of humor. Once I took her to a company party and all anybody could talk about the next day was how beautiful and amazing my wife was. That was when it began to bother me. That people didn't think I deserved her. That they thought I was somehow less than her.

I don't think she understood the protocol of being a good wife. "Let's go into the city and eat at a nice place," she used to say. Why? So I could feel more out of place not being able to read the menu? No thank you.

But without her, there would be no daughter, Wendy. There's that to consider.

Now that I'm older, I see my theory prove itself day after day. Until illness and then death, life is indeed the result of a series of algorithms being executed. I didn't need a coach to learn how to play tennis, because before I even stepped onto the court, I understood the fundamental math of the game through theory. I know that the GPS in my car is using an algorithm, taking into its calculations a satellite moving through space, transmitting down to me to tell me where my car is.

So right now I need to make an algorithm to solve the problem of Wendy. My only daughter, who I somehow managed to drive away from me—door slamming and little eyes pooling up during dinner.

I wish to concentrate on the relevant details of our relationship, from tonight and beyond, in order to break down our problem into something that can be decoded, processed, and used to save our relationship. How did I hurt her? Will she ever come back to me?

The evening was one of those calm, snowless December evenings in Westchester County. My daughter, whom I hadn't seen in nearly a year, was home on vacation from studying in England and planned to spend two weeks living in her old bedroom. I had already prepped the pigs feet to throw in the pressure cooker, and defrosted tofu skins I'd smuggled in from my last trip to Jilin. When she walked through the door, pink-nosed and taller than I remembered, I felt such a rush of affection for the girl that I went right up to her and pinched her arm really hard.

I broke down these two weeks into pseudocode just to see how it was going to work out in my mind:

> If (daughter comes to stay)
>   then (if (temperature = cold))
>   then (enjoy home cooking)
>   else (watch movies)
>   else (buy her consumer electronics)

"*Baba,* is it your goal to make me obese?" she asked when I showed her the five-pound bag of uncured bacon shoved in my fridge. I replied, "Oh, come on, little fatty, you know you crave my pork stew," and she laughed. She hadn't changed very much, had the same chubby little hands that I love squeezing. She still had my smile, the one that was all gums.

Even before I had finished putting out all the vegetables and meats on the counter for prepping, Wendy was already showing me pictures of all her weekend trips. She'd been to France, Italy, and Spain. I pulled my head back so that the countries got into focus.

"Where are pictures of you?" I asked as she clicked.

"I was too busy documenting the landscape." She went through the snapshots slowly, importantly, lifting her computer to show me pictures of bus stops, lampposts, jars of pickles.

"How do you have so much time to travel when you're supposed to be studying?" I asked.

"You think I went all the way to England just to sit in my room? Besides, all the Brits do it too."

For me, she speaks Mandarin, which had gotten rusty. She mispronounced words and made up her own metaphors. But I loved hearing her talk, just like when she was a child, telling me stories while I tried to teach her how to make a good steamed fish. While her mother would be out taking real estate courses or painting a still life, Wendy would always keep me company in the kitchen. I didn't want to look at the pictures, but I was happy having her voice fill up the house. I gutted a red snapper and stuffed it with ginger.

"Can't say I have the same attitude toward education," I said. I handed her a potato peeler and she finally put away her laptop.

"Of course, I studied too, Dad, and I made a ton of friends from all over the world," she said.

"That's good, expanding your horizons," I said.

"There were Chinese students at my school too. Bunch of wackos. They just stayed in their dorm rooms and made dumplings all the time. It looked fun I guess, but *all* the time." I nodded, and she went on, "In England. Can you imagine?"

"And they were your friends too?" I asked.

"No, they never talked to me. Probably because I spoke English and didn't study engineering." She started chopping the carrots into strips, and I showed her how to make them into stars, "but I didn't go over to England to pretend like I lived in China, you know?"

"Probably good you weren't friends with them," I said solemnly. "The only Chinese kids that get to study in England have to come from crooked families with embezzled money."

"Maybe…but I can't imagine it would be all of them," she said, squinting at me. "There was this one crazy thing that happened while I was there. There's a lake in the middle of campus where the university raised exotic geese from all over the world. Then one day, the caretakers noticed that one of the Egyptian geese was missing its mate."

She stopped talking until I gave her my full attention. "Turns out this Chinese student had killed it! Goose dumplings." She put down her chopping and with great affect said, "The University expelled him."

"That's a pity."

"Isn't it? I heard the guy was from Anhui." She said. "And I just kept thinking, why did he do it? Even if he didn't know they were pets. What makes him see a beautiful bird and immediately want to kill it?"

"I wouldn't worry about it, Wendy," I said. "Here, help me over here." How would she know that my brothers and I used to kill sparrows with slingshots as food to eat. How we shot so many sparrows the birds couldn't land, so exhausted they began falling out of the sky, dead.

"It's just so typical of Chinese people too, not to even protest their friend's expulsion." She went over to the sink and began peeling the potatoes with great indignation.

If anything, I thought, it was she who protested too much. Always concerned with things that she has zero control over. Like missing her SATs for a hunger strike against the Iraq War, something she had nothing to do with.

Maybe I should have told her, the happy dinners where those little birds filled up my little brothers' swollen, wanting bellies. Maybe a little American like her might have understood after all. The water boiled and the fish was steamed.

Then there was the wine.

"I brought you this wine, Baba, carried it on my back through three border crossings," she said. "It's from Ravello, below Naples, on the way to this beautiful town called Amalfi." I nodded at the unlabeled bottle, which was made of heavy green glass.

"It was a family vineyard. The vintner said it was the best wine he's ever made. The vines grew on the cliffs facing the ocean. I had to hitchhike just to get this bottle for you." The girl kept going, excitedly, her hands remembering Italy.

Right then the phone rang, it was Charles and Old Ping, my two divorced and now bachelor buddies. They were wondering what I was doing for Christmas dinner. These buddies and I cut each other's hair once a month. They had nowhere to go that night, so naturally, I invited them over.

"Come! We are going to have great food, and Wendy's here," I said.

I smiled at Wendy and she shrugged and went about opening the wine. She couldn't have been upset about that, could she? Having my best friends over to share our Christmas dinner? No way, she wouldn't be that selfish. In fact, even though she's not very logical, she was always a remarkably reasonable, well-behaved child.

My ex-wife and I, we never hid things from her; she shared equal partnership in the family.

Maybe there were some things we shouldn't have told her. She probably shouldn't have been at the lawyer's during the divorce agreement where I probably shouldn't have yelled at her crying mother, "What are you going to actually miss? Me or the money?" That was probably a mistake, but I can't do anything about that now.

Was it the wine? I bet it had something to do with that wine. As we were preparing the last of the food, we had a rather unpleasant conversation about the fundamentals that make up a good bottle. "The most popular cocktail in China right now is the Zhong Nan Hai no. 5," I said. "They say it was created by former Premier Jiang Zemin himself: wine with Sprite."

"*Ba,* let me tell you some of the basics. So the most common red wines are Merlot, Cabernet Sauvignon, and Syrah," she said. She continued on like an expert, "Wine is not supposed to be *ganbei*-ed, the way you do it. It's supposed to be tasted and sipped, since it's about the appearance, the smell, the aftertaste."

"That sounds like a needless hassle to me," I said. "It's a drink."

"You know, you were probably destined to be a lonely migrant farmer, but instead you were blessed with me and you don't even know how to appreciate it!"

She circled around the kitchen counter and stood facing me. "Come on, I thought you'd like knowing about this," she said, as she slowly opened the bottle. "While I'm here, maybe I can take you to a wine tasting in the city. It'll be really fun!"

"You can save your energy, Wendy. Your old man is not fancy, and

I'm not going to sniff booze like a snob. I'm a working-class guy, in case you forgot," I said with a sniff, "while you were in Europe."

I took a sip from the glass she poured me and said, "I feel that in my experience, the best wine is wine that is over 14 percent alcohol content, with a wide neck; preferably the bottle should have a large indent at the bottom."

I thought I saw her roll her eyes at me, so I said, "When did you get so stuck up? Did you learn that from your mother?" and she turned away from me.

The previous situation can be broken down into pseudocode:
> If (daughter is frustrating) then (compare her to her mother)
> While (daughter shuts up) do (change the subject)

When the doorbell rang, Wendy skipped over to answer and I assumed everything was back to normal. She was very polite to both of them, like a good daughter. I didn't even have to ask her to help unpack the two cases of beer into the fridge. What a sight my friends must have been to her! Old Ping was as unwashed as ever, but he had changed out of his work overalls for the occasion. Charles still had paint splatters above his eyebrow, and his hair had grown long everywhere that was not bald.

When I tried to offer them Wendy's wine, both of them initially refused.

"I don't know about foreign liquors. Most things white people like give me the runs," said Charles.

"I'll stick to my *baijiu*, but thanks, little Wendy," said Old Ping, whose eyes were already rimmed with red. He must have started drinking in the car.

Wendy set up the table while I finished cooking. It was one of my most sumptuous spreads. There were five dishes, fish done two ways, and a soup. All the colors satisfied, every plate still hot. Old Ping opened twelve bottles of beer and clinked them against the plates. Now we could eat.

"A toast," Old Ping said, "for little Wendy giving us the honor of her presence. We owe it all to you for this nice meal we are having."

"Don't pay attention to your Uncle Ping, he has no education like you," said Charles.

Old Ping pointed a chopstick at Wendy, "Be nice to your old Dad, don't neglect him."

"*Chi Chi* Eat Eat!" I said, digging into the brisket.

The table was quiet with eating, until Ping started talking again: "Say, Wendy Wendy Wendy, when are you going to get married?"

"Ah, don't bother the girl, Ping, she's going to get a PhD, isn't she?" Charles asked me.

"You know!" Old Ping cut in, "They have a saying in China, there are three genders: men, women, and women with PhDs."

"Well this isn't China, last time I checked," she replied.

"Don't take too long is my advice," said Old Ping. "Make sure you find a boyfriend before your PhD scares all the boys away!"

I jumped in, "She doesn't have to worry about that. If she doesn't want to get married or can't get married, or whatever, she can always live here with her old dad. I'll pay the bills."

Then, what the heck, they decided to give the wine a shot. Charles asked her, "Wendy, you really think this tastes good? I'm not going to lie. I'm ignorant."

"It's from a family vineyard in Italy," I said, but not wanting to make my friends feel out of place, I added with a laugh, "Not that *I* could taste the difference."

"It's a little too sweet," Old Ping said as he wobbled toward my refrigerator and cracked a few ice cubes from the ice tray with his hands. He sauntered back to the table with a fist full of ice cubes and I reached out my glass.

I drank a big gulp and made a satisfied sigh.

It happened sometime after that. Charles had made us all take some shots of baijiu, and we were laughing when I noticed Wendy had stopped eating. She pushed her bowl away from her and was blinking at the ceiling light.

"Have some fish," I said to her. Her eyes glistened.

"Dad, why am I here?" she said, getting up from the table, "I flew back just to spend time with you, but it's like you don't need me at all. You have no interest in me. It's like I'm…"

"Oh, so if you're going to have to spend time with me, it should be all about you."

"I'm not saying that."

"I should be honored that you came back."

"Jessica's dad said her first verb was 'scurry!' What was my first *verb?*" she asked me.

"How am I supposed to remember a word from twenty years ago?" I laughed. I should have just made something up on the spot, like "eat!"

"Don't be a brat, Wendy, we have guests here."

"Come on, come on," Charles said. He pressed his lips together and rubbed his hands together. He had his own grown daughter that he was afraid of.

Knocking against the table, she struggled to put on her jacket.

"Hey, you can't be mad at your Dad," I said. "I raised you, you can't just throw a tantrum over nothing," I said, and somehow I accidentally ripped a few hairs from her head in trying to stop her from getting up and putting on her jacket.

She yanked away from me and went into the kitchen. I got up and the ground moved below me.

"Think of all the stuff I bought you. Think of all the sacrifices I've made for you. Now you come here with a bottle of wine and ask me questions? Make demands on *me?*" I said, yelling now, "Do you know how much of my money it cost to raise a little bratty girl like you all these years?"

She stopped by the kitchen door and looked at me. "You calculated the exact amount of money it cost to raise me?"

Old Ping cleared his throat, "Hey, Ma, stop it now."

"Yeah, it's 150,000 US dollars, not including all your tuition," I said to her, the blood rushing to my head as if I was hung upside down. "How about I act like Jessica's American Dad, and ask you to pay me back?"

"Yeah, why don't you pay me my money back?" I said as I banged my hand on the table. "Why don't you think about that?"

She left. Charles and Old Ping left soon after that too, leaving the table a mess of bottles and bones. An hour passed before I realized she was not going to take responsibility for her disrespectful behavior and return to apologize. Fine, have it her way. If she was going to be an ungrateful little brat, then that's her code of operation. I don't get it. My mind works best in bytes, in data, in things permanently and irrevocably true. I'm not even going to pretend that I understand women at all.

It's possible that I might have said some things in bad taste. I might have drunk a little too much as well. Thus, I had a problem on my hands.

I am aware there are limits to the capabilities of the human mind. That's why solving complicated algorithms is difficult; it requires a person to keep track of so many interrelated concepts. The solution couldn't possibly be figured out that very night. The last of the wine tasted bitter in my mouth, but I drank it anyway. Birds went up into their nests and I went to bed.

Wendy didn't call that night. She is still young, self-important, and takes her hurt feelings seriously. Even though she knows, at least should know, that I'd simply lost my temper. But even though I am asleep in bed, things will start happening. That's the phenomenon of problem solving; the mysterious wells of inspiration will often follow a period of incubation. Often the most difficult problems are solved only after one has formally given up on them.

So while I sleep, my mind will be incubating. The subconscious part of my brain will continue working on a problem previously met without success. Even after I wake up, work my mindless eight-hour shift in the assembly line of a computer repair shop, then watch basketball with Charles and Ping, I'll be trying subconsciously to get to the mysterious inspiration to solve my yet unfathomable problem. Once I do, the solution will be forced into my conscious mind.

Everything makes logical sense in computer science. Computers know not to get sentimental; they can rise above and work in symbols and codes. The world of imagination, uncertainty, and doubt can be managed through entities, HEX notations, and sooner or later, everything becomes representational and quite manageable. You don't need to worry about the specifics, once you figure out the abstract.

My favorite is the Nondeterministic Polynomial, which is simply a case in which someone or something, a magic bird perhaps, shows up out of nowhere and simply gives you the "answer" to a difficult problem. The answer is "yes." This is the only thing you need to do to find a way to check if the answer is correct, that the circumstances of the problem actually exist, and to be able to do so in a reasonable amount of time.

At one point in the past, I thought I had all the answers already. It happened before moving to America, before the marriage, before the daughter, before I'd even attended college. It was the summer I hitched a train to Guangzhou, then bought the cheapest ticket to Hainan. I was eighteen years old with a shaved head and twenty yuan in my pocket, but I just wanted to see the ocean, to float above the water and see the sand below. I still remember it now, that water reflecting a million perfectly placed petals, lifted up to meet the moon. Those birds that lined the trees like big white fruit, who transformed back into birds when I approached them and then flew away to become clouds. Those clouds reaching down to meet the sea, like a lock of wet hair on a girl's neck.

It was then I realized that the reflection on the sand looked like the electricity in a light bulb, like the mysterious maps of marble. I thought I knew the answer to a question I hadn't even asked, that there was some order in this universe.

Life happened so quickly. My hair thinned and I developed a paunch. The years melted and quietly pooled at my feet. Before I was at all prepared, I was married to an ambitious woman, with a precocious daughter, giving up my professorship and moving to New Jersey to become another immigrant American living an ordinary immigrant life.

Now that I think about it, those years were like watching a sunrise. It was not at all like the pleasant vision I had in mind. It was too much to handle, the great sun peering out from the distance: warm and comforting for a moment, and then brilliant, too brilliant to bear. The soft halo of light quickly became a flare and it stung. And yet, by the time I learned to turn away, most of my life was over.

Some nights I wake up in a panic and wonder: Why did everything that I worked for turn into things I despised? How did I become an old man? How did I end up with no one?

Algorithm discovery is the most challenging part of algorithmic problem solving. The phases themselves are unambiguous, but it is *determining* them that is the art. To actually solve a problem, I must first take the initiative.

Phase 1. Define and understand the problem

Phase 2. Develop a plan for problem solving

Phase 3: Execute the developed plan

Phase 4: Evaluate the solution for accuracy, and for its potential as a tool for solving other problems

Phase 1: Define the Problem: The daughter herself

I always knew this daughter was going to be trouble. The first inkling of it was sparked when I used to take her on my bike around my old campus. Because we didn't have any children's seats, I sat her on the pole directly behind the handlebars of my bike. The first thing I told her was to never, ever, get her feet close to the wheels. They would get caught and the wheel would cut her feet badly. I told her the only thing to do was concentrate on keeping her feet as far from the wheel as possible.

So the first thing she did was get her feet caught in the wheel. Cold sweat beaded on my face when I bandaged her bloodied little feet, but she barely cried. It was as if she was testing me, as if she had gone against my warning just to be sure I was telling the truth.

Phase 2: ? No, let's go back.

Phase 1: Understand the Problem: Immigration

Maybe it began soon after Wendy was born, after my wife and I boarded a plane from Beijing to JFK. Probably right after I took my first bite of ham and peanut butter sandwich and liked it. The problem might have arisen following decades of listening to the same Chinese songs, driving to Queens to be surrounded by other transplanted Chinese people, craving the same food we left behind. Perhaps it was sparked during the last twenty years of watching television, how I could never understand enough of the dialogue to chuckle along with the laugh track.

Phase 2: Could it have begun because TV wasn't funny? No, let's try again.

Phase 1: Understand the Problem: Unfair and unexpected reversal of roles

When I pictured myself being a father, I'd always assumed I'd take the lead in the relationship. I'd teach her how to read, how to ride a bike, how not to talk to strangers, and all that, but a lot of these opportunities at fatherhood have been robbed from me. It was she who taught me how to read English, when she was eleven. When she was twelve, she helped me pass my citizenship exam by making up acronyms. When she was sixteen, I taught her how to drive, but it was my daughter who helped me renew my license. I never got to console her over some little punk kid breaking her heart, but she held my hand when I cried, after her mother left me.

Is that all there is? It can't be. Cannot proceed to Phase 2.

I must admit, there are some ultimate limitations of algorithms. A difference does exist between problems whose answers can be obtained algorithmically and problems whose answers lie beyond the capabilities of algorithmic systems.

A problem solved algorithmically would be my temperamental attitude. I have since stymied the urge to physically threaten teenage boys being assholes in public, and I no longer pay for car damage due to routine road rage. It was logical reasoning.

However, there is ultimately a line to be drawn between processes that culminate in an answer and those that merely proceed forever without a result, which in this case might be:

1. The problem of wine
2. The problem of daughters

But this can't be the end, not for Wendy and me. We used to have a good relationship, a great relationship, with some all-involving grace that didn't need problem solving. When I watched her ride away on her first bicycle, her ponytail flapping back and forth like a bird's wing; or as I listened to her sing in the school choir, my heart skipped when she spotted me in the crowd and waved. That's my girl! I made her! Like when I visited her third grade open house and she showed me that in her bio, she had written "hiking with father" under hobbies, and "father" under heroes. That's got to be worth something.

So I can't give up. There has to be a solution.

And so, a portion of my unconscious mind will go on translating ideas from abstraction to pseudocode and laying it out systematically in algorithmic notations. It will be an ever-slowing process. Once I wake up, life will bring about more arguments and disappointments; small trespasses in this long life to live.

My relationship with my daughter might never fully recover from this night. We might miss a lot of holiday cooking together, and my hair will thin even more and she will grow just a little taller. Maybe out of the blue, some years from now, she will introduce me to a boyfriend, a strange-looking but polite boy. It might take even more years, but maybe she will come home and apologize and wash my dirty pillowcases and overeat in order to please me. I wouldn't be able to know how unhappy I had been until she returned.

She cannot abandon me. She loves me and thus will be able to anticipate my indignation and put my hurt feelings before her own. Those are some of the concessions made. There will be others. These sequences of instructions are programmed within her; that is her heritage.

Ah, but the solution, and there is one, will come to me years later. Perhaps when I am on a fishing boat in Baja, or in the middle of my honeymoon with my second wife, or in the hospital room at the birth of my new baby daughter, Lana. When it comes to me, and it will, I will remember this:

One afternoon, not long after we immigrated, when my daughter was still outgrowing her baby teeth, I came home from work early and found her walking alone around the dim apartment. Holding a hand mirror, face up at her waist, she walked from room to room while peering down into the reflection.

"What are you doing?" I asked.

"I am walking on the ceiling," she replied.

I was about to tell her to stop fooling around, to do her homework, but instead I paused and allowed myself to go with her imagination. I tried to picture what she might have seen up there. What magical inexplicable things could have been walking on the ceiling with my lovely fat-faced daughter, who spoke no English, sensitive and shy, and so often alone.

KEVIN WILSON

An Arc Welder, a Molotov Cocktail, a Bowie Knife

It was almost midnight when my girlfriend got a call about her sister who had been arrested for taking a kebab skewer at a cookout and stabbing her husband so close to his dick that it was probably going to affect its long-term functioning. Though I did not like the guy at all, the prognosis for his dick had been my immediate concern upon hearing of the altercation, not the fact that his wife was now in jail.

Even though it was over an hour away, I drove my girlfriend to their house so she could watch her nieces and nephews until their parents found a way to get back home. "If they end up killing each other," my girlfriend told me, "I think I'm the one who gets custody of the kids." I didn't have to say anything in response, because she knew as well as I did that I would not be around if that scenario ever became a reality.

The kids were as close to feral as you can get, like animals dressed up in camouflage jumpsuits. Someone had dumped an entire box of frozen corn dogs onto a pan and was warming them on top of a kerosene heater in the living room. The younger boy, who was five, and the two girls, eight and ten, were tearing open packets of Pop-Tarts even though there were already dozens of half-eaten Pop-Tarts all over the house. There were three or four kittens, their eyes oozing pus, running up and down the hallways, and my eyes burned from the smell of piss that saturated the air. In what was ostensibly the dining room, there were, I shit you not, six broken, outdated computers in plain sight.

The older boy, who I think was fourteen but looked older, was playing a videogame about the apocalypse, but all he kept doing was scrolling through the available weapons in his possession while the game was on pause. I couldn't stand still in the house, because the toxins in the air would settle on me, so I kept pacing through the rooms, afraid to stop moving. In the kitchen, there was a person-size puddle of grape soda that had turned solid, imprints of the kids' bare feet tracking it all over the vinyl floor.

My girlfriend took the girls into the bathroom and turned the shower on them and got them ready for bed. Then she made a bed on the sofa for the little boy, and we watched him hump a pillow for nearly fifteen minutes before he finally fell into something that was barely sleep. The oldest kid, a fucking giant, more than six feet, three inches tall, just kept scrolling through all the weapons he could, if he wanted to, use on any number of irradiated mutants. My girlfriend went into the kitchen to clean up a little, and I watched the hypnotic clicking of the game as the boy went back and forth between items: brass knuckles, pieces of brick, a baseball bat with nails in it, a BB gun, a 9mm pistol, a sniper rifle, a sawed-off shotgun, an arc welder, a Molotov cocktail, a bowie knife, a sledgehammer, an empty two-liter of Mountain Dew, a plasma rifle, and on and on and on.

Finally, without even looking at me, he said, "People always talk, but then, when you do something, they shut up."

I had no idea if he was threatening me or if this was connected to the paused game, but I did not, for one second, think about responding.

"Bitches today, they are everywhere," he said without any emotion whatsoever.

"OK," I said.

He finally unpaused the game, having selected a plasma rifle, and it was not more than five seconds before a zombie jumped from a tree overhead and ripped out his throat. He restarted the game, paused it, and scrolled again through the list of available weapons. The cat-piss smell was starting to settle on my clothes, particles of it like snowflakes on my eyelashes, and so I got up and did another round through the house.

"I found a bone beside the toilet," my girlfriend said to me, holding up something white and hard; it was not a fragment of a bone, but an intact bone of unknown provenance. Human or animal, we did not know, and both seemed equally likely based on the other evidence in the house. We had to keep our voices down because the older boy was still in the living room, gnawing on the wooden corn dog sticks until they splintered in his mouth, still trying to decide how best to kill something imaginary.

"He split her lip once," she said to me, as if there wasn't a bone on the edge of the sink in front of us, like we were just going to table the unknown bone and talk about what we already knew, that her sister and brother-in-law were not going to resolve anything anytime soon.

"Do you think the skewer is a direct, like, retaliation for getting her lip split?"

"I don't know," she said, seriously considering it. "It was, like, almost a year ago."

"You think your sister could take a split lip, hold onto that moment for almost a year, waiting for the right time and weapon, and stab him in the dick?"

"Yes," she replied, her eyes like a kaleidoscope with the realization of how right she was.

"Then, it's just going to escalate, I think," I told her, as if this were the kind of shit I had any experience with.

"What do I do?" she asked me, and I was shocked to see her crying. She was crying about her fucked up, always drunk, sarcastic sister. She was scared because her sister was in jail and she was probably going to have to pay the bail and her sister would probably be released from jail at the same time her brother-in-law would be released from the hospital and they would probably just walk right back into this shitty house and fuck everything up again. My girlfriend was crying because her sister, who hated her, would need help, and my girlfriend would try to figure out how to give it.

I leaned across the sink to pull her close to me, and I knocked the bone into the sink and it made a clattering sound that made my teeth grind. But I held onto her and tried to calm her until I heard the little boy moaning, half awake and needing some kind of assistance. She started to get up, but I set her on the edge of the bathtub, right next to a giant hole in the ceramic that looked as if someone had dropped a bowling ball on it, and told her I would take care of it.

Before I had even completely kneeled down to look at the boy, he had his arms around my neck. "Are you having a bad dream, buddy?" I asked, and he whimpered and nodded. "It's OK," I said, and I am not lying when I say that I was suppressing my gag reflex the entire time I was holding him, this sweet little boy who was in no way responsible for all the awful shit that swirled around him on a daily basis. I thought back to what my girlfriend had said about custody if the parents killed each other and I thought, fuck it, maybe I'd take this one and light out for parts unknown. I'd never held a baby, a toddler, or any child really, but I was getting used to being needed by something powerless. The boy had snot running down his nose, and I didn't even think about it when I took the sleeve of my shirt and cleaned up his face. I lowered him back onto the sofa and he, like a black belt in jujitsu, snatched my hand and pulled my entire left arm underneath his body, right up against his crotch, and he humped my arm for what felt like a long time until the battery inside of him wore out and he was asleep again. I looked over at the older boy, the giant, still scrolling, still obsessed with finding some kind of A-bomb of a weapon that automatically ended the game in his favor, and he was smirking, shaking his head as if I'd just been Punk'd, like he'd set this all in motion and now I had done something embarrassing for him.

"You ever kill a fucking thing in this game?" I asked him, my face hot with embarrassment.

"More than you ever could," he said.

My hand was tingling, as if it had some kind of special power that the little kid had imparted in the course of his humping.

"In real life," I said, "I don't think you can just pause the action until you find the right weapon."

"That's why I'm practicing with this game," he said. "When I go into the Marines, I'll be ready."

"You going to be a Marine," I said, my voice lacking the slightest bit of surprise or suspicion.

"I'm gonna be a sniper," he replied, "or a light machine gunner, or on the back of a fifty cal, and I'm gonna be the best." He was wearing snake boots that went to his knees, and he'd duct-taped a butterfly knife to one of them.

"Fair enough," I said.

I went back into the bathroom to find my girlfriend now on her knees, scrubbing the tub with scouring agents that had not been utilized once in the house's history. I told her that it was too late to even think about cleaning this place. She replied that she was going to sleep in the bathtub, its surface offering the quickest possibility of cleanliness. "The sheets," she said, shuddering, "require more than I can handle right now." I asked her what about me. I could not fit in the tub with her. She suggested that, it being summer, I could sleep on the front porch. Now that the tub had been scraped clean and disinfected, she settled into it and twisted her body into the shape of sleep. I leaned over and kissed her. "We'll figure this out," I told her, and I hoped that she noticed that I had said we. I wanted her to know that, despite her questionable genetics, whatever hidden DNA contributed to the inhabitants of this house, I was a part of this now. I wanted her to know that if we ever combined our genes, the good would outweigh the bad. But she was already snoring, so who knows if my intentions were understood.

Back in the living room, the oldest kid was asleep, his gums bleeding from the corn dog sticks, his hand in some state of rigor mortis, his thumb depressing the controller so that, all night long, he would be scrolling through his weapons. I walked out of the house, across the lawn, and slept in my car, the windows rolled up, already reeking of my new circumstances.

I woke the next morning to find the two girls sitting in the passenger-side front seat. One of them had twisted off the stereo knobs and the other one was trying, and failing, to get the car's electric cigarette lighter to ignite. The younger one, her teeth a crooked mess that, at her age, seemed sweet enough, said, "Are you going to marry Sassy?" I asked her if my girlfriend was Sassy. They said yes, and I said yes in reply without hesitation. They asked what they could call me. "Just call me Cam for now," I told them. "We're hungry, Cam," the older one said. I looked around the car, but I kept it clean, so there wasn't any food around. I said we should go inside and find something, but they said they were out of food and that Sassy wanted me to drive them to the Creekside Market and get some food. They were in their underwear, or maybe it was their pajamas. "Fine," I said, and I sped off without telling them to put on seatbelts. They shared the front seat and leaned out the window. If a car crash had maimed them, I would have been shocked into a coma.

At the market, I handcuffed my hands around their wrists and led them up and down the tight aisles of the market. The air in that building was humid and smelled of crickets and worms from the bait boxes near the register. We got some cans of Vienna sausages and some more Pop-Tarts and gallon jugs of fruit punch. I did not trust the eggs or milk in this place, where the refrigerated section was humming smoke and rot. The girls asked for some boxes of macaroni and cheese, and so we got four of them. They also asked for some kind of powder candy that turned their mouths shocking shades of blue. Fine with me. I bought whatever they asked for. The total was more than I had expected, but that's what life is like with four kids, I supposed. It seemed as if anything more than two kids was resigning yourself to a life of food in bulk and lack of funds. I figured, now that I was so sure I was going to marry my girlfriend, when, the previous night, I imagined the ease of leaving her, that if we did come into custody of the kids, we could choose two of them to keep and send the other two into foster care. I knew this was wrong, but I also knew the rest of my time with these kids was going to be a silent audition for my grace. We bagged up the goods and sped home, their mouths toxic with the candy they had not saved for their brothers.

Back at the house, I found the older boy removed from the couch for the first time in our short history together. He was standing in the utility room and holding a garbage bag while my girlfriend, her nostrils plugged with tissue paper, shoved her gloved hand into the dryer. "What's going on?" I asked. The boy just shrugged and, when he saw the girls skipping into the kitchen with the food, dropped the garbage bag and shuffled, his body getting closer to the kitchen without any apparent ambulation, toward them. My girlfriend gagged and turned quickly away from the dryer. "Where the fuck did he go?" she said. I motioned toward the kitchen without moving my gaze from the dryer. "What's going on?" I asked again.

"All of their clothes smell like…like this house," she said. "So I told them we needed to wash their clothes, and they said the washing machine was broken. And it is, I think, or maybe a fuse is blown. But when I looked in the dryer, which does work by the way, there was… this thing in it."

I picked up the garbage bag and held it out for her. She gathered her courage, took a sharp intake of breath, and then retrieved a dead squirrel from the mouth of the dryer with her thumb and index finger. Half of the squirrel was fur and half of it was bone. It was flattened. She weakly tossed it toward me, toward the garbage bag I realized too late, and it fell to the floor, right at my feet. We both danced out of the room, into the hallway, and stared at the corpse.

"Do you think it died in there?" she asked.

"Or what?" I asked.

"Or do you think someone put it in there?" she said.

One of the kittens started pawing at the squirrel. Its claws got caught in the fur and it shook its paw to disengage itself. My girl-friend picked up the squirrel and dropped it like a grenade into the bag. I twirled the bag shut and took it into the backyard. The less said about the backyard, the better. Fire pit. Rusted tractor. Foam block archery targets.

"OK," my girlfriend said to the kids, who were eating, of course, every last one of the Pop-Tarts. "I want each one of you to pick three outfits: shirts, pants, socks, underwear, plus one pair of pajamas, and your bedsheets. We're going to the laundromat."

The little boy cheered, the frosting and fruit filling between his teeth like something caught in a bear trap.

I played Old Maid with the kids while my girlfriend got the washing machines whirring into the early stages of shocking all the death out of those tainted fabrics. She had a plastic bag filled with quarters from the change machine, and they were rapidly declining. I shuffled the cards and discovered the pattern of play; they cheated. Without hesitation or attempt to hide it. I dealt the cards. The child who received the Old Maid card would quickly pretend that it was one of a pair and place it, face down, on the table. After about fifteen minutes of the game, with only one card, a Two of Clubs or a Jack of Hearts, left, we would real-ize that someone had lied. I then had to flip everyone's cards over until the cheater was discovered. Only then did someone lose and someone else win. At first, I was pissed off. I would explain how receiving the Old Maid card would not mean that you ended up with it at the end. But the kids did not want to take this chance. They wanted to cheat their way to freedom as quickly as possible. After a few hands, I simply gave up. I took cards and then let someone else take them from me. I let the kids sort it out on their own and the game became nothing more than an incredibly inefficient way to shuffle cards. "Are you guys having fun?" I asked them. The little boy cheered, excited to be doing anything. The other kids didn't answer, trying to figure out who had already lost and who would lose again.

I emptied a snack machine and let the kids fight over the contents. I sat with my girlfriend while she watched the dryers flash fry the clothes. "I don't know if I can walk back into that house," she said. I asked her why we needed to go back at all.

"Let's just take them back to our place," I said.

"It's an hour away, for starters," she replied. "And it's a one-bedroom apartment."

"It doesn't smell like cat piss and dead squirrels, though," I offered.

"I just..." she said, "I don't want them to do to our place what they did to that house."

"They can't possibly. Not in a day or two," I said.

"I think they can," she said, staring at the kids, who had sugared themselves into what looked zombie enough to be called resting. Their internal batteries, leaking fluid and electrons, were simply recharging themselves for another backbreaking surge.

"What do we do then?" I said. "We can't clean that whole house. It's not possible. It needs government assistance."

"We do the best we can," she finally said. "We do just enough to keep them alive."

"If we could get rid of the cats," I offered.

"That would help," she agreed.

We got the kids to fold their own clothes, which had the same effect as asking them to turn their clothes into origami tumbleweeds. It was hypnotic, to watch their folding, somehow, become unfolding. But my girlfriend walked them through the steps, as if she were in a training video for The Gap, and the kids got it mostly right and we placed them all in some garbage bags and I felt like Santa Claus, carrying a sack of things that, though maybe not what they'd explicitly asked for, would make their lives happier than they were before.

Their father was at the house when we returned. One of his friends was sitting in an idling truck and the kids seemed happy to see their dad, who was shoving some of his clothes, and a twelve pack of beer, into yet another garbage bag. The house, I determined, was 30 percent garbage bags. The kids wanted to hug him, but he turned slightly away. "I'm injured," he told them. "No heavy lifting for a good long while, kiddies."

I didn't want to look full on, but I was curious as to the exact state of his incapacitation. He looked sheepish and a little peeved, but that might easily be his default state. He was a tiny man, skinny to the point of breaking in half, and his teeth had that brown rot of chewing tobacco.

"I have to recuperate," he told us. "I'm staying with Jerry for a few days, until I can get back to work."

"What about Cindy?" my girlfriend asked.

"She's still in jail, I think," he told her.

"Could we maybe talk about this on the porch," I said, trying to be a grownup. "Away from the kids?"

"They've heard so much worse," he said.

"I believe it," I told him.

"But are you going to press charges?" she asked him.

"Not up to me," he replied.

"Really?"

"Well," he continued, "I don't pretend to be a lawyer. I don't think it's up to me, though. She brought this all on herself, so she's got to clean it up by herself."

"And what about the kids?" my girlfriend asked him.

"Can't you just keep watching them?"

"Until when?" I asked.

"Until Cindy comes back," he said, getting irritated.

"Fine," my girlfriend said. "Fine, go get drunk and ice your dick."

"This is all your sister's fault," he said, and then he pushed past us and hobbled outside. He turned, noticed the garbage bags I was holding, and asked, "What's in those?"

"We washed some clothes for the kids," I said.

"Did you do any of my laundry?" he asked.

We shook our heads. If there had been a kebab skewer anywhere in reach, my girlfriend would have stabbed him with it.

"Well, thanks a lot," he said, and eased into the truck before they drove off, leaving us alone, again, with the kids.

The kids fought. They shared the same spaces, made paths in each other's footprints. It was necessary, to keep your space singular, to place an elbow in someone's mouth, teeth on an ankle, knuckles digging into someone's back like rough stones. After twenty or thirty attempts to keep the magnets of their feet and fists from attracting another's, I gave up and let the ruin come down on top of me. I noticed that this happened without much resistance on my part. This was life, I imagined. Or, rather, this was a terrible life, the way you slowly gave in to your surroundings and let them wash over you. I did not completely notice the smell of the house by this point, honestly.

Finally, what we had been expecting since the moment we entered the house happened; my girlfriend's sister called from jail. I kept the kids away from the phone, left my girlfriend to her pained privacy. One of the cats peed on a magazine that was lying on the floor and one of the girls picked up the magazine and simply moved it to the coffee table. I noticed that not a single toy of theirs was intact. This was, I began to understand, by design. If you ruined your own toys enough, no one else would try to steal them.

"OK," my girlfriend said when she returned only a few minutes later. "It's complicated."

I walked into the bathroom with her and she discussed the basics, which was all she could get out of her sister. Bail was set, and the charges weren't as bad as they could have been, mostly regarding the shit she gave the police who arrested her, not the skewer/dick business. My girlfriend needed to come up with five hundred bucks for bail. It was a lot of money for us. I do tattoos and my girlfriend does piercings at the same shop, but we're not rich. We are not in a single dollar of debt, and the reason for this is that we didn't put up bail for every idiot we knew who got locked up. Then I thought about the four kids, all of them in our apartment, all the breakfast cereal they would inhale, and it seemed like five hundred was a fair price for our freedom.

"What about the kids?" I asked.

"I imagine she'll get to keep them for now," she said. "Maybe child services will be involved at some point, but who knows. I think they get to keep the kids as long as the kids don't get hurt."

"I'm happy," I admitted, "but it still seems kind of fucked up. It seems like a stabbing should invite some sort of inquiry into your fitness as a parent."

"The deeper you get into this shit," my girlfriend said, "the more you realize that nobody is keeping anyone else from fucking things up."

I bought a boatload of pizzas and brought them back to the house, where I found the kids helping to straighten up the living room. There were eight garbage bags filled with detritus and old food and what may or may not have been actual shit. There was a landfill of cheese-curl dust between the cushions of the sofa. Heavy objects, like broken furniture and boxes of rain-diseased textbooks, had been moved from the middle of the room, like hostages in a negotiation, and pushed against the walls, as if to keep the house propped up. It gave space to the room and allowed some measure of air to circulate. My girlfriend emptied the remains of a can of Febreze into the air and the room just swallowed it whole.

In their newly laundered clothes with their hair combed, the children merely looked like freaks in a carnival show instead of wild animals. They were on the floor, huddled around the stack of pizza boxes like it was a campfire, and the youngest one said a short blessing that started off as a prayer and ended as a death metal intonation, the other kids simply kneeling on the floor as if expecting benediction, against all signs that suggested the opposite. We ate and it felt, for the first time, like an actual family and not adventurers in an inhospitable, unstable region. We smiled and our teeth were not scary. They were just the quickest way to show happiness. I imagined my girlfriend and me ten years down the line, the faces of the children replaced with those of our own design. It made me long for the future, which I never, ever, did in real life.

The same routine as the night before, my girlfriend got the girls ready for bed. They lined up and gave me a hug. They smelled like kids, powdered sugar and belly lint, and it made me tender toward them. They scrambled into their bedroom, and it wasn't long before they were asleep. I rocked the little boy against my chest until his head lolled to the side, and I transferred him awkwardly to one of the sofas. He twitched as if his foot was keeping a kick drum time to his own unsteady heartbeat. His dreams, I could not imagine.

My girlfriend and I sat on the floor and watched the oldest do his thing with the video game, finding no weapon to his liking, eventually giving in to his inevitable and quick death. He wanted, I now understood, to be stronger than anything evil. But he never would.

Eventually, my girlfriend yawned and retired to the bathtub. I kissed her and continued to watch the oldest kid nervously scroll through the weapons for the millionth time: an arc welder, a Molotov cocktail, a bowie knife. It would never end, the possibilities for ruination. He eventually chose the bowie knife and tried to hack a zombie into bite sizes, but it got the jump on him and it was game over.

"Fuck," he finally said.

"This is a hard board," I said without conviction.

"No duh," he responded. "It's the hardest board in all video games. I got the cheat code off the Internet just to get here. I used some of my own money to buy all the weapons that don't even come with the actual game. I've done all the shit I'm supposed to and I just keep getting ass-killed like some chump. Nobody on the message boards will even talk about this board."

"What are you supposed to do?" I asked.

"Not get killed."

"That's it?" I asked.

"I guess so."

It made sense enough to me. Surrounded by death and decay and no hope of anything getting better, all you could hope for was not to fall into the same fate.

"Just run," I finally said.

"Yeah, OK," he said, making a wanking motion with his free hand.

"I'm serious," I said. "Don't fight them. Just run as fast as you can."

He considered this, wondered if he was being mocked. "I do have some boots somewhere in this game that make me run really fast."

"Use them. Just run and don't stop running."

He got the boots from the inventory. He restarted the game. Before the zombie dropped out of the tree, he was already digging into the earth and pushing himself forward. The zombie fell out of the frame.

"Shit," the kid said, alive for as long as he'd ever been alive. "Fucking shit."

"Keep running," I said. On the little map in the upper left-hand corner, I could see a swarm of red dots forming behind him. They moved not quickly but with singular purpose.

"I'm running," he said. He ran and ran and ran, and the territory evaporated under his feet. He jumped over any non-living impediment. Any time his route was cut off, he changed directions and kept running. It was like the Pied Piper, trailing an unending line of zombies. He ran and ran and scorched the earth behind him until, finally, nearly an hour later, there was nothing left.

"Fucking shit," he said, looking over at me. The game suddenly shut down and the screen had returned to the title. "I beat that shit," he said.

I offered him my extended hand for a high five, but he just smirked and shook his head. He restarted the game and went back into his inventory. I knew what was coming. Even when you've smashed through the people who want to fuck you over, you still want to keep tabs on the things that might keep you safe. I stood up, my bones popping.

"Good night," I said, and he nodded, his eyes that blue glaze of reflected screens.

I walked into the bathroom and knelt over the tub. My girlfriend was asleep but just barely. It was easy enough, just with my presence, to bring her back to me.

"It'll be fine tomorrow," she said, still half asleep.

"Not for them," I said.

"I guess not," she replied.

After a few moments of silence, she said, "I asked my sister and she said that they had never finished the paperwork for custody."

"So what does that mean?"

"The kids don't go to me. They go somewhere, and I guess it could maybe be me, but it's not the law."

She adjusted her body, pulling tighter into herself, and I kicked off my shoes and squeezed into what was left of the tub. We were jammed into each other, sharing a foxhole, and we held each other tight against the constant presence of unhappiness that infiltrated the air around us. We would tear out our fingernails digging our way to something good. The world would try to fuck us and we would stab it with whatever weapon was available to us. We would make every object a weapon that would protect us from anything that tried to convince us that we would not live forever in happiness.

CHRISTIAN WINN
Arco, Idaho

"Please, Sylvia, give me a moment to think."

These are the last words you hear your father speak. You are eleven, and the two of you are traveling midsummer through eastern Idaho headed for Glacier National Park. It's the year your mother passed, and so much has been hard and empty since the long suffering was finally over in March, a week before your birthday, a week after hers. She was supposed to make this trip too, and you're learning that not everything that wants to be gets to be.

It's bright and dry and hot, and the air conditioner's been spotty since Boise, so things are tense and tired. Your bare legs stick like warm, weak tape to the vinyl bench seat. It's 3:00 p.m. and your father has grown weary of your questions about geology and history and the Wild West, and as you cross into the city limits of tiny Arco, he pulls into a gas station/café around the corner from the Sawtooth Club and says he's going to get himself a beer and unwind.

He tells you to pump gas and squeegee the dust and bugs off all the windows. You ask what he thinks Mom's opinion of Arco, Idaho, would be. He stares at you, his eyes tired but steady. He bites his lip, then says, "I won't be long, Sly," and then those final quiet words with his eyes shut; then he strides his tall, thin frame across the lot, around the corner, and disappears into the wavering heat without looking back.

You step out, go to the pumps, look out across the wide main street, and up at craggy hills rising as backdrop. A sandstone building up the block tells you this is Arco, Idaho, "The First City In The World Lit By Atomic Power."

"Wow..." you whisper, which seems the only sound alive anywhere near this place.

You think about a giant, glowing turbine beneath you. You think about the kids in science club back home, and impressing them with just the fact that you were here, atop that atomic coil.

Everything is a bell of silence, and then you clatter the pump into the tank, and a sweet wave of petroleum rises. Across the lot in the café, you think you can see the silhouette of a waitress and a man kiss at the counter behind the shaded front window.

You find the water pail and squeegee and slosh gray, soapy water across the windshield and back window. You peel it off with the purple blade of rubber, but the wind is too dry, the day too hot, and the dirty water glazes the glass. You wet it again, and move quickly this time. You want to leave no lines at all, to make it perfect so your dad will be impressed and happy and know you are his sweet capable daughter, Sylvia, again. You pull the water off, use an old towel to dry the crooked lines and rub the bugs away. But soon enough, you realize that no matter, there will always be something left staining the glass. Besides, there's just more dirt and flies waiting to find your windshield once you leave this place. You finish, and feel the whir and tremble of that turbine alive beneath this city once more. The heat waves across the street pulse with its heart.

No one comes for money. No cars pass. You think your dad is likely talking with the bartender, maybe touching glasses and telling stories about you, and this road trip, and plans for catching cutthroats along Henrys Fork like he did with his dad.

You lean against the Buick in the lowering sun, tracing hearts with your bare toes on the dusty cement, and wait. Your father does this sometimes back home in Sunnyvale—picks you up after school clubs, or soccer, needs to unwind, drives to Crabby's Tavern out near the dump. Even before mom got sick, but more often after. Even though you wish you could, you're never allowed to join him in Crabby's, because he says it's no place for a good kid like you.

Minutes pass, and still not a person around. You find a ballpoint Bic in the glove box. It looks like one of those new erasable kinds, but soon enough you find out it's not.

The first word you write along the soft, pale inside of your forearm is your name. Sylvia. Neatly. In cursive. Like your mom taught over and over. Sloppy writing was one of her pet peeves.

You trace it, and trace it again—again, again. Harder each time, because of your wish for your father to just get back so you can get to the campground sometime tonight. Again. Again. The blue ink nearly turning black.

Then you start in on the word *Please.* You whisper the name of each letter, like in a spelling bee. You're the best speller your age in Santa

Clara County, three years running. That's something your dad's even proud about, but your mom was the one who trained you up.

By the time you finish writing and retracing those eight words many times, your father still isn't there. It must be half an hour. So you walk around that corner toward the Sawtooth Club.

Inside the low, open space of the tavern sits a long polished bar, a red-glowing jukebox, a wall full of glassware, and old metal beer signs. Two tall, thin men shoot pool. The bartender is a blond, pretty woman who reminds you for a moment of your mother in years-old photos. This woman cocks her head to the side and watches silently as you approach the bar. It smells like cigarettes and bread and Pine-Sol all stirred up.

"Well, hello, sweet thing," she says too loud, only half smiling.

"Is he in here?" You put your hands on the bar, which is warmer than you expected and is vibrating, humming. You are certain the atomic heart is churning far below, controlling the mood and spirit of everything here.

"Who?" She puts her hands beside yours on the bar, and you stare at the smooth, tan fingers.

"He's about as tall as that guy?" You point to one of the pool-shooting men, and he points back, smiling as if he knows you. Though you want to, you cannot look away for long moments.

"That's not him?"

"He's too old to be my dad."

"That's who you're looking for? Your dad?" She reaches for a pint glass, fills it with ice and Coke, and hands it across. "It's too fucking hot out there today, if you'll pardon my French."

"Was he in here?" You take a big swallow and it's so cold and sweet it nearly hurts. "Just a bit ago?"

"Jackson! Roy! You seen this girl's—what's your name...?"

"Sylvia," you whisper, a hole within your chest slowly widening. "Dad calls me Sly."

"You boys seen Sylvia's dad in here?"

They shake their heads, no, and go back to their game. As the balls clack and thud against the rail, the jukebox starts up "American Pie," one your father sings along to after Crabby's.

The heart beneath the city coils tighter, louder, a sound beyond sound. You sit up at the bar, press your palms into your bare thighs, feel the icy wash of air conditioning. You bow your head, somehow knowing—though it takes years to understand that this is the moment—he is gone, you are alone.

As a teenager, a graduate student, a mother, a widow, a doctor, a pensive quiet old lady, you will know that this moment in the Sawtooth Club, at the bar, the taste of sugar and dust in your mouth and nose, the air conditioner loudly clattering, Don Mclean singing the only story ever told, this is the fracture, this is the divide, the what was and what will be still visible, but retreating.

"Sly," the bartender whispers. "Honey, you can't sit up at the bar. We could get into trouble." There is a knowing in her voice. But you know you will never know it too, that knowing.

"What happened?" You slide off the stool, lean into the bar. "He just needed a minute."

She smiles, fine wrinkles and laugh lines blooming.

"Let's go out back," she says. "Have a look around. Have a talk. You can bring your soda."

In the open back lot there is no shade. She takes your wrist, turns your arm gently, her breath acrid and smoky and sweet.

"What's all this?" She runs a finger over the dark-blue cursive.

"It's all he wanted, a minute." You squint across the lot, down the side alley, up into the dry foothills, hoping to see him walking along, looking for you, or simply looking for a moment to figure out everything. "And a cold beer, or something."

"Your dad." She nods, and you know she knows. And the low whine of the heart spreads as a halo above the city.

"I've been tracing it so I can remember."

And as she stands and slips a cigarette from her pack, you also stand and sip that quickly warming soda. You hold her eyes, and you know just what will happen next:

She will say, Well, let's find him, let's get ourselves a little plan together.

You will return to the car, where still there will be no one.

You will return to the Sawtooth Club, where Roy and Jackson will be at the bar drinking new tall beers and the jukebox is silent and the lights will flicker for several long moments. You will ask about atomic power, about the big heart-shaped source below the city, and if your father has returned. And along with the bartender, they will laugh, and laugh some more as you walk out to find the only two policemen in town, and proceed to look everywhere, and nowhere—restaurants and churches and tiny neighborhoods and grocery stores.

They will ask questions—was your father happy? did he often leave you alone? how much and often did he drink? did he ever speak of suicide?—so many questions.

They will form lists of small theories—he stumbled into a bad situation in the bar; he hopped a ride with a long-hauler; he met a woman traveling through; he simply wandered into the hills.

In the end they will know nothing, no one will, and they will phone your aunt and find you a place to stay for the two nights it will take for her to arrive from Florida.

The next week will be spent looking, questioning, and looking farther out.

Everyone will be confounded.

You will walk and ride across every dry inch of Arco, Idaho, and everywhere the swallowing heartbeat is deep beneath you, and the taste of ions and the friction of atoms being pulled apart, all of it what we are made of too.

What happens to us? Where do we go when everything that was us disappears, evaporates leaving only shadows and the trace of words?

Your aunt will try to explain, to create a salve of understanding as you drive east and south, then south some more, where a new life hunches, waiting for you to inhabit it.

You will pen your father's words into your arm for weeks, and they will become a permanent blue smudge that only you know the meaning of. People will see it as a birthmark, a bruise.

You will tell the man you marry half the truth of the smudge, never all. This man will have your father's name and your father's kind, earnest eyes, his long lean frame, and so often you will lie next to this man in the late, late hours, and the quiet of dawn, and you will put your arm over his slow-breathing chest, and you will pretend you are your mother, and he is your father. You will whisper his name, and "I love you," and, "You're here, it's OK, you made it home…" Your husband will never ask for any more than this.

Only once will you return to Arco, thirty-two years later, not long before you lose your husband too.

You and your daughter are on your way to Seattle, road-tripping to her wedding, and you will share several beers in the Sawtooth Club, where, impossibly, the same bartender is pouring, the same tall, crooked men are shooting pool, "American Pie" is still playing, the same smells seep from the bathrooms, the same bright turbine heart wheels and pulses below the two of you.

Your daughter knows the story of this place, of you in it, but she will not ask you to tell it—not here, not now. You will toast, watch the men shoot pool, laugh a little at what lies ahead and what has been, and she will wait, wait and tell that story herself in the years scrolling blindly ahead of you both.

ABOUT LAUREN GROFF
A Profile by Elliott Holt

Last summer on Martha's Vineyard, Lauren Groff and I went running. I have a lot of endurance—I ran a marathon back in 2001—but my usual pace is middling: I tend to run nine-minute miles. But my first mile with Lauren clocked in at 6:52 (I know because I have an app on my phone that tracks such things). It was the fastest mile I've ever run and it almost killed me. After that, I told her to go on ahead. She sprinted off as I watched her blond ponytail disappear down the sandy trail.

Lauren Groff is an athlete. She is tall and majestic; she carries herself with strength and poise. She was a competitive swimmer when she was young and she rowed at Amherst (where she met her husband, Clay, on the crew team). When I asked her about the relationship of sports to her writing, she said, "I think writing is intensely physical, and the stereotype of writers being nerdy weaklings is more false than true: almost every good writer I know is committed to being healthy. I love the discipline of training; at a certain point, youthful zest gets spent, and what you have left is the daily discipline of sitting down with it, no matter what. And there's nothing that gets me unstuck more than a very long run without music in the heat, because I stop thinking, and my subconscious is left to wander its own way. If I sit down for three hours and can't do much more than read, I go for a run or walk or swim, and by the time I get back, I have some small glimmer of truth to use."

At thirty-six, she has used those glimmers of truth in four books: The Monsters of Templeton, her bestselling debut novel, which was shortlisted for the Orange prize for new writers; Delicate Edible Birds, a collection that showcased Groff's brilliant range as a short-story writer (her stories have appeared in The New Yorker, Harper's, Ploughshares, and in Best American Short Stories, The O. Henry Prize Stories, and The Pushcart Prize anthology); Arcadia, a New York Times Notable Book, finalist for the Los Angeles Times Book Award and one of the Washington Post's 10 Best Books of 2012; and the dazzling Fates and Furies, which will be published by Riverhead in September of this year. It's an impressive output for someone so young, but Lauren Groff is one of the hardest-working writers I know.

Groff was born in 1978 and raised in Cooperstown, New York (fictionalized as Templeton in her first novel), but she has lived for the past nine years in Gainesville, Florida, with her husband and two young sons. I asked her where she feels like home and she said, "The truth is that I'm in a sort of limbo, perpetually between places, and I think it's part of my nature to feel a little lost, a little uncomfortable, always at the edges, looking longingly at other people who are happy and calm in the center. It's excellent training for being a writer, I think. You never want to be too comfortable, you never want to feel as if you've made it, you don't want to know what you're doing. Writers are perennially lonely, and a writer's longing to connect is what fills her work with urgency. I don't mind feeling uncomfortable, feeling a little lonely, if it means that I get the great joy of continuing to write." That longing to connect is present in her work. Community—the way people are tied together by history, by place, by love—is often a theme in Groff's novels. In The Monsters of Templeton, the town and its mythic history connect its residents; Arcadia, her second novel, concerns an intentional community; and Fates and Furies is about a luminous couple and their close-knit group of friends.

Before I met Groff, I fell in love with a story she wrote. "L. Debard and Aliette" appeared in The Atlantic Monthly and then in The Best American Short Stories in 2007. The alliterative first sentence knocked me out: "He is at first a distant wave, the wake-wedge of a loon as it surfaces." I'd never heard of Lauren Groff when I read that, but knew I was in the presence of supreme talent. "L. Debard and Aliette" is a smart retelling of Abelard and Heloise, the twelfth-century story about Heloise d'Argenteuil and her relationship with philosopher Peter Abelard. Groff's story is one I teach regularly; I continue to be impressed by its lyricism, its wit, and its omniscient voice. There are few contemporary writers who use omniscience, and I can't think of any who do so as well as Groff. In "L. Debard and Aliette," she artfully dips in and out of her characters' perspectives, but she also sweeps out, giving the story scope without sacrificing intimacy. (Speaking of omniscience, I sometimes think that Groff is, in fact, all-knowing. She has read everything and is an astute critic.) She also uses an omniscient narrative voice to beautiful effect in Fates and Furies, an epic novel about a marriage that has the urgency of Greek tragedy and the sly humor that permeates all of Groff's work. (She is funny, on and off the page.)

Fates and Furies is about Lotto Satterwhite and his wife, Mathilde. They marry young, right after they graduate from Vassar, and though it is Lotto who eventually becomes a famous playwright, Mathilde is crucial to his success. Mathilde is editor, dramaturge, and muse. She is also one of the fiercest, most compelling characters I've ever encountered. Fates, the half of the novel focused on her perspective, reads like a kommos, a lamentation so lyrical and powerful that it had me weeping by the end. Fates and Furies asks how well we can ever know another person; it is also about art, ego, desire, and the creative process. Groff writes of Lotto Satterwhite, "He was enough of a lover of forms to understand the allure of such a strict life, how much internal wildness it could release." (p. 125)

Groff's life is also strict. "I'm from taciturn hardworking Pennsylvania Dutch farming stock," she told me, "and work is what we delight in, and we feel at a loss if we're not being anchored by daily sweat." She writes early drafts by hand, on legal pads. Once she has a complete draft of a novel, she throws the pages away, and begins again, writing the new draft (again by hand) from memory. "The handwriting/ legal pads technique developed because I tend to overthink, overwrite, overstress my drafts, and it gives me a gorgeous amount of freedom to fuck up without consequences," she said. "You figure out pretty quickly what the structural flaws are if you bullet through a first draft in a few months. After a few drafts written this way, the story begins to feel like an item that has been 3-D printed, the material built up little by little to become something multidimensional in my mind. My very favorite draft is always the last one, when I do the delicious, deeply satisfying work of just playing with sentences, because the joy of sentence-making is what got me into writing to begin with. It's the frosting to the equally satisfying cake."

And what stunning sentences they are. Groff is a wonderful storyteller, in the vein of Charles Dickens, but she is also a prose stylist, who counts Virginia Woolf among her many influences. Groff's sentences are those of a writer attuned to the sound of words. I admired those sentences long before I knew their author, but knowing Groff gives me even more appreciation for them. Lauren Groff is a woman of intellect and integrity; she is generous and warm; and she's hard to keep up with. Watch her; she's already gone far, but she's only just begun.

Elliott Holt is the author of You Are One of Them *(Penguin Press, 2013). Her short fiction and essays have appeared or are forthcoming in* The New York Times, Slate, Time, Virginia Quarterly Review, Guernica, the Pushcart Prize anthology, *and elsewhere.*

FIRST LOVES
A Plan B Essay by Thomas H. Pruiksma

My career as a kid magician reached its height in eighth grade in the Eckstein Middle School Talent Show. I'd gone from performing in church basements and private homes to the cavernous auditorium at the heart of our school, with its banks of colored lights, its gargantuan raked balcony, and its rows of fold-down wooden seats. The previous year, I had built my own illusions, making Charie Vathanaprida appear from an empty box, levitating Karen Sollek in the middle of the stage, and vanishing myself from behind a white cloth—only to reappear in the very center of the audience, balanced on the armrests of a chair. The girls around me all screamed. It was as if I'd walked through the screen of our television to enter the TV magic shows I lived for.

In eighth grade, I planned to go further. I wanted the new act to be darker, more somber, more serious. More like a work of art. Out went the music from adventure film soundtracks, in came Dead Can Dance, Depeche Mode, Pink Floyd. I rehearsed on the stage with my hand-picked assistants, getting them out of class with the help of the Vice Principal. (Mr. Salvino liked my magic so much he supplied me with my own hall passes, gave me the key to the storage cage, and insisted on introducing me in the show.) As the great day approached, my mother sent a press release to the local stations. I dreamed I might make the evening news.

Magic was my first love—before music, before books, before writing. At Meadowbrook Co-op Preschool, near our home in north Seattle, I happened to see a magician do a trick with colored scarves. He stuffed one inside the other, waved his hands, said some words, and revealed that the scarf had vanished. The preschoolers squealed their amazement. I was convinced, however, he had pulled it through a hole, and I spent the next several weeks raiding my mother's sewing drawers. The fabric that worked best was a blue translucent rayon that would seem to float if you threw it in the air. Its weave was so loose you could make a hole anywhere. I opened one off-center in the first of my two "scarves," where I could work the second one through it by shoving it with my finger. Sometimes the fabric got caught and

I had to loosen my fist, revealing in the process the scarf's hiding place. My parents weren't too impressed, but at Christmas that year I found magic sets among the presents beneath the tree. My interest grew from there.

One of my favorite tricks was the so-called Chinese Linking Rings, which actually comes from Europe. Almost everyone has seen it somewhere: eight metal rings join together and interpenetrate, forming pairs, chains, and geometric shapes. I can still remember my delight, before I learned the secret, at watching the gleaming rings seem to melt through one another in the hands of Seattle's myriad magicians. In fourth grade, on a family trip to San Francisco, I bought my first set at the "World of the Unexplained" magic shop on Fisherman's Wharf. (The shop, like many others, has long since disappeared.) The young demonstrator behind the counter didn't want me to buy it. "You'll be disappointed, kid, I promise," he said. I bought it anyway.

Back in the hotel, after the disappointment, I began studying the routine he had given me with the trick, a series of typed notes and drawings on blue paper, folded in half to form a little booklet. I still have it. It was my first full routine, and I annotated several pages with early attempts at cursive. Already I was making changes and adding bits of "patter" that I'd picked up from magicians I'd seen. "Ladies and gentlemen," I told myself to say, "here I have eight solid rings." Not very original, but it got the thing started.

The biggest change I made was the addition of "figures," different shapes I could form with four or more rings—a flower, a globe, a waterfall. Some experts, I learned, didn't see them as real magic. In his textbook *Rings in Your Fingers*, Dariel Fitzkee proclaimed no taste for them at all: "Without benefit of wedlock, this illegimate [sic] child of art gone psychopathic and magic with delirium tremens has somehow crept into *The Chinese Linking Rings*." I thought, however, that they were pretty. I selected my favorites and found a place in the routine where I could slip them in more or less logically (if such things can be said to have logic). The rings featured in the shows that I performed at church potlucks, company picnics, school assemblies, and family gatherings. Soon I had earned enough to purchase a larger set, with more durable and professional-looking rings. While other tricks came and went, depending on the venue, the rings held their place in my shows.

That is, until I hit middle school. There, in place of pretty, I gave spectacle center stage, with flash pots, fog machines, and plenty of teen angst. For the act in eighth grade, after Mr. Salvino's introduction, I cut myself in half, removing a chunk of my middle without the benefit of a box. Then I performed what I hoped would be the highlight of the whole talent show: an escape in the style of Houdini. My assistants covered my eyes with bandages and bound my hands, strapping me to an electrocution device in an upright curtained cabinet. Karen Sollek explained the details through the loudspeakers: I had ninety seconds to escape or get fried. (By this point, I no longer spoke in my acts, doing everything instead to music. "From where I lie," went the lyrics we played for the escape, "I want to die, I want to live, I want to die.")

Of course, the effect was rigged. As the tension in the auditorium ratcheted upward, the device went off prematurely. Sparks flew from the timer, lights flashed overhead, Charie Vathanaprida fainted to the floor, and red smoke rose in the air. I could hear classmates in the audience scream. But when Opokua Oduro brought up the lights, and Eli Semke, Andy Chaffin, and Danny Zebelman opened the cabinet, everyone saw that it was empty. Then, as before, I appeared in the audience, but this time in a new change of clothes. It was even better than the year before.

Or so I thought. After the performance, as I congratulated my assistants, some friends approached me from the wings. "Caitlin is crying," they said. "She's in the corner." Caitlin Milner was the first person to ever ask me to a dance, a heavy-set and sensual and spirited young woman. Now she was crumpled near the curtains.

"Caitlin?" I asked, approaching.

She stood up with some effort and accepted a hug, her arms and hands still shaking. "I thought you had died," she said. "I thought you got killed. Never, ever, do that again."

And like that, my euphoria vanished. I'd gone too far. At the encore for family and friends that evening, I could hardly bear to go through the motions. What had once seemed like my life's highest aim and purpose now felt fraudulent, hollow, false.

I can't blame either Caitlin or my angst-ridden act for the end of my childhood career. In a way, it had already ended. Adolescence was now turning my mind to other things: schoolwork, music, preparing for college, the tumult of coming out as gay. I was also growing painfully aware of the ecological and social turmoil I could see around me. Doing magic shows began to feel like a previous existence, a little boy's hobby, nothing more. It wasn't serious enough, wasn't useful in the world. For over a decade, I gave it no thought.

Then my sister Emily surprised me with an invitation. I had moved to Vashon Island, just outside Seattle, where I was living on a farm, working for food and board, memorizing poetry, and trying to write about my years living in south India. Emily, who'd moved to Vashon for reasons of her own, managed the island's farmers market and wanted me to perform for their Harvest Fair. It wasn't at all what I'd moved there to do, but I figured the extra money couldn't hurt. Maybe it could even support my writing in the winter.

I unpacked my tricks from their old cardboard boxes, fashioned a short show, and made some new business cards, just in case. At the Harvest Fair itself, the performance went well enough, kids watching from the grass, parents standing with crossed arms along the edges. I could still manage to surprise them with a few of my tricks and even introduced a new set of magic words: "ZUcchini, ZUcchini, TROMbocchini!" At the close of the show, I brought out my linking rings, the patter coming back to me as if I'd never stopped doing it. But what had worked for a child of seven or eight didn't work as well for an adult. I could no longer count on the cute factor. When I said, "Ladies and Gentlemen, I have eight solid rings," I could almost hear people thinking, "Why does he have to *say* they're solid?"

And although I did get some bookings from the show, they were hardly enough for me to rely on. An apprentice doesn't get the luxury of daily pay.

But several years later, my friend Merna Hecht, a poet and storyteller working in the schools, made another unexpected invitation. In one of her classes of fifth graders in Seattle, she'd discovered an aspiring magician. Could I come perform for them on her last day? She could pay me, she explained, a little, not much, but it would mean so much to her students. Without giving it much thought, I said yes.

But as I prepared on late winter afternoons, a new possibility occurred to me: why not combine magic with my apprenticeship to poetry? Instead of doing tricks the way I'd done them as a child, I could use them as metaphors for the magic of words, for the ways they return us to ourselves. Instead of my old patter, I could share poems I'd come to love. Maybe, as my partner, David, repeatedly insisted, I could even write a few of them myself.

I decided to start with the rings. And it's here I saw that the "figures" of my childhood might serve to make the effect more meaningful. The rings, as circles, the oldest of symbols, might stand for the ways that stories, poems, and songs do not really end when they end. Instead, they continue in unending patterns that return us, repeatedly, to origins. Song links with song, story links with story; together they form figures in our hearts and our minds. So I wrote a little poem to accompany the figures, weaving it between the flowers and falling waters. "Rings of Song," I called it. The effect and its poem culminate in a single long chain, "where all that we've learned / and all we've become / join in one chorus / with the moon and the sun." It might not be a masterpiece, but it's memorable. Beyond that, it's uniquely my own.

As a child, I had aped other performers and magicians, copying their patter, their persona. Many of them had done the same thing themselves, carrying on the same jokes, repeating the same bits, doing the same tricks time after time. It comes with the territory, I suppose. But now I am learning to strip things away that properly belong to others: phrases, assumptions, old habits.

This past spring I premiered a new show, not for schools or families, but for adults—*By Heart: A Celebration of Words, Magic, and Memory*. In it I tell the story of how living in south India and learning the Tamil language led me, at last, to love poetry—after years of being mystified by the way it was taught in school. I describe how I learned to hear the music of words by learning certain poems by heart. And I share how these poems brought me in turn to meeting my beloved and life partner, David. This time the show moved its audience to tears, not out of fear or anger, but joy.

And at the heart of the piece, my old rings make their appearance, only now they are wedding rings, borrowed from the audience, to speak about the words that we give to each other, the promises we make visible with deeds.

I take the two rings, bring them together, and hold them for everyone to see. "Saying our vows and then giving our rings is a way of showing what cannot be seen, the word that we say in our hearts. Yes—yes—yes," I say. "Yes to the pleasures, yes to the pains, yes to the whole beyond pleasure and pain, that joins us to everyone everywhere."

And the wedding rings link as the words come together, joining not only the words and the deeds, but the boy I once was, and the man I am now, and the things we want to say and sing.

Thomas H. Pruiksma is a poet, magician, writer, translator, teacher, musician, and lover of life. His books include Give, Eat, and Live: Poems of Avvaiyar; Body and Earth: Notes from a Conversation *(with the artist C. F. John); and* A Feast for the Tongue *(with the Tamil scholar Dr. K. V. Ramakoti). He lives on Vashon Island, Washington, with his partner, David Mielke. www.poetsmagic.com*

ANTHONY AYCOCK

How to Appreciate an Exploding Cigar: A Look2 Essay on Peter De Vries

Anthony Burgess called him "one of the great prose virtuosos of modern America." Harper Lee lauded him as "the Evelyn Waugh of our time." Kingsley Amis said he was "the funniest serious writer to be found on either side of the Atlantic." He wrote 27 books plus gobs of stories and essays, collecting two honorary doctorates and a spot in the American Academy of Arts and Letters. Yet by 1993, the year of his death, Peter De Vries could not walk into a bookstore and buy one word he had written (well, maybe off the remainder table). A New England writer, he is overshadowed by other New England writers—John Updike, John Cheever, Wallace Stevens. A satirist, he takes a backseat to other satirists—Dorothy Parker, Robert Benchley, James Thurber, Kurt Vonnegut. A 43-year veteran of *The New Yorker,* he is less remembered than other *New Yorker* writers—E. B. White, J. D. Salinger, Truman Capote, Philip Roth, and everyone else, just about. With two of his books, *The Blood of the Lamb* and *Slouching Towards Kalamazoo,* back in print thanks to the University of Chicago Press, it seems a good time to look deeper at the person Daniel Dennett called "the funniest writer on religion ever."

I remember my first time with De Vries (rhymes with "kiss"). It was in August of 1993, the day before my senior year of college. I was driving my girlfriend, Michelle, home when traffic came to a stop. An eighteen-wheeler had overturned, blocking both lanes. The late afternoon sun was nasturtium-orange, and sitting on a mountainside, a valley yawning beneath us, we seemed sky-high, like that bright ball. People were shutting off their cars to stand on the road, and Michelle did the same. We had been to a used bookstore, so I pulled out the book I had just bought, *The Prick of Noon* by Peter De Vries, which tells the story of Eddie Teeters, a young man who moves from Backbone, Arkansas, to Merrymount, Connecticut, with the hope of charming his way into the upper crust. To that end, he sets his sights on the beautiful socialite Cynthia Pickles.

Eddie woos Cynthia, is rebuffed, tries again, ends up in bed with her, meets her friends, meets her mother, and, thinking himself set for life, buys a big house for them to live in. One problem: Eddie is also Monte Carlo, producer of a line of sexual-technique instructional videos (read: porno flicks), and when the bluenoses of Merrymount find out, he ends up charged with the crime of "transporting obscene material across state lines and through the mails." He is found guilty, loses his company (while avoiding jail), gets a job as a limo driver, and marries Toby Snapper, a waitress he got pregnant on the rebound from Cynthia, who dumped him earlier for one of those upper-crust friends whose pageantry had attracted Eddie in the first place. It is lost to me now why I bought a book by an unfamiliar writer, but on that stand-still summer evening, as I read Eddie's awkward pursuit of Cynthia, I laughed. Snorted, in fact. When Michelle sat back down in the car, I said, "Here, listen to this." Two hours later, when traffic finally moved, I was still reading aloud and still laughing. Actually, we both were.

It is time to read Peter De Vries again. Some of his stuff has aged well, and some hasn't, but this is generally true of comedy. Modern comic writers—Sloane Crosley, Sarah Vowell, Patton Oswalt, Laurie Notaro, Chelsea Handler, and David Sedaris—mostly write "casuals," short fiction and sketches of the type made famous by *New Yorker* writers of the 1920s and '30s. In a world of shrinking attention spans, the comic novel, which has to be funny for 200 or more pages, is a dying breed. De Vries made it look easy. He wrote funny better than Hemingway wrote Hemingwayesque.

And he was more than a farceur. De Vries' son Derek has mused that his father was "in a lot of pain." His 1961 novel *The Blood of the Lamb*, about a man, Don Wanderhope, who suffers one loss after another culminating in his daughter's death, is often cited as proof of that pain. Did De Vries hurt worse than most people? Hard to say. No memoir, volume of letters, or book-length biography has ever appeared. He was born in Chicago in 1910 into a Dutch immigrant community that, as he told an interviewer in 1964, "still preserved its old-world ways."

> *My origins would have been little different had my parents never come to America at all, but remained in Holland. I still feel somewhat like a foreigner, and not only for ethnic reasons. Our insularity was two-fold, being a matter of religion as well as nationality.*

In addition to being immigrant, and not able to mix well with the Chicago Americans around us, we were Dutch Reformed Calvinists who weren't supposed to mix—who, in fact, had considerable trouble mixing with one another. We were the elect, and the elect are barred from everything, you know, except heaven.

Calvinists are a hard-working, humorless lot, and young Peter was brought up to avoid most secular pursuits—movies, dancing, playing cards. Sundays saw his family in church, usually all day. Everyone, even the kids, sat around and "engaged in doctrinal disputation." Such a scene opens *Blood*. Don Wanderhope's brother Louie, who "lost his faith during his medical studies at the University of Chicago," pans religion at every opportunity. At one family gathering, he opines that the biblical account of the virgin birth "was slipped in by a later writer, prolly, after the doctrine had been cooked up by the church," which gets the hoped-for reaction.

A gasp went around the kitchen table, at which now a small congregation sat. Men stiffened in their black suits, and women shook their heads as heresy darkened into blasphemy. Here under one roof were two candidates for the dread afgescheidenen, *a term as dire as "purge" to citizens of a later absolutism. My mother poured coffee with a trembling hand; my nearly blind grandmother, who lived with us at the time, was busily trying to sweep cigar burns in the oilcloth into a crumber; my grandfather went out to the front porch, where he stood scratching himself in a manner said to be depreciating property values. My uncle shook a finger threateningly in Louie's face. "I'll pray for you."*

After spending his childhood in church schools, De Vries went to Calvin College in Grand Rapids, Michigan, finishing in 1931 with a degree not in religion, as his parents had wanted, but in English. He worked odd jobs—candy seller, radio actor, furniture mover, ad copywriter—before selling a few poems to *Poetry* magazine (yes, that *Poetry*). By 1938, he was an associate editor, moving up to coeditor in 1942, which let him meet high-profile creative types, like Robert Penn Warren, Frank Lloyd Wright, and James Thurber. De Vries had written an essay, "James Thurber: The Comic Prufrock," arguing that Thurber had more in common with poets than other humorists. It is a sincere appreciation of Thurber's literary feats that also wears the robes of lit-crit ("If Eliot symbolizes his spiritual intricacies in terms of mythological beings…Thurber can personify his own modest nemeses in figures as concrete"), which De Vries would later don as farce. He sent Thurber a copy of the essay in November of 1943, a gesture equal parts hero worship and audition.

Thurber was flattered—most critics didn't take him seriously—and he admired De Vries' style. The friendship grew in April of 1944, when Thurber gave a benefit lecture for *Poetry* at the Chicago Arts Club. An underconfident speaker, he prepped with De Vries the night before. The talk went so well that Thurber persuaded Harold Ross, famous founder of *The New Yorker*, to read some of De Vries' work. An incomparable spotter of talent, but no great writer himself, Ross replied, "I have gone over [De Vries' pieces] and find, to my astonishment, that they are what can readily be described, in the language of this office, as very promising." He hired De Vries as poetry editor while allowing him to write other stuff. De Vries also helped in the art department, writing captions for cartoons or reworking a cartoon's premise, a job he kept until the 1980s.

De Vries' first novel, *But Who Wakes the Bugler?*, appeared in 1940 to little acclaim. Two more ho-hummers followed plus a collection of casuals, *No But I Saw the Movie* (1952). Then, in 1954, he wrote his fourth novel, *The Tunnel of Love*, about an unlikely friendship between Dick, a magazine editor, and Augie Poole, a would-be cartoonist. Augie's wife, Isolde, can't have children, so when the couple decide to adopt a baby, they ask Dick and his wife, Audrey, to be their references. Problem is, Augie is a serial cheater, and when his latest bedmate, Cornelia Bly, turns up pregnant and gives the baby to the same agency that approved the Pooles, Augie unwittingly adopts his own love child. Augmenting this comic plot is what De Vries is perhaps best known for: wit. Responding to his wife's complaint that her back is "stiff as a board," Dick says, "It's supposed to be stiff as a board there. That's called the lumbar region." Elsewhere, Audrey chides him for telling their son to take up the shoehorn because "[n]ow the child thinks you can play on one." Dick replies, "You can—footnotes." A daydreamer, Dick checks out to "an imaginary lodge" on "a remote promontory of the Maine Coast" that he calls Moot Point (a real punhouse, that one).

Tunnel became a bestseller. Two years later, De Vries adapted it for

Broadway, where it ran for 417 performances until 1958, when Hollywood had its turn. The Gene Kelly–directed film, his first in which he did not also appear, starred Doris Day and Richard Widmark. The plot was punched up in places (tranquilizers, financial chicanery, mistaken identity) and reversed in others (Dick, not Augie, becomes the philanderer), and at least one critic thought Widmark miscast, saying his performance "drops like a lead bassinet." Yet it is recognizable as the story that made De Vries a mid-century celebrity, along with Salinger, Philip Roth, Joseph Heller, Kurt Vonnegut, Allen Ginsberg, and Jack Kerouac. Those fellows took on the big questions of life, while De Vries kept his plots close to home—marriage, adultery, social climbing, the battle of the sexes.

More than plots, humorists are known for comic personas—think of David Sedaris' "Weird Little Gay Guy," in the words of one critic. The fiction writer, again, has it harder, coating that persona with a glaze of invention and shipping it to a made-up world. In 1927, when James Thurber published his story "An American Romance," a story whose opening words are "The little man in an overcoat that fitted him badly at the shoulders had had a distressing scene with his wife," he created "Little Man" humor, which *New Yorker* editor David Remnick describes as "tales of ineffectual men victimized by the world, by women, by nagging suspicions of their own absurdity." De Vries added a twist to the Little Man shtick, creating male characters who are losers but fancy themselves urbane. The typical De Vries protagonist is smug, a bit of a rake, and not troubled by ethical lapses. We usually find him rebelling against, escaping from, and ultimately accepting society and convention. The books can be dark, but not in the *Slaughterhouse-Five* sense. They can be surreal, but not in the *Gravity's Rainbow* sense. Sex is central to some of his plots—Augie's love child in *Tunnel*, Eddie's smut films in *Prick*, Maggie Doubloon's pregnancy at the hands (so to speak) of her student Anthony Thrasher in *Slouching Towards Kalamazoo*—and figures into many of his best bon mots. A decade before the sexual revolution, he had Cornelia Bly happily hooking up with Augie Poole, which shows his progressivism. And when he wrote about the act itself, it was without an ounce of tawdriness.

Lying down, [Rena] offered up two small breasts as white as the snow. Bent to those, I heard her moan my name on the pillow.

Beneath my journeying hand her slim body arched in a convulsion about which there could be no mistake.
  "I won't ask whether I'm a virgin any longer after that."

De Vries spent most of his adult life in Westport, Connecticut, where he had moved in 1948 with his wife, the poet Katinka Loeser. Then, as now, Westport was an accomplished burg. Robert Penn Warren was a neighbor, and J. D. Salinger lived nearby. John Hersey and Jean Stafford were sometime dinner guests. De Vries' son Jon recalls awaking one night to "a fantastic voice booming away" in the living room, which turned out to be Dylan Thomas reading parts of *King Lear.* Westport-like towns became the settings of most of his books, establishing him as "the suburbs' comic laureate," a view he encouraged. Humor to him was serious business; it is to most comedians. The trick, he knew, is to make the jokes seem unforced. He often quoted Charlie Chaplin on this subject—"If what you're doing is funny, don't be funny doing it"—which reminds me of Elmore Leonard's admission that "[i] f it sounds like writing, I rewrite it." Put the two together, and you have Peter De Vries: character-driven stories, effortless style, and when you reach page 20, you've been laughing for—well, you don't know how long.

De Vries' fame grew in the 1950s with more comic masterpieces, notably *The Mackerel Plaza* and *The Tents of Wickedness.* Then came 1960 and the death of his ten-year-old daughter, Emily, of leukemia. The novel that followed, *The Blood of the Lamb,* was startling—"a furious tract about the impossibility of religious faith written by a man who wanted desperately to believe," as one critic wrote. It is the story of Don Wanderhope, a young Dutch Calvinist from Chicago chafing under his parents' faith. He moves to Connecticut for a chance to sip from a secular cup, but he can't seem to stay on the right side of fortune. His brother dies of pneumonia, his girlfriend of tuberculosis. Then his father goes mad. A few years later, his wife commits suicide. His beacon through this darkfall is his little girl, Carol, who gets struck down at age 11 by, of all things, leukemia. De Vries teases Wanderhope, and us, by having Carol rally under chemotherapy only to get a staph infection that "ravage[s] her bloodstream" and "[breaks] out on her body surface in septicemic discolorations." Finally, with her father by her hospital bed, Carol dies.

Blood is called "autobiographical"—a gratuitous caption. Many of De Vries' books have autobiographical elements. A wine connoisseur, he wrote about wine connoisseurs. A cartoon doctor, he made Augie Poole a cartoonist and Dick the editor of *The Townsman,* a derivative of *The New Yorker.* When De Vries' physician told him in the 1980s that he had a heart condition, his next protagonist had the same scourge. And his characters' one-liners were sometimes heard originating in De Vries' own mouth. Woody Allen, who has long been thought of as Hollywood's confessional poet, said in a 1987 *Rolling Stone* interview: "[T]he stuff that people insist is autobiographical is almost invariably not, and it's so exaggerated that it's virtually meaningless." This is how I imagine De Vries would answer questions of source material in his books. A writer's life, he might say, is the ingredients, not the recipe.

Blood is also thought of as De Vries' "religious" novel, though he had written about faith and despair before. Indeed, according to the critic Jeff Evans, religion "appears as subject matter, object of satire, or repository of former values in virtually all the novels," even the early ones. In just his third book, *Angels Can't Do Better* (1944), a character explains his faith by saying,

> *I believe that the sky is high, that blood is a river of miracles mul-tiplying questions faster than you can answer them, I believe that faith is a kite in a cloud, that it is insolent of you to scatter the dust of your platitudes across the incomprehensible riddle that is the Universe, that death is neither a question mark nor a semi-colon but a period, that bugs are in earnest, and I believe that it is now a quarter to one.*

Note the fanciful tone of this passage. The high-flown language. And the quip at the end. Reminds me of Robin Williams' character in *Mrs. Doubtfire:* the Man Who Can't Be Serious (even when his wife leaves him). Now look at the Wanderhope creed.

> *I believe that man must learn to live without those consolations called religious, which his own intelligence must by now have told him belong to the childhood of the race. Philosophy can really give us nothing permanent to believe either; it is too rich in answers, each canceling out the rest. The quest for Meaning is foredoomed.*

Human life "means" nothing. But that is not to say that it is not worth living.

Sounds different, right? Less campy, more earnest? According to Calvin De Vries,* "[t]he religious dimension in De Vries' books is traced out especially in the struggle between belief and unbelief." Evans echoes this by calling a scene in *Blood* "a classic illustration of the ambivalence of belief and unbelief." In the scene, Wanderhope leaves the hospital after Carol's death, carrying a cake he had brought for her. Passing a church, he notices a statue of Christ. Furious, grieving, he throws the cake at Christ, splattering His face.

Evans dwells on this episode. Expounds on it. Uses terms like "stoic honesty" and "literary foil" and "epistemological." De Vries would have snickered at this. The nature of his faith was up for grabs, but there is no misconstruing what he thought of academe. To one interviewer, he said, "I have recently read a couple of serious-type articles about what I am actually up to, and I can only conclude that my stuff is really over my head." To another, after discussing the "learned theses" that graduate students write on his books, he mused, "Of course, I was the last to know."

It is clear that Emily's death turned him inward, at least for a while. In his obituary, Paul Theroux recalled "a darkness and a kind of morbidity entering De Vries' work" around this time. *Blood* also contains one of De Vries' rawest speeches, which Wanderhope delivers after Carol's death.

How I hate this world. I would like to tear it apart with my own two hands if I could. I would like to dismantle the universe star by star, like a treeful of rotten fruit. Nor do I believe in progress. A vermin-eaten saint scratching his filth in the hope of heaven is better off than you damned in clean linen...

To me, though, and I think to De Vries as well, humor is the key to *Blood*—humor amid tragedy, because the two are conjoined. "[L]ife is a tragedy," De Vries told an interviewer, "which entails, however, no need to banish gaiety."

---

* No relation, but Peter would have loved the absurdity of being critiqued by another De Vries, especially one named Calvin. Loved it so much he would probably have used it in a book. How's that for autobiography?

Thus the importance of De Vries' cake-faced Christ is that it is hilarious, slapstick, and entirely in keeping with Wanderhope's character. De Vries made him a smartass, and desserting the Savior is exactly what you would expect from someone who, lying abed with his high-school girlfriend, raises her skirt and muses, "Sometimes I think this leg is the most beautiful thing in the world, and sometimes the other. I suppose the truth lies somewhere in between." Or who, being asked by a later girlfriend if he is an atheist, replies, "Not a very devout one." She goes on to ask what he would do if he were God. His answer: "Put a stop to all this theology."

This does not mean that De Vries had nothing serious to say. Remember Evans' note of a religious undercurrent in "virtually all the novels." Why, if that subject was so dear to him, did he become a novelist instead of a philosopher or theologian? His sense of humor? People of the cloth can be funny. His joy in wordplay? Academics can have a compelling style—think Stephen Jay Gould (who is also funny).

No, I think it comes down to the distance that fiction imposes between writer and subject. Don Wanderhope may be similar to Peter De Vries, but he can't *be* De Vries, nor would De Vries want him to. If De Vries had been comfortable speaking directly to the world, he would have. Think of it this way: you can't stand right next to a bonfire. Too hot. Better to stand ten to fifteen feet away, where you can enjoy the fire without melting your belt buckle. Those feet are fiction. And even from a distance, don't look directly at the fire. You'll see those not-really-there fireflies everywhere you look afterward, which means your vision has been compromised. Better to look just to the side of the fire. That looking-to-the-side is comic fiction.

I think De Vries *did* have a lot to say on faith and morals, and he chose to say it through, in the words of one critic, "one-liners, situation comedies, satire, farce, and burlesque." This means either that he didn't trust his beliefs or that the play's the thing. I go with the latter. A more dire worldview might have led him to speak to us directly, but I guess he saw that there was time for humor. There was time, so he didn't rush to prophecy. No need for burning bushes or pillars of salt or bellies of fishes. Or maybe things *were* bad but De Vries knew the same thing as Jesus of Nazareth: parables work better than preaching.

De Vries left us parables. Lots of them. Critics say sad ones like *The Blood of the Lamb* are autobiographical, and they may be, but I imagine him more like the husband in his story "The High Ground, or Look, Ma, I'm Explicating." The husband is asked by his wife to be more talkative at dinner parties, theater outings, and the like, so at the opening of an art gallery, he says about one painting, "What we have here seems to me to be an organic fusion of form and content...one in which linear and compositional values are also happily resolved." After a few minutes of this blather, his wife hisses to him, "Go back to the way you were." But the husband can't, or won't, stop. He gets more bombastic with each party, alienating his wife's friends until she turns on him, shouting that he "mask[s] a genuine aggression under a façade of compliance and vice versa—a sort of basic insecurity inside this husk of independence," which leads him to muse, "Ah, well, it's an age of criticism, isn't it?"

Peter De Vries is who he is. He wrote humor, not literature. He recycled his plots. Some of his characters are stereotypes, some are shallow, and some are despicable. He was slow to update his language, meaning *The Prick of Noon* sounds like *The Tunnel of Love*. And, yes, some of the jokes aren't funny. Critics wanted him to change, be more serious, but he refused; he wanted to be known as a raconteur.

Some writers who have this gift renounce it. Mark Twain tried. In an 1865 letter to his brother and sister-in-law, he wrote

> *I never had but two powerful ambitions in my life. One was to be a pilot, & the other a preacher of the gospel. I accomplished the one & failed in the other, because I could not supply myself with the necessary stock in trade—i.e., religion. I have given it up forever. I never had a "call" in that direction, anyhow, & my aspirations were the very ecstasy of presumption. But I have had a "call" to literature, of a low order—i.e., humorous. It is nothing to be proud of, but it is my strongest suit, & if I were to listen to that maxim of stern duty which says that to do right you must multiply the one or the two or the three talents which the Almighty entrusts to your keeping, I would long ago have ceased to meddle with things for which I was by nature unfitted & turned my attention to seriously scribbling to excite the laughter of God's creatures.*

If Twain was ashamed of comedic skill, De Vries celebrated it. Indeed, it seemed to be his raison d'ecrire. He was buffeted by his daughter's death, which amped up the faith and morals in his work, but it never stopped making people laugh. So sit back. Enjoy. You can look deeper, and there is plenty to see. Or you can let him be refreshment. Sometimes an exploding cigar is just an exploding cigar.

Anthony Aycock is a former librarian, an occasional humorist, and bewildered by faith himself: his father is a retired Baptist pastor. He has published a book, The Accidental Law Librarian, *plus essays in* The Gettysburg Review, The Missouri Review, Creative Nonfiction, Information Today, *and* Library Journal. *He is also an assistant editor at www. conventionscene.com. He lives in North Carolina with his wife, daughter, wife's hermit crabs, daughter's corn snake, and a group of cats belonging to all of them (and, in the manner of cats, none of them).*

Alice Hoffman Prize for Fiction · Summer 2015

The Alice Hoffman Prize for Fiction

Ploughshares is pleased to present Nick Arvin with the fourth annual Alice Hoffman Prize for Fiction for his short story "The Crying Man," which appeared in the Fall 2014 issue of *Ploughshares*, guest-edited by Percival Everett. The $1,000 award, given by acclaimed writer and *Ploughshares* advisory editor Alice Hoffman, honors the best piece of fiction published in the journal during the previous year.

About Nick Arvin and "The Crying Man"

Nick Arvin has published three books of fiction, *In the Electric Eden* (Penguin, 2003), *Articles of War* (Anchor, 2006), and *The Reconstructionist* (Harper Perennial, 2012). His writing has been honored with awards from the American Academy of Arts and Letters, the NEA, and others. He is also an engineer, involved in the design of power plants, and oil, gas, and biogas facilities. He lives in Colorado.

What inspired "The Crying Man"?

Like a lot of men, I think, I've had a complicated relationship with crying. I remember when I was a kid, a friend of mine was spanked for crying, and I thought, Well, if he gets spanked for crying, I better not do it either. I took that very much to heart. For years and years, I never let myself cry. Eventually, I realized how messed up this was, but even then it took me a long time to relearn how to cry.

So I was thinking about these things, and my problem was that I couldn't cry, but it occurred to me that the opposite situation—an inability to stop crying—would be a problem too. That was the germ of the story.

How did the story find its final form? What did you discover or grapple with while writing it?

I just started writing little bits here and there, revolving around that original idea. It seemed to me that crying at work would be especially awkward, and I wanted to include that. My son was three or four at the time, and he loved to look at these books full of reptiles and amphibians, which have wonderful names, so that found its way in. At some point it struck me that all this crying was awfully sad, and I started injecting as much humor as I could. I was struggling to pull the threads together at the end of the story, and at that time my wife and I used to make up stories for my son when he went to bed, stories that often went into weird directions, and I thought maybe I could do something with that. I hesitated over it for a long time, though, because it seemed such a strange direction to go in a short story.

How does this story fit with the rest of your work?

I'm an engineer, and the characters in my short stories are often engineers, like the narrator of "The Crying Man." They keep trying to work through things in the systematic mindset of an engineer, but the world and their own foibles keep thwarting their efforts. My most recent novel, *The Reconstructionist,* is about two engineers who work on forensic reconstructions of car crashes.

On the other hand, my first novel, *Articles of War,* is a war story, set in Europe during World War II. It might not seem related to "The Crying Man," except that *Articles of War* is very much concerned with masculine notions of honor, duty, courage, and cowardice. "The Crying Man," and *Articles of War* involve some interrelated questions. What if you are a man who cannot fight? What if you are a man who cannot stop crying? What kind of man are you, then?

*Book Recommendations from
Our Advisory Editors*

Neil Astley recommends *Visiting Indira Gandhi's Palmist* by Kirun Kapur: "Kirun Kapur has taken many years to produce a first collection which is so assured and lyrically compelling that it reads nothing like a debut volume. Her poems draw on family history, myth, and people's stories to dramatize how the past informs the present, and how the child inherits a living legacy from mother (a former nun) and father (an Indian who found refuge in the US after the genocide caused by the 1947 Partition of British India, the subject of one of her book's central sequences). This is a remarkably mature and coherent collection of poems, which tell of horrors and heartache, as well as love, wisdom, and affirmation." (Elixir Press, January 2015)

Robert Boswell recommends *All Things Tending Towards the Eternal* by Kathleen Lee: "This is a beautiful novel about a woman traveling across China just after a large historical event (Tiananmen Square) and a very private tragedy (the mysterious death of her brother). She accumulates a wonderful cadre of companions, and the narrative becomes larger than any of their individual stories. Here's a tiny sample of the writing: 'Under the darkening sky, she went up on deck and stared out to sea, the expanse of dark water shiny with moonlight, surging softly. Here was the reason people rejoiced at setting sail: a ship's deck to look out from, the curve of the earth to roll over, a spit of land to round. The seen to the unseen, the known to the unknown; the unfamiliar turning by mysterious alchemy into her own experience before sliding into the past. Far from home, riding the watery flanks of the world.'"

Robert Boswell also recommends *Father Brother Keeper* by Nathan Poole: "Heartfelt, lyrical, and moving, these stories make you feel the texture of your life alter while you're immersed in them. The narrative's claim on its landscape is astounding. This is a remarkable book, and it announces the arrival of a brilliant young writer. Here's a tiny sample of the writing: 'Now the decades had become a problem. Now time could compress and dance, it could wobble and reverse like a rattle-back toy. He was getting worse and sooner than he expected.'"

Peter Ho Davies recommends *Gold, Fame, Citrus* by Claire Vaye Watkins: "This near-future vision of an evacuated, drought-stricken Southwest is as gripping as it is grimly persuasive. Restlessly formally inventive, as perhaps befits characters trying to scavenge and salvage what they can to survive, the book is also steeped in a deep sense of the past, walking backwards in the footsteps of westward pilgrims from Lewis and Clark to Tom Joad."

Margot Livesey recommends *Contenders* by Erika Krouse: "The author has written a novel as hard paced and surprising as her heroine, the inimitable Nina Black who can beat almost any man in an unfair fight. But *Contenders* isn't only about street fighting. It's also about the spiritual life and the life of the affections, within and beyond family. Can Nina come back from the edge of darkness? These brilliant pages offer several possible answers."

Thomas Lux recommends *We Deserve the Gods We Ask For* by Seth Brady Tucker, Gival Press: "Some of the best war (Tucker was a paratrooper in the first Gulf War) poems and some of the best love poems I've read in a long time."

Joyce Peseroff recommends *Furs Not Mine* by Andrea Cohen: "Grief at her mother's death is the grit forming the pearl of Andrea Cohen's new book, but grief doesn't temper her signature wit. In the title poem, loss is 'an inmost // Siberia made more Siberian by one / who basks nearby, oblivious in her Bolivia.' Terse, tart, piercing, and tender, the poems develop a language to cope with 'the central O / of loss going on'"

Rosanna Warren recommends Michael Longley's *Collected Poems*, especially the volumes from *The Ghost Orchid* (1995) onward: "These poems are gravely strange, kinetic in their seeing, alive to mourning and horror but also to celebration. Longley's rhythms float out upon the air with great subtlety. And what a vocabulary for birds and plants."

Eleanor Wilner recommends *The Corpse Washer* by Sinan Antoon: "An essential novel that invites us into the soul-wearying attrition and bottomless sorrow of Baghdad's broken world, through the daily life (and constant nightmares) of a man intended by talent and desire to be an artist, but forced by war and its surfeit of corpses into the family trade of the Shi'ite ritual washing of the dead. As the book portrays what ordinary Iraqis endure, it becomes itself a rite of mourning for the dead and for all that is lost." (translated from the Arabic by the author, Yale University Press, 2013).

Tobias Wolff recommends *H Is for Hawk* by Helen Macdonald: "Beautifully written, it is all at once a meditation on loss and grief, a story of seduction giving way to love, and a stern but deeply sympathetic portrait of the life of another writer, the troubled T. H. White."

EDITORS' CORNER
New Works by Our Advisory Editors

Jane Hirshfield, *Ten Windows: How Great Poems Transform the World,* essays (Knopf, March 2015)

Jane Hirshfield, *The Beauty,* poems (Kopf, March 2015)

Martin Espada, *The Meaning of the Shovel,* poems (Dufour Editions, 2016)

Major Jackson, *Roll Deep,* poems (W.W. Norton & Company, 2015)

CONTRIBUTORS' NOTES
Summer 2015

Osama Alomar was born in Damascus, Syria, in 1968. A well-known writer of short stories, poetry, and essays in Arabic, Alomar published *Fullblood Arabian* (New Directions, 2014), his first volume in English translation. A Norwegian edition of *Fullblood Arabian* was published this year. His writing has been published in *Coffin Factory, The Literary Review, Gigantic, Dissent, TriQuarterly,* and on the *New Yorker* website. He lives in Chicago.

Ramona Ausubel is the author of the novel *No One Is Here Except All of Us* (Riverhead Books, 2013) and the story collection *A Guide to Being Born* (Riverhead Books, 2014). Her work has appeared in the *New Yorker, One Story, Electric Literature* and elsewhere. She is currently a faculty member of the Low-Residency MFA program at the Institute of American Indian Arts.

Jesse Ball (1978-) has written many books. His work is thought to be absurd.

C. J. Collins is a librarian and Arabic translator based in Queens, New York. He translated *Fullblood Arabian* (New Directions, 2014) in collaboration with its author, Osama Alomar, whom he first met in 2007, when Collins was living in Syria on a Fulbright grant.

Lydia Davis is the author of *The Collected Stories of Lydia Davis* (Farrar, Straus & Giroux, 2009), a translation of Flaubert's *Madame Bovary* (Viking Penguin, 2010), a chapbook entitled *The Cows* (Sarabande Press, 2011), and a poem entitled "Our Village" in *Two American Scenes* (New Directions, 2013). In 2013, she was awarded the Man Booker International Prize for Fiction, and her most recent collection of stories, *Can't and Won't,* was published last year by Farrar, Straus & Giroux.

Alex Epstein was born in Leningrad (St. Petersburg) in 1971 and moved to Israel when he was eight. He is the author of ten works of fiction in Hebrew, and in 2003 was awarded the Israeli Prime Minister's Prize for Literature. His work has appeared in *Guernica, Iowa Review, Electric Literature, Kenyon Review, PEN America,* and elsewhere. He lives in Tel Aviv. Two of his collections of micro-fiction, *Blue Has No South* (2010) and *Lunar Savings Time* (2011), are available in English from Clockroot Books.

Kevin A. González is the author of a collection of poems, *Cultural Studies* (Carnegie Mellon, 2009), and the coeditor of *The New Census: An Anthology of Contemporary American Poetry.* His stories have been awarded the Narrative Prize, the Playboy College Fiction Prize, and the Michener-Copernicus Award, and they have appeared in *Narrative, Playboy, Virginia Quarterly Review, Ploughshares Solos, Mississippi Review, Best American Nonrequired Reading,* and in two editions of *Best*

New American Voices. He teaches at Carnegie Mellon University and serves as editor of *jubilat.*

Yardenne Greenspan has an MFA in Fiction and Translation from Columbia University. In 2011 she received the American Literary Translators' Association Fellowship. Her translation of *Some Day* by Shemi Zarhin (New Vessel Press, 2013) was chosen for *World Literature Today's* 2013 list of notable translations. Her full-length translations also include *Tel Aviv Noir*, edited by Etgar Keret and Assaf Gavron (Akashic Books, 2014), and *Alexandrian Summer* by Yitzhak Gormezano Goren (New Vessel Press, 2015). Greenspan's writing and translations can be found in *The New Yorker*, *Haaretz*, *Guernica*, *Words Without Borders*, and *Asymptote*, among other publications.

Eliana Hechter (1987–2014) began taking graduate creative writing classes at the University of Washington at the age of 15. She graduated with a major in mathematics at 17. A Rhodes Scholar, she received her DPhil in Statistics at the University of Oxford. She did genome research at the Broad Institute of Harvard and MIT, and was in the Health Sciences and Technology Program at Harvard Medical School. "Extremities" is her only published work of fiction.

Vladislava Kolosova was born in 1987 in St. Petersburg. She grew up in unruly Perestroika-Russia, during the so-called wild nineties. In 2014, she received an MFA in creative writing from New York University, where she studied with Jonathan Safran Foer

and Zadie Smith, among others. She works as a journalist in Germany and has previously published only nonfiction books.

Fiona Maazel is the author of the novels *Last Last Chance* (Picador, 2009) and *Woke Up Lonely* (Graywolf Press, 2013). Her third novel, *What Kind of a Man*, is forthcoming from Graywolf Press in the fall of 2016.

Rebecca Makkai is the author of the new story collection *Music for Wartime* (Viking, 2015), of which this story is part; four pieces from the collection were selected for *The Best American Short Stories*. She has two novels, *The Hundred-Year House* (Viking, 2014) and *The Borrower* (Penguin, 2012), and this fall she'll be visiting faculty at the Iowa Writers' Workshop. She lives in Chicago.

Ander Monson's most recent book is *Letter to a Future Lover* (Graywolf, 2015).

Helen Oyeyemi is author of five novels, including *White Is for Witching* (Riverhead Books, 2014), which won a 2010 Somerset Maugham Award, *Mr Fox*, which won a 2012 Hurston/Wright Legacy Award, and, most recently, *Boy, Snow, Bird*. In 2013, Oyeyemi was named one of Granta's Best Young British Novelists. "'Sorry' Doesn't Sweeten Her Tea" forms part of her story collection *What Is Not Yours Is Not Yours*, forthcoming from Riverhead in 2016.

Daniel Peña is a Fulbright-Garcia Robles Scholar based in Mexico City. He graduated from the MFA program at Cornell University and is at work on his first book. His writing can be seen in *Kenyon Review Online*, *Huizache*, *Callaloo*, and *The Rumpus*, among other outlets. He's originally from Austin, Texas.

Alex Shakar's latest novel, *Luminarium* (Soho Press, 2011), won the 2011 *Los Angeles Times* Book Prize for Fiction. It was also named a *Washington Post* Notable Book, a *New York Times* Editor's Choice, and a best book of the year by *Publishers Weekly*, *Booklist*, and other periodicals. His novel *The Savage Girl* was a *New York Times* Notable Book. His story collection "City in Love" won the FC2 National Fiction Competition. A Brooklyn native, he now lives in Chicago and is a professor at the University of Illinois at Urbana-Champaign.

Sjón is a celebrated Icelandic novelist who was born in Reykjavík in 1962. He won the Nordic Council's Literary Prize (the equivalent of the Man Booker Prize) for his novel *The Blue Fox* (Bjartur, 2003), and the novel *From the Mouth of the Whale* (Bjartur, 2008) was shortlisted for both the International IMPAC Dublin Literary Award and the Independent Foreign Fiction Prize. His latest novel, *Moonstone – The Boy Who Never Was* was awarded the 2013 Icelandic Literary Prize and will be published by Farrar, Straus & Giroux in 2016. Also a poet, playwright, librettist, and lyricist, he has frequently worked with his countrywoman Björk and has written a number of opera librettos. Sjón is the president of the Icelandic PEN Centre and former chairman of the

board of Reykjavík, UNESCO city of Literature. His novels have been published in thirty-five languages.

Xuan Juliana Wang was a 2011–2013 Wallace Stegner Fellow at Stanford University. She was born in Heilongjiang, China, but after age seven, did most of her growing up in Los Angeles. She has lived and worked in Paris, New York, and Beijing. www.xuanjulianawang.com

Kevin Wilson is the author of a story collection, *Tunneling to the Center of the Earth* (Deckle Edge, 2009), which won the Shirley Jackson Award, and a novel, *The Family Fang* (Ecco, 2012). His stories have appeared in *Ploughshares*, *Tin House*, *A Public Space*, *One Story*, and elsewhere. He teaches in the English Department at Sewanee: The University of the South.

Christian Winn is a fiction writer and teacher of creative writing living and working in Boise, Idaho. His fiction has appeared in *McSweeney's*, *The Chicago Tribune's Printers Row Journal*, *Hayden's Ferry Review*, *Greensboro Review*, *Chattahoochee Review*, *Gulf Coast*, *Bat City Review*, *Every Day Fiction*, *The Pinch*, *Santa Monica Review*, *Handful of Dust*, *The Strip*, *Revolver*, and *cold-drill*. His debut collection of short stories, *NA-KED ME*, is recently out from Dock Street Press - dockstreetpress.com. Find his work, reviews, and updates at christianwinn.com.

GUEST EDITOR POLICY

Ploughshares is published three times a year: mixed issues of poetry and prose in the spring and winter and a prose issue in the fall. The spring and fall issues are guest-edited by different writers of prominence, and winter issues are staff-edited. Guest editors are invited to solicit up to half of their issues, with the other half selected from unsolicited manuscripts screened for them by staff editors. This guest editor policy is designed to introduce readers to different literary circles and tastes, and to offer a fuller representation of the range and diversity of contemporary letters than would be possible with a single editorship. Yet, at the same time, we expect every issue to reflect our overall standards of literary excellence.

SUBMISSION POLICIES

We welcome unsolicited manuscripts from June 1 to January 15 (postmark dates). We also accept submissions online. Please see our website (pshares. org) for more information and guidelines. All submissions postmarked from January 16 to May 31 will be recycled or returned (if SASE is included) unread. From March 1 to May 15, we also accept submissions online for our Emerging Writer's Contest.

Our backlog is unpredictable, and staff editors ultimately have the responsibility of determining for which editor a work is most appropriate. If a manuscript is not timely for one issue, it will be considered for another. Unsolicited work sent directly to a guest editor's home or office will be ignored and discarded.

All mailed manuscripts and correspondence regarding submissions should be accompanied by a self-addressed, stamped envelope (s.a.s.e.). No replies will be given by email (exceptions are made for international submissions). Expect three to five months for a decision. We now receive well over a thousand manuscripts a month.

For stories and essays that are significantly longer than 5,000 words, we are now accepting submissions for *Ploughshares Solos* (formerly *Pshares Singles*), which will be published as e-books. Pieces for this series, which can be either fiction or nonfiction, can stretch to novella length and range from 6,000 to 25,000 words. The series is edited by Ladette Randolph, *Ploughshares* editor-in-chief.

Simultaneous submissions are amenable as long as they are indicated as such and we are notified immediately upon acceptance elsewhere. We do not reprint previously published work. Translations are welcome if permission has been granted. We cannot be responsible for delay, loss, or damage. Payment is upon publication: $25/printed page, $50 minimum and $250 maximum per author, with two copies of the issue and a one-year subscription. For *Ploughshares Solos,* payment is $250 for long stories and $500 for work that is closer to a novella. The prize for our Emerging Writer's Contest is $1,000 for the winner in each genre: fiction, poetry, and nonfiction.

PEN AMERICA

A JOURNAL FOR WRITERS AND READERS

ISSUE #18: IN TRANSIT

FEATURING CONVERSATIONS, ESSAYS, FICTION, POETRY, AND ART BY

LYDIA DAVIS	MANA NEYASTANI	FRANK BIDART
XIAOLU GUO	OSAMA ALOMAR	JUSTIN VIVIAN BOND
JUDITH BUTLER	ANTHONY MARRA	and many more...

www.PEN.org/journal

UNIVERSITY OF WYOMING

Assistantships,
summer stipends,

publication support,

travel funding,

The University of Wyoming   MFA Program   Department of English 3353   1000 E. University Av

MFA PROGRAM IN CREATIVE WRITING

A fully funded two-year studio program in
fiction, nonfiction, & poetry

FACULTY: Andy Fitch, Alyson Hagy, Harvey Hix,
Mark Jenkins, Frieda Knobloch,
Rattawut Lapcharoensap, Jeff Lockwood,
Beth Loffreda, Kate Northrop, Danielle Pafunda,
David Romtvedt, Brad Watson, Joy Williams

roam. RECENT VISITING WRITERS:
Dinaw Mengestu, Sherwin Bitsui,
Claudia Rankine, Mark Nowak,
Ed Roberson, Kent Nelson

2015-2016 WRITER IN RESIDENCE:
NAM LE

nie, WY 82071   307.766.6453   cw@uwyo.edu   www.uwyo.edu/creativewriting

Health Affairs
Narrative Matters

Stories on the human side of health policy

Personal stories about experiences with the health care system and the people in it, using the power of literary nonfiction to highlight important public policy issues.

Delve into first hand encounters with the health system

READ ▸ Personal stories

LISTEN ▸ To authors telling their stories via podcast

SUBMIT ▸ Your compelling, first-person story to *Health Affairs* Narrative Matters Editorial team for consideration. Stories should explore health care delivery, roles of providers or patients, system redesign, or needed changes in public policy.

Where to find *Health Affairs* Narrative Matters

WEB ▸ healthaffairs.org/narrative-matters

FACEBOOK ▸ facebook.com/HealthAffairs

PLOUGHSHARES

Stories and poems for literary aficionados

Known for its compelling fiction and poetry, *Ploughshares* is widely regarded as one of America's most influential literary journals. Most issues are guest-edited by a different writer for a fresh, personal vision, and contributors include both well-known and emerging writers. *Ploughshares* has become a premier proving ground for new talent, showcasing the early works of Sue Miller, Edward P. Jones, Tim O'Brien, and countless others. Past guest editors include Raymond Carver, Kathryn Harrison, Seamus Heaney, Lorrie Moore, Derek Walcott, and Tobias Wolff. This unique editorial format has made *Ploughshares* a dynamic anthology series— one that has established a tradition of quality and prescience. *Ploughshares* is published in April, July, and January, usually with a prose issue in the fall and mixed issues of poetry and fiction in the spring and winter. Subscribers also receive an annual Omnibus that gathers together our Solos—longer form stories and essays originally published in digital form.

Subscribe online at pshares.org.

☐ Send me a one-year subscription for $35.
    I save $27 off the cover price (3 issues and Omnibus).

☐ Send me a two-year subscription for $55.
    I save $69 off the cover price (6 issues and two Omnibuses).

Name _____

Address _____

_____

E-mail _____

Mail with check to: Ploughshares · Emerson College
                  120 Boylston St. · Boston, MA 02116

Add $35 per year for international postage ($15 for Canada).